George Ferguson Bowen

Thirty Years of Colonial Government

Vol. I

George Ferguson Bowen

Thirty Years of Colonial Government
Vol. I

ISBN/EAN: 9783744715829

Printed in Europe, USA, Canada, Australia, Japan

Cover: Foto ©ninafisch / pixelio.de

More available books at **www.hansebooks.com**

THIRTY YEARS

OF

COLONIAL GOVERNMENT

A SELECTION FROM THE DESPATCHES AND
LETTERS OF THE RIGHT HON.

SIR GEORGE FERGUSON BOWEN, G.C.M.G.

HON. D.C.L. OXON., HON. LL.D. CANTAB.

GOVERNOR SUCCESSIVELY OF
QUEENSLAND, NEW ZEALAND, VICTORIA, MAURITIUS, AND HONG KONG

EDITED BY

STANLEY LANE-POOLE

With Portrait

TWO VOLUMES—VOL. I.

LONDON
LONGMANS, GREEN, AND CO.
AND NEW YORK: 15 EAST 16ᵗʰ STREET
1889

CONTENTS

OF

THE FIRST VOLUME.

—◦◦—

PART I.

PREFATORY MEMOIR.

PART II.

THE FOUNDING OF QUEENSLAND : 1859-1868.

CHAPTER VI.

CHAPTER VII.

CHAPTER VIII.

CHAPTER IX.

CHAPTER X.

PART III.

NEW ZEALAND : 1868-1873.

CHAPTER XIV.

CHAPTER XV.

PART I.

PREFATORY MEMOIR

CHAPTER I.

INTRODUCTORY — IMPORTANCE OF THE COLONIES — ALTERED STATE OF PUBLIC OPINION ON THIS SUBJECT—VIEWS OF ADAM SMITH—MR. W. E. FORSTER—LORD ROSEBERY—IMPERIAL FEDERATION—COLONIES GOVERNED BY SIR G. BOWEN.

THERE are few subjects in the arena of political debate upon which the minds of the majority of Englishmen have so completely changed in recent years as that of the relations of the Colonies towards the mother-country. There was a time when the so-called Manchester school of politicians, together with many of their allies among the Statesmen of the day, could talk complacently of the final separation of Canada, Australasia, and South Africa, from a parent who seemed anxious to rid herself of her encumbrances. What is still stranger, similar ideas were then prevalent even among the bureaucracy of the Colonial Office. From the Autobiography of Sir Henry Taylor,[1] long one of the most prominent and influential members of that Department, it appears that he was strongly in favour of getting rid of the greater Colonies, and that Sir Frederic Rogers (now Lord Blachford), then the Permanent Under-Secretary of State, wrote to him, 'I go very far with you in the desire to shake off all responsibly governed Colonies; and as to North America, I think if we abandon one,

[1] Vol. II. chap. 17.

we had better abandon all.' Nay more, we find Sir H. Taylor writing (in February 1864) to the Colonial Minister, the Duke of Newcastle; 'As to our American possessions, I have long held, and often expressed, the opinion that they are a sort of *damnosa hæreditas*; and when your Grace and the Prince of Wales were employing yourselves so successfully in conciliating the Colonists, I thought you were drawing closer ties which might better be slackened.'

The time when such sentiments could be openly professed is gone for ever. The politicians and officials once hostile or indifferent to the Colonies now feel that, in the altered state of public opinion, they must (as one of the most prominent among them recently admitted) 'assume a virtue, if they have it not.' The distant provinces of the British Empire are no longer in their struggling infancy : they have grown, and are still growing, in wealth and population, so fast that they have already left behind them, in most elements of material prosperity and importance, the secondary kingdoms of Europe. The rapid development of steam communication has brought our most remote provinces practically nearer to us than the Hebrides were a hundred years ago ; and the old country has begun to realise that distance is not disintegration, and that a great colonial city twelve thousand miles away is as much British as if it were situated in Yorkshire or in Midlothian. Those of us whose work lies in Canada or Australia are so frequently revisiting the ever-welcoming white cliffs, that we who stay at home readily forget the space of ocean which parts us from the scene of their labours; and there is a general feeling of kinship and common loyalty among us all, wherever our place may be in the Empire, which hardly existed a generation ago. England has at last awoke to the sense of her own greatness.

Many causes have contributed to this awakening. Not the least of these has been the example of our powerful neighbours in Europe, who have taught us that what we used to undervalue is to them above all things to be desired. 'The nations of Europe,' said the late Mr. W. E. Forster, in 1885, 'begin to find out how important it is for England to have great possessions in different parts of the world, and try to have their share in such possessions.' Germany and France in recent years have striven at immense cost to establish themselves on such spots of the globe as still remain open to colonisation. Tongking, the New Hebrides, New Guinea, East and West Africa, Madagascar, are names which testify to the colonising ambition of these powers; and Italy, the newest of European kingdoms, has not waited long before making an effort in the same direction. Emulation is the soul of enterprise, and these endeavours of foreign nations have keenly aroused the pride and interest of Great Britain in her far-off provinces.

Even if the example of our neighbours had not stirred us, other reasons led towards the same happy result. The Colonial and Indian Exhibition of 1886, and the Colonial Conference of 1887, have exercised a salutary influence on the public mind. Moreover, the statistics of recent years have proved beyond doubt that the maxim that 'trade follows the flag' is true; and we have learnt that in the fierce and ever-increasing competition of commerce our colonial kinsmen are our best customers. And if this be thought a somewhat sordid, however necessary, consideration, let us remember that our Colonies have shown themselves one with us not in commercial interests only, but in national spirit. They have heartily responded to the enthusiasm which the idea of a United Empire has aroused in England, which is still to every colonist his 'home'; and they showed their eagerness to share in the dangers as well as in the glories of the mother-country when they sent their volunteers to help us in our war in the Soudan; when they contributed with their customary generosity to the relief of Indian famines; and responded in many other ways to calls for assistance, often but indistinctly heard across half the globe. 'But as relates to the great question of the future, it would be impossible to use more impressive language than that of Sir Edward Bulwer Lytton,[1] while Secretary of State for the Colonies, in a speech worthy of himself and of the subject, delivered on the occasion of a celebration in London of the foundation of the Australian Colonies. "You, gentlemen of Australia,"said the brilliant orator, " took with you from this country no bitter or angry resolutions, no associations of the reigns of the Stuarts; but, on the contrary, you carried with you the feelings of affection for a free country, and the tie has been all the stronger because it has been more gently felt. The time will come when these new Colonies will be great States; when they will find it easier to raise fleets and armies than they now find it to raise a police; when they will have in their harbours forests of masts and navies of their own. It may so happen that in that distant day England may be in danger, that the great

_____
[1] Afterwards the first Lord Lytton.

despotic and military powers of Europe may then rise up against the venerable mother of many free Commonwealths. If that day should ever arrive I believe that her children will not be unmindful of her, and that to her rescue, across the wide ocean, ships will come thick and fast, among which there will be but one cry, " While Australia lasts, England shall not perish." '[1]

Lord Lytton did not live to see the general awakening of the national spirit which now presses more and more eagerly towards the realisation of some such settled scheme of unification as is conveyed in the words Imperial Federation,—words which have stirred the imagination and roused the sympathies and enlisted the energies and thought of many of the leading Statesmen in all parts of the Empire. Mr. W. E. Forster, whose closing years were much occupied with this great subject, defined this Federation to be 'such a union of the mother-country with the Colonies as will keep the British Empire one State in relation to other States, through the agency of (1) an organisation for common defence, and (2) a joint foreign policy.' So the Earl of Rosebery, who succeeded Mr. Forster as President of the Imperial Federation League, said in a recent speech : 'The cause which we call Imperial Federation is worthy of the devotion of the individual lives of the people of this country. . . . Ever since I traversed those great regions which own the sway of the British Crown outside these islands, I have felt that it was a cause which merited all the enthusiasm and energy that man could give to it. It is a cause for which any

[1] *Quarterly Review*, 1863, art. ' Australian Colonies.'

one might be content to live : it is a cause for which
any one might be content to die.'   .

In one of the latest letters which Mr. Forster ever
wrote (in August, 1885), he exhorted his friend Sir
George Bowen to throw into the scale of Imperial
Federation 'the weight of his unmatched experience
in colonial administration.'   This prompting was
in accordance with all that the veteran Proconsul
had felt during his long career ; but coming when
it did, almost as a voice from the grave of the
departed Statesman, it moved him deeply. Since
then, at many public meetings, and especially before
the Royal Colonial Institute, he has set forth his
views on the nature and limitations of the future
Federation to which so many people, both in England
and in the ' Greater Britain,' look forward with patriotic hope.   This is the main reason for the present
work.   Many public men have given their opinion
that, in view of the present increasing interest and appreciation of the Imperial relations of Great Britain,
it would be useful to lay before the British people an
outline of the work of Colonial government, illustrated
by despatches and letters, and reaching over many
years and a wide extent of the Empire, together with
a summary of the official career of one who may
justly be regarded as the type of a Colonial Governor.
Five of our chief Colonies have seen Sir George Bowen
in the highest command ; for more than a quarter of
a century he has aimed at binding our kindred across
the seas closer to the Crown and the mother-country ;
and the record of his official work cannot but throw
light upon the varied phases of colonial government,
and upon some of the problems which still await

complete solution. Above all, this book will have achieved its chief object if it helps to promote the movement towards Imperial Federation. The difficulties which surround this grandest of colonial problems are manifold : but assuredly they ought not to be beyond the powers of British statesmanship. [1]

In the pregnant words of Adam Smith : ' There is not the least probability that the British constitution would be hurt by the union of Great Britain with her Colonies. That constitution, on the contrary, would be completed by it, and seems to be imperfect without it. The Assembly which deliberates and decides concerning the affairs of every part of the Empire ought certainly to have representatives from every part of it. That this union, however, could be easily effectuated, or that difficulties, and great difficulties, might not occur in the execution, I do not pretend. I have yet heard of none, however, which appear unsurmountable. The principal, perhaps, arise, not from the nature of things, but from the prejudices and opinions of the people both on this and on the other side of the Atlantic.' [2]

In the same spirit, Professor Seeley observes : ' The old colonial system is gone. But in place of it no clear and reasoned system has been adopted. The wrong theory is given up, but what is the right theory ? There is only one alternative. As the Colonies are not, in the old phrase, *possessions* of

---

[1] The question of Imperial Federation, and of the relations of the mother-country and the 'Greater Britain,' are ably discussed in Mr. Froude's *Oceana*, chap. 21.

[2] *Wealth of Nations*, Book IV. chap. 7.

England, they must be a part of England ; and we must adopt this view in earnest. We must cease altogether to say that England is an island off the north-western coast of Europe, that it has an area of 120,000 square miles, and a population of thirty odd millions. We must cease to think that emigrants, when they go to the Colonies, leave England, or are lost to England. We must cease to think that the history of England is the history of the Parliament that sits at Westminster, and that affairs which are not discussed there cannot belong to English history. When we have accustomed ourselves to contemplate the whole Empire together, and to call it all England, we shall see that here, too, is a United States. Here, too, is a great homogeneous people, one in blood, language, religion, and laws, but dispersed over a boundless space. We shall see that, though it is held together by strong moral ties, it has little that can be called a constitution, no system that seems capable of resisting any severe shock. But if we are disposed to doubt whether any system can be devised capable of holding together communities so distant from each other, then is the time to recollect the history of the United States of America. For they have such a system. They have solved this problem. They have shown that, in the present age of the world, political unions may exist on a vaster scale than was possible in former times. No doubt our problem has difficulties of its own, immense difficulties. But the greatest of these difficulties is one that we make ourselves. It is the false preconception which we bring to the question, that the problem is insoluble, that no such thing ever was done, or ever will be done ; it is our misinterpretation of the American Revolution. From that Revolution we infer that all distant Colonies, sooner or later, secede from the mother-country. We ought to infer only that they secede when they are held under the old colonial system.'[1]

'Those persons,' said Sir George Bowen, in his address at the Royal Colonial Institute in 1886,[2] ' who still insist that the Federation of the British Empire is *impossible*, even hereafter and in the fulness of time, would do well to ponder on the striking precedents of Germany and America. The federal Constitution of the United States was long despaired of by its strongest advocates, and was not carried until 1789, thirteen years after the Declaration of Independence in 1776. Again, ten short years before the proclamation, in 1871, of the federal Empire of Germany, before the victory of Sadowa and the capitulation of Sedan—that Empire which now throws its gigantic shadow across Europe was generally regarded as a dream of a few patriotic enthusiasts. Finally, thousands of those who recently witnessed the opening by the Queen-Empress of the Imperial Exhibition (as it may justly be called), which owes so much to the Prince of Wales, the President of this Institute, hoped and prayed that this grand national spectacle may prove a foreshadowing of permanent union and of future Imperial Federation. Thus we should be brought nearer to the prophetic vision of Burke, when " the

[1] *Expansion of England*, p. 158.
[2] Republished in a pamphlet form by Messrs. Kegan Paul, Trench, & Co., *Second Edition*, 1889.

spirit of the English Constitution, infused through
the mighty mass, shall pervade, vivify, unite, and
invigorate every part of the Empire." [1]

A preliminary glance at the sphere in which the
work of Sir George Bowen has been carried on will
help towards the realisation of what is meant by ' the
Greater Britain.' The Ionian Isles, Queensland, New
Zealand, Victoria, Mauritius, Hong Kong, Malta—the
varied scenes of his public life—comprise a large portion of our Colonial Empire, and severally illustrate
many of the salient points of our Imperial rule. Corfu
and Malta, of which the former marked the commencement of his career of colonial administration thirty-
five years ago, while the latter was but last year
(1888) the theatre of his latest appearance in that
field—are both striking landmarks in England's
route to India, China, and Australia by way of the
Mediterranean.   Mauritius, which Thiers called the
' Malta of the Indian Ocean,' is an essential link in
our alternative chain of communications with our
Eastern dominions by way of the Cape of Good
Hope. Queensland, the latest formed, and Victoria,
long the most wealthy and prosperous of the Australian provinces, afford typical illustrations of the enor-
mous extent, of the rapid progress, and of the constitutional system of government on the parent model,
which characterise the British Empire in Australia.
In New Zealand we see the ' Great Britain of the
South '; but with glaciers and snowy peaks resembling those of Switzerland ; with geysers and hot

[1] *Cf.* Virgil, *Æn.* VI. 726.

> *Spiritus intus alit, totamque infusa per artus*
> *Mens agitat molem, et magno se corpore miscet.*

lakes worthy of Iceland; and with arms of the sea winding among lofty mountains and precipices, surpassing the fjords of Norway. And here we are brought into contact with the Maoris, the noblest race of savages that has ever been absorbed by civilisation. Finally, Hong Kong, at once a great emporium of trade and a commanding naval and military station, brings more especially into prominence one of the principal factors in our national greatness, the commercial as distinct from the Imperial and Colonial element in the British Empire. As our main stronghold in a quarter of the globe which contains one-fourth of the entire human race, but which long resisted all intercourse with the western world, and as the channel through which passes the vast trade of the teeming millions of China and Japan, the Crown Colony of Hong Kong illustrates, perhaps to a fuller degree than any other British dependency, the commercial instinct which has so powerfully pervaded and strengthened the expansion of England.

Thus it will be seen at the outset that a comprehensive view of those portions of the Queen's dominions with which Sir George Bowen has been officially connected tends to bring before the mind many of the most important considerations and problems affecting the past and future history and progress of the British Empire. Before, however, entering upon the detailed record of his administration of these varied seats of colonising and commercial enterprise, it may be useful to set down the chief incidents of his life in brief outline.

CHAPTER II.

SIR G. BOWEN'S EARLY YEARS—OXFORD—THE IONIAN ISLANDS
—PUBLICATIONS ON GREECE, ETC. — TRAVELS IN EASTERN
EUROPE—VIENNA IN 1848—WAR IN HUNGARY—LORD STRAT·
FORD DE REDCLIFFE—APPOINTED SECRETARY OF GOVERNMENT
AT CORFU — MARRIAGE — LORD PALMERSTON AND MODERN
GREEK—MR. DISRAELI ON EASTERN QUESTIONS.

GEORGE FERGUSON BOWEN, though descended from
an old Pembrokeshire family (Ap-Owen), was born in
Ireland in 1821. He is the eldest son of the late Rev.
Edward Bowen, rector of Taughboyne in Donegal,
and is brother of the present Dean of Raphoe. He is
wont to state that the earliest public event which he
remembers was the battle of Navarino in 1827, which
led to the independence of Greece, and to ascribe
partly to that fact his active sympathy throughout life
with the progress and welfare of the modern Greeks.

His education was the good old-fashioned training
of an English public school and university—Charter-
house, and Trinity College, Oxford, where he gained
an open scholarship in 1840, at the side of the late
Rt. Hon. Montague Bernard, of the present Bishop
(Jones) of St. David's, and of Henry Coleridge,
brother of the Chief Justice. During his career at
the university he formed many life-long friendships.
Like many other men who have won success in after
life, he was a prominent member of the Union, and

he enjoyed the rare distinction of having been twice
elected President of that society. His long vacations
were generally spent abroad. As a child he had lived
with his family for two years in the south of France ;
and this experience, matured by later rambles in
Brittany, Germany, Italy, and Sicily, explains his
fluency in European languages. In 1844 he took
his degree in the first class in classical honours,
having with him in the same class the present Deans
of Westminster (Bradley) and Wells (Plumptre) ; and
in the same year he was elected to an open Fellowship at Brasenose College. The political activity of
his after life has not obliterated the stamp of his old
Oxford days. Classical studies have always retained
for him their early charm, and have been his solace
amid official cares. Nor is it unreasonable to presume
that sympathy with the history of the Greeks, the chief
colonisers of the ancient world, and of the Romans,
the first practical exponents of imperial rule—ever
mindful of the stimulating counsels of Anchises—

> *Tu regere imperio populos, Romane, memento ;*
> *Hæ tibi erunt artes, pacisque imponere morem,*
> *Parcere subjectis, et debellare superbos,—*[1]

may have contributed to his appreciation of the dignity of Colonial and Imperial administration. The
first Lord Lytton once wrote to him : ' It requires a
Scholar as well as a Statesman fully to appreciate
what Bacon calls " the heroic work of Colonisation." '
The same remark might be extended to the appreciation of Lord Beaconsfield's maxim that the British
Empire should be founded on the principles alike of
Imperium and *Libertas* ;—that is, Imperial control in

[1] *Æn.* VI. 851-3.

matters of Imperial concern, and local self-government in matters of local concern.

After taking his degree, Sir G. Bowen became a member of Lincoln's Inn, but he never practised at the Bar; his tastes and special capabilities lay elsewhere. In 1847 he was offered a post congenial to his Oxford training, the task of reorganising, as President, the Ionian University, which had been founded at Corfu in 1820 by an eminent scholar and philhellene, Frederick North, Earl of Guilford, as the chief centre of education for regenerate Greece. In congratulating him on this appointment, Dr. Liddell, the present Dean of Christ Church, wrote : ' for an Englishman to preside over the destinies of a Greek University is indeed a picture in the words of Æschylus [1] ' of great and hyperborean felicity.' The manner in which he performed his duties at Corfu on this temporary mission gained him the approval of the English Government and the thanks of the Ionian Senate. During his residence there he acquired a thorough knowledge of both the Italian and modern Greek languages, and made himself acquainted with Greece and the Greek provinces of Turkey, through which he made two extensive tours on horseback. The knowledge which he thus acquired of these regions and their various peoples was embodied in a practical form in the ' Handbook for Greece ' which he contributed to Mr. Murray's series; and which, like Ford's ' Handbook for Spain,' was intended for readers at home as well as for travellers abroad. Prefixed to this volume are several essays on Greek archæology, the Greek Church, and the history and language of

[1] Æschylus, *Choeph.* 373.

modern Greece. Another result of his quasi-Greek residence was his 'Ithaca in 1850,' which has been recognised by Mr. Gladstone and other Homeric scholars as a conclusive identification of that island with the island of Odysseus; while his 'Mount Athos, Thessaly, and Epirus,' was a graphic journal of a ride, in 1849, from Constantinople to Corfu across the principal provinces of European Turkey, including a visit to the celebrated monastic communities of Mount Athos, and Meteora, and to many parts of Albania, of which it was truly said by Gibbon, 'a country within sight of Italy is less known than the interior of America.' [1]

Several articles on these countries in the chief periodicals of the day were contributed by Sir George Bowen; and, at a later period, after a visit to the Prince of Montenegro, he wrote an article for the 'Edinburgh Review' (April 1859) which first drew general attention in England to the peculiar position of that principality, which has maintained its independence for more than four centuries against the Turks, 'rising, like Ararat, above the overwhelming flood of Mohammedan conquest.'

In 1848 occurred one of the most remarkable incidents of his life. Having suffered severely from Greek fever,[2] he was sent, on medical advice, for

---

[1] This book was favourably noticed in the *Edinburgh Review* for January, 1855.

[2] It is curious that Sir G. Bowen has ascended the three famous classical mountains of Ætna, Olympus, and Parnassus; and that the man who went up Ætna with him, a Polish Count, was afterwards hanged by the Russians for treason; the man who went up Olympus with him, an English colonel, afterwards died of fever; and that he himself barely escaped the same fate after going up Parnassus. He attributed his recovery to the friendly care of Sir Edmund (afterwards the first Lord)

change of air to Austria; and in October 1848 he witnessed the celebrated insurrection in Vienna and its capture by the Imperial troops under Prince Win-dischgrätz, and Baron Jellachich, the Ban of Croatia, who led to the rescue of the House of Hapsburg his wild levies from the Debatable Land between Christendom and Islam. They were looked upon in Vienna much as the Scotch Highlanders who followed Prince Charles Edward in 1745 were regarded in England. Sir G. Bowen's narrative of the events of which he was an eye-witness was contained in a letter to the Principal of Brasenose, who communicated it to the 'Times,' wherein it was published, with the editorial comment 'admirably graphic.' Extracts from it were reprinted in the 'Annual Register' for 1848, and a few passages may here be quoted.

'The Jägerzeile, the beautiful street leading to the Prater, had been the scene of the hardest fighting of all, as it had been fortified by the insurgents with a succession of barricades, built up to the first-floor windows in a half-moon shape, with regular embra-

Lyons, then British Minister at Athens, with whom he ever afterwards maintained a cordial friendship. A striking incident of the Crimean War was related to him by Lord Lyons when he visited Corfu in 1858 in command of the Mediterranean Fleet. He had always advo-cated a prompt attack instead of a regular siege of Sebastopol after the battle of the Alma. In confirmation of this policy, he recited a conversation with an old friend, a Russian Admiral, who described in graphic language how the chief Russian Commanders had stood watching the advance of the Allies from Balaklava, and expecting an immediate occupation of the town, which was then almost wholly unfortified on the south side; when suddenly the enemy was seen to halt and to begin his trenches and parallels instead of marching directly to the assault. Then Todleben threw his cap into the air, ex-claiming, 'Nous sommes sauvés! We are to have a regular siege. I will raise defences that will be hard to take.' And how he did it the history of that weary siege forcibly attests.

sures, and planted with cannon. This street was strewn with the dead bodies of men and horses; but they and the pools of blood all about did not strike us so much as the horrid smell of roast flesh, arising from the half-burnt bodies of insurgents killed in the houses fired by Congreve rockets, which we saw used by the Imperial troops with terrible effect. Half of the houses in this suburb were thus burnt down, while the other half were mostly riddled with shot and shell. On every side we could see weeping wives, sisters, and daughters picking literally piecemeal out of the ruins the mutilated bodies of their relatives.

'On Sunday evening, the 29th October, the city, dreading a bombardment from the Imperial batteries, agreed to surrender; but the capitulation was violated, when, early the next morning, the approach of the revolted Hungarians to raise the siege was signalled from the tower of St. Stephen's cathedral. Then came the real crisis. Most of the Imperial troops and guns were removed from the Leopoldstadt to meet the Hungarian enemy in the rear; while the remainder set to work to barricade the bridge which connects the suburb with the city, so as to prevent a sortie. There was a steady fire from the ramparts; and I, for the first time, literally tasted blood, which was dashed over my face and clothes when a round shot carried off the head of an artillery-man by my side. . . . Meanwhile the roar of cannon and the rattle of musketry in our rear told us that the Hungarians had joined battle to raise the siege; while in our front, from the ramparts and the roofs of the houses and churches, the insurgents were firing signal guns and waving flags to cheer them on. It was a dark, lowering autumn day, and all felt that there were trembling in the balance not only the fate of the grand old Austrian Empire, *An Siegen und an Ehren reich*,[1] the monarchy of Charles V. and of Maria Theresa, and long the bulwark of Christendom against the Turks—but with it the peace and safety of Europe. High above the roar of battle and the shouts of the combatants swung the solemn peal of the great bell of St. Stephen's, never before tolled except at the death of an Emperor, but which now seemed, when rung as a tocsin by the insurgents, to toll the knell of the Empire. . . .

'At length the firing behind us gradually slackened and then died away; and towards sunset the victorious Imperialists marched back from the field of battle, having utterly routed the Hungarians and driven three thousand of them into the Danube, which will roll their bodies down to Pesth—fearful tidings of their defeat. You may fancy what cheers now arose from the Imperialists, and what yells of despair from the insurgents, whose offers of a conditional surrender were scornfully rejected.

'All that night and the ensuing morning were devoted to the rest of the troops, wearied by the incessant fighting of the last week. But in the afternoon a fierce bombardment began from the batteries opposite the Burg Thor; and as it grew dark, Jellachich forced his way over the ramparts, his soldiers arriving in time to save the priceless treasures of art and science in the Imperial Palace, to which the rebels had set fire in their baffled rage and spite. . . . On

---

[1] 'Rich in victories and honours': so Austria is described in Arndt's famous national song, *Was ist des Deutschen Vaterland?*

that dreadful night of October 31st I saw Jellachich, a tall and magnificent-looking man, by the blaze of the burning houses and the flashing of a hundred cannon, lead his wild Croats to the storm, his white plume shining, like Henry IV's at Ivry, as the pole-star of the whole army. He seems to be one of those remarkable men who are raised up from time to time to sway the destinies of nations.'[1]

Hardly less impressive was Sir G. Bowen's journey across Hungary in 1849, at the great crisis in the history of Eastern Europe when that country was re-conquered by the Austrian and Russian armies after a resistance of nearly two years. He witnessed the siege of Comorn (then held by the Magyars under Klapka), and noted the strange variety of tongues spoken by the composite Austrian army; for the military orders of the day were printed in some twelve languages and dialects of languages—German, Italian, Hungarian, Roumanian, Polish, Bohemian, Croatian, Dalmatian, Servian, &c. From Buda-Pesth he proceeded down the Danube to Constantinople. At Vidin he found Kossuth and the other chief

[1] When Sir G. Bowen again visited Vienna, forty years later, in May 1888, he accompanied the English Ambassador to the grand inaugural ceremony of the monument of Maria Theresa, erected in front of the Palace Gate (Burg Thor), near the very spot where, in 1848, he had seen planted the Imperial batteries for the bombardment of the insurgent city. A generation had passed away, and in that vast and glittering assemblage where the Emperor and Empress stood encircled by all that is fair and noble in Vienna, it seemed that there were few but he who could explain the traces of the cannon-balls still visible on the huge blocks of stone which form the Burg Thor. Here too Sir G. Bowen renewed his old acquaintance with Dr. Smolka, still President, as he had been in 1848, of the Austrian Chamber of Deputies. The cordial greeting of these two survivors of a social and political state of affairs which had well-nigh disappeared, was noticed with interest in the Press of Vienna.

Hungarian leaders, who had fled into Turkey after the close of the war in Hungary.   The Austrians and Russians demanded their extradition, to which the Turks might have yielded had it not been for the energetic interposition of Sir Stratford Canning (afterwards Lord Stratford de Redcliffe), then the British Ambassador at the Porte.   Hearing that there was an Englishman on board the steamer, several of the refugees at Vidin came off with their wives and daughters, and implored him to take charge of a letter for the Ambassador, for, they pleaded, it was a matter of life or death.   He consented, at some personal risk, to take charge of this letter, and delivered it to the Ambassador, whose guest he became at his summer residence at Therapia on the Bosphorus. The result of Sir Stratford's action is well known. Aided by the French Ambassador, he saved the refugees, with vast and far-reaching consequences to the eastern world.[1]

In 1854 Sir George Bowen received his first political appointment.   He was recommended to the Queen by the Earl of Aberdeen, then Prime Minister, and the Duke of Newcastle, then Secretary of State for the Colonies, for the post, especially important at that crisis, of Chief Secretary of Government (under the Lord High Commissioner) in the Ionian Islands, which were then under the British protectorate.   His appointment shortly preceded the outbreak of the Crimean War in 1854; and during that struggle Corfu became the chief *point d'appui* and *place d'armes* of England in the Levant.   The normal difficulties of the protectorate of the Ionian Islands

---

[1] See S. Lane-Poole, *Life of Stratford Canning*, Vol. II., chap. 22.

conferred on the English Sovereign by the European Treaties of 1815,—always 'a tough and unprofitable job' (as the Duke of Wellington foretold it would prove),—were greatly increased by the excitement caused throughout the Greek nation by the war undertaken by England and France in defence of its hereditary foes, the Turks, and against its co-religionists and hereditary friends, the Russians. The strong feeling in favour of national union was further promoted in Greece by the similar feeling prevalent in Italy, Germany, and elsewhere. All fair-minded Ionians admitted that their English government was a just and efficient rule, and had conferred many material and social benefits on their country. But they preferred the chance of being even less well governed by their own countrymen to any rule whatsoever by foreigners. The Ionians argued somewhat in this fashion: 'We are thankful to England for undertaking our protection at a period when without such protection we should have fallen under the dominion of the Turks. But now that England has herself powerfully assisted, by her cannon at Pylos (Navarino) and by her influence in the councils of Europe, to create an independent Kingdom of Greece, we pray that we may be permitted to throw in our lot with our countrymen.'

This was practically the purport of the Address to the Queen unanimously adopted by the Ionian Parliament in 1858, when Mr. Gladstone was sent out as 'Lord High Commissioner Extraordinary,' to inquire and report on this complicated question. Sir George Bowen strongly advocated, in official reports and otherwise, that (if possible, and consistent with the faith of treaties), the proper course for England to pursue would be to give up to the Kingdom of Greece the southern Ionian Islands (Cephalonia, Ithaca, Leucadia, Zante, and Cerigo) which lay along the coasts of that kingdom, and where the population and their sympathies were purely Hellenic ; and to incorporate with the British Empire (like Malta and Gibraltar), Corfu, with, of course, its tiny satellite Paxo, which lay off the coast of the Turkish province of Albania, and where all the upper classes and a considerable part of the general population were Italian rather than Hellenic in language, feeling, and customs. Moreover, large sums of money had been spent on the fortifications of Corfu, whereas there were practically no strongholds in the southern islands. Again, he urged an argument which, in the light of later events, is a proof of political foresight. He showed that Corfu had always been of supreme importance, both in ancient and modern times, as a commanding naval and military station, controlling the entrance to the Adriatic Sea. Corfu, the Corcyra of old, in the most brilliant period of Greek history was the greatest naval power in Western Greece, and the natural base of operations between Athens and the Greek colonies in Italy and Sicily. Here assembled the famous expedition of Athens and her allies against Syracuse, which was the turning point of the Peloponnesian War. Here was the rendezvous of the fleets of Augustus before the battle of Actium, and of Don John of Austria before the battle of Lepanto—two of the most decisive battles of the world. So, in Roman times, Corcyra became the chief connecting link, with its opposite and neighbouring port of Brundusium (Brindisi) between Italy and Greece, the West and the East. In 1859, and for many years afterwards, Marseilles was the point of departure and arrival for mails and passengers to the East; the Suez Canal had not been completed ; and railways did not exist in Southern Italy. But Sir G. Bowen foretold that the time would come when the overland route to Egypt and the East would resume its ancient channel by Brindisi, and that then the possession by England of the beautiful and historic island of Corfu would mean the practical control of that route. The importance of such a position to England needs no demonstration. The ultimate result of Mr. Gladstone's mission, however, was the surrender of Corfu, together with the southern Ionian Islands, to Greece in 1864. Doubtless there were grave diplomatic difficulties, arising from the jealousy of the other great Powers, which obstructed the course preferable for the interests of England.[1]

While Secretary of Government in the Ionian Islands, Sir George Bowen married the Countess Diamantina Roma, daughter of His Highness Count Candiano Roma, G.C.M.G., President of the Ionian Senate—a nobleman of an ancient Venetian family, possessed of large estates in the island of Zante. Lady Bowen's name is a ' household word ' in the Colonies which her husband has ruled, and is held in grateful remembrance in consequence of her exertions in support of charitable institutions, and of the grace

[1] Moreover, much difficulty was created by the premature publication in a London journal of a copy (purloined from the Colonial Office) of a despatch from the Lord High Commissioner (Sir John Young, afterwards Lord Lisgar), in which the above-mentioned views were advocated.

with which she presided over the constant hospitalities of the Government Houses.

During his wedding tour in England, Sir George wrote as follows:

To a political Friend.

London: July, 1856.

The most interesting event of my brief stay in London was the interview to which I was invited by the Prime Minister, Lord Palmerston. As I had travelled so much in Greece and in the Greek provinces of Turkey, and as my official position in the Ionian Isles has given me peculiar opportunities of observation, I was enabled to answer fully the acute questions put to me by him concerning Greek and Turkish affairs. He referred also to the famous Pacifico case, concerning which his policy and action were so powerfully attacked in Parliament in 1850, and were regarded unfavourably by many even of his political adherents. In his earlier career, when connected with Canning, the constant friend of Greece, he seemed inclined to Philhellenic views; but he has now been long ill-disposed towards the Greeks, and determined, from policy rather than from personal feeling, and from hostility to Russia rather than from friendship for Turkey, to support the Turks. I do not think it right to place on record, even in a private letter, the details of our conversation on political subjects; but there can be no reason why I should not tell you that, after he had finished picking my brains on Greek politics, he turned the conversation to questions of Greek scholarship. He remarked, very truly, on the many points of similarity between the ancient and the modern Greeks; but did not go so far as the French Consul at Athens, who assured Lord Byron in 1810, that 'the Greeks are the same *canaille* as in the days of Themistocles!' He was also far in advance of most English scholars of the present day in agreeing with me that the modern Greek language is practically the same with the ancient language, and not a different language, as Italian differs from Latin.

I pointed out, moreover, that it can be proved by many arguments, that the ancient Greeks must have pronounced the vowels and diphthongs in the same way as the moderns; and that the only real difficulty is respecting the accents, for modern Greeks pronounce according to accent and not according to quantity. But then, as a Greek scholar once remarked to me, 'the accents were first invented in the decline of the language, and must have been invented to preserve the right pronunciation. Englishmen talk as if they were invented only to puzzle English schoolboys!' Lord Palmerston related to me, with much glee, the controversy which had arisen about the proper pronunciation of the name of his mare Ilione, well known on the English turf. He himself pronounced it in the Greek way, Ilióne, whereas large bets had been laid that it should be pronounced Ilíone, and an amusing ballad had been written on the subject by, of all people, a Scotch judge (Lord Neave).

I observed that we must necessarily pronounce either by quantity or by accent ; so Ilíone, on English principles, must be wrong: we must say either Iliŏnē according to quantity, or Ilióne according to accent. In reply to other queries, I explained that the modern Greeks pronounce η, ι, ει, οι, υ, υι, all like the Italian *i*, and that consequently ἡμεῖς, *we*, and ὑμεῖς, *you*, are pronounced identically. ' Ah ! they confound *we* and *you*, do they ? ' said Lord Palmerston ; ' I fear that is not the only way in which modern Greeks confound *meum* and *tuum* ! '

I think this is as good a *mot* as even the best of those ascribed to Lord Palmerston ; as, for instance, when he advocated granting permission to marry a deceased wife's sister on the ground that ' a man might thus have two wives and only one mother-in-law ' ; or when he defended putting some pictures in the basement story, or cellars, of the National Gallery, on the principle that *ars est celare artem.*

I may here mention that, in discussing the question of Greek pronunciation with Bishop Wilberforce, he told me that he recently had as a candidate at one of his ordinations, Mr. M., the son of an English merchant settled in Greece. ' I examined him myself,' said the Bishop, ' in the Greek Testament, when he used what to me was an unknown pronunciation. " Oh ! Mr. M.," I cried, " where *did* you learn Greek ? " " *At Athens,* my lord," faltered out the trembling candidate.'

For other information about the modern Greek

language, I would refer you to my remarks on that subject in the introduction to the 'Handbook for Greece.' It will be seen that the English mode of pronouncing Greek was invented by Erasmus early in the sixteenth century, and as a badge of Protestantism ; for our Universities were then divided into parties calling themselves *Greeks* and *Trojans*—i.e. *Catholics* and *Protestants* respectively. Since that time, says honest old Fuller, ' We English speak Greek, and understand each other, which nobody else in the world can.'

Differing widely as I do from much of Lord Palmerston's policy, my practical acquaintance with the Levant enables me to agree with Mr. Disraeli, who remarks in 'Tancred,'[1] that 'whatever difference of opinion may exist as to the policy pursued by the Foreign Minister of England with respect to the settlement of the Turkish Empire in 1840–1, none can be permitted, by those at least competent to decide upon such questions, as to the ability with which that policy was accomplished.' The policy of 1840–1 sounded the key-note of Lord Palmerston's subsequent policy in the Levant.

À propos of 'Tancred,' I may mention that Disraeli considered that book to contain the best record of his views on the Eastern questions therein discussed ; for when a political friend of mine, and supporter of his, asked him some question on the subject, he replied, ' You should read what I say in " Tancred " on that point.'

[1] Book III. chap. 6.

CHAPTER III.

PROMOTION TO G.C.M.G.—TO QUEENSLAND—TO NEW ZEALAND—
TO VICTORIA—ON LEAVE IN ITALY—KING VICTOR EMMANUEL
—PIUS IX.—GARIBALDI—KING HUMBERT—LEO XIII.—THE
VATICAN AND IRELAND—ITALIAN POLITICS.

IN recognition of his services in the Ionian Islands, Sir George Bowen, who had in 1856 been created a K.C.M.G., was appointed on the recommendation of the then Secretary of State for the Colonies, Sir E. Bulwer Lytton, to be the first Governor of the new Colony of Queensland in Australia. We shall show in subsequent chapters how he helped to raise that country from small beginnings to a noble growth. In 1860 the Queen promoted him to the Grand Cross of St. Michael and St. George in token of approval of the manner in which he had organised the new Colony ; and he enjoyed the rare honour of having the usual term of a Governor's office (six years) extended to eight years. At the close of 1867, on the recommendation of the Colonial Minister (the late Duke of Buckingham), he was promoted from Queensland to New Zealand, then the most difficult of our Colonial Governments ; where the Maori War, which had virtually lasted for ten years (1860–1870), was brought to a close under his auspices, and a durable peace was established between the contending races. From 1873 to 1879 he was Governor of Victoria, long the most energetic, populous, and progressive of the Australian Colonies, which passed safely during his administration through a very severe political crisis and parliamentary deadlock, caused by a prolonged dispute between the two Houses of the Legislature.

As the Secretary of State, Lord Knutsford, observed in Parliament in 1887, Sir George Bowen was absent on leave for only eighteen months in the aggregate during the first twenty-nine years of his service abroad. He left Corfu for six months in 1856, on his marriage tour, and he took a year's leave from Victoria in 1875, when his presence in England was required on urgent private affairs after a continued absence of sixteen years. On his way home from Melbourne, in 1875, he spent ten days with the Governor of Bombay (Sir Philip Wodehouse), visiting Poona, the Caves of Elephanta, &c., and then proceeded to England by Brindisi and Rome. In the Italian capital he was received cordially by Victor Emmanuel and by the present King and Queen, then Prince and Princess of Piedmont, in consequence of his having entertained at Melbourne the Duke of Genoa (Prince Thomas of Savoy, the nephew of the King, and brother of the Princess Margaret), when in 1873 he visited Australia as an officer of the Italian frigate 'Garibaldi.'[1]

---

[1] When Sir G. Bowen visited Spezzia, in the spring of 1887, the Duke of Genoa was there in command of an Italian ironclad, and showed him much courtesy and hospitality, He also telegraphed to his Duchess (a Bavarian princess) to invite his friend to dinner at Turin when he passed through that city on his return to England. The Palace of the Duke of Genoa and the Opera House occupy opposite sides of the Royal Palace, untenanted since the King and Queen have resided at Rome, but famous for its armoury, probably the finest in Europe after that at Madrid. After dinner the Duchess invited Sir George to accompany her to the opera in a very striking procession,

One of Sir George's interviews with Victor Emmanuel was characteristic of the *Re Galantuomo*. At 8 A.M. he found the King dressed in a shooting-jacket in his roughly furnished room on the ground floor of the Quirinal. After his usual bluff and hearty greeting, he made him sit down beside him on two common wooden chairs—which, with a plain table and two benches for the Ministers when they attend the Council, formed the only furniture. The conversation that ensued was carried on in Italian, and was very frank and friendly. His Majesty remarked that he had followed the example of the Queen of England with regard to her son (the Duke of Edinburgh) in putting his nephew the Duke of Genoa into the Royal Navy, which he hoped would soon revive the old maritime glory of Italy. He added that he was entirely satisfied with both his army and navy; that he was aware that some foreigners were of opinion that both those forces were maintained on too large and expensive a scale for the revenue of the new Kingdom; but that the fact was that they were required not only to secure the recently consolidated State in its proper position as one of the Great Powers of Europe, but also as a school of Italian nationality, in which the various component parts of the nation, the Piedmontese, Lombards, Venetians, Genoese, Tuscans, Romans, Modenese, Neapolitans, and Sicilians, should learn to speak and feel like one people. His visitor here remarked that it was delightful for

preceded by several soldiers of the Guard bearing *flambeaux*, along the dark and silent halls of the Royal Palace, the light of the torches playing fitfully on the arms and banners—until the Princess with her guest reached the full blaze of the illuminated theatre.

him, as a sincere friend of Italy, to return to Rome after
an absence of twenty years, and find the country which
he had formerly known when divided into seven separate States, now united in one.—' Yes,' said the King,
'our House of Savoy has had great good fortune.' 'Will
your Majesty permit me to say that the House of Savoy
has had great merit ?' 'Ah !' said the King, 'we have
been bold (*siamo stati audaci*).' Here Sir George remarked : 'What says the great Italian poet Virgil,
Audaces Fortuna——' '*Juvat*,' added the King. He
spoke with deep respect of Pope Pius IX., saying 'We
are Italians, but we are also Catholics, and we revere the
Pope as the head of our religion.' Reference having
been made to the measures then (1875) being taken
by Prince Bismarck against the Roman Catholic clergy
in Prussia, the King observed with a smile, ' I fear
Bismarck does not know how to treat priests as well
as I do. One should treat priests much as one treats
women (*Bisogna trattare i Preti come si tratta le
donne*); one should treat them with perfect respect,
courtesy, and indulgence, but one should not allow
them to have too much money or too much political
influence.' When Sir George observed that he supposed that Bismarck was more hot-tempered (*passionato*) than Cavour, the King replied, ' Cavour also
was *passionato*, but I reined him in '—making a
gesture with his hands as if curbing a mettlesome
horse. The conversation then turned to the Franco-
German war and the fall of Napoleon III. The King
lamented the imprudent conduct of M. Benedetti, the
French Ambassador at Berlin in 1870—*quel benedetto
Benedetti*, as he styled him. 'I warned my friend the
Emperor,' continued his Majesty, ' that his army was

not in a fit state to cope with the Prussian veterans
who conquered at Sadowa ; a large portion of the
French troops had been employed in hunting Arabs
in Algeria, which really is little better as a preparation for European warfare than your hunting kangaroos in Australia.' At this point, the Ministers
arrived for a Council, and Victor Emmanuel dismissed his visitor with a hearty shake of the hand,
saying, ' *Mio caro amico*, I thank you once more for
your kindness to my nephew.'

This interview with the King was followed by a
dinner at the Quirinal. On the next day Sir George
Bowen had interviews with the Pope and with Garibaldi. The hours fixed for these only allowed just
time enough to drive from the Vatican to the villa
outside the walls which was then inhabited by the
great patriot. So on his visit to Rome in 1881, it
happened that both King Humbert and Pope Leo
XIII. fixed the same day for receiving him, and he
had only just time to drive direct from the Vatican
to the Quirinal.

Sir George Bowen had always maintained friendly
relations alike with the Anglican and with the Roman
Catholic Bishops in the several Colonies over which
he had presided. Some of these latter had mentioned
his name favourably in their correspondence with the
Vatican, and the consequence was his admission to
a private interview with Pius IX. in 1875 and with
Leo XIII. in 1881. On entering the ante-chamber
to the former's private audience-room he was courteously received by several Cardinals and other dignitaries. On his remarking on the fine view over the
city and the Campagna to the Alban and Sabine

mountains from the windows of the Vatican, 'the most interesting palace in Europe,' a prelate who from the accent with which he spoke Italian seemed to be a foreigner, exclaimed, ' Formerly it was a palace, now it is a prison' (*Prima era palazzo, adesso è prigione*). But this exclamation was courteously rebuked or excused by the Italian Cardinals and Prelates standing by. They seemed to feel that it was improper to introduce papal politics in the presence of a foreigner, whose personal feelings might be *froissés*, and who was for the moment the guest of the Holy Father. Sir George related that he remembered how, on one of his earlier visits to the Eternal City, in 1846, at the time of the election of Pio Nono, the walls were covered with huge placards bearing the words *Grati nomi, Amnistia e Ferrovia* (Pleasant words, amnesty and railroad), which form an anagram on the name of the new Pope, *Giovanni Maria Mastaï-Ferretti* (as the name of *Horatio Nelson* makes ' *Honor est a Nilo*'); and alluded to His Holiness having granted two most popular boons, refused by his predecessor, a political amnesty and permission to construct railways in the Papal States. One of the Cardinals said, ' I hope your Excellency will repeat that to the Holy Father at your audience, for it will please him.' Accordingly, when admitted, and asked by the Pope the inevitable question, 'Have you been at Rome before?' his visitor repeated the reminiscence, at which the Pope smiled, but said merely: ' You have a good memory.' Pius IX. was then fully eighty years of age, but he was still vigorous in mind and body—*di stupenda salute*, as an Italian statesman said. He asked several questions about Australia, and showed more acquaintance with that country than is possessed by most English Bishops. It is believed that the reports of the Roman Catholic Bishops abroad to the Vatican are very complete. Leo XIII., Cardinals Howard, Jacobini, and many other Roman dignitaries, displayed similarly accurate knowledge of the British Colonies.

It was a sudden and striking change to drive in less than an hour from the historic Vatican, and the Pope and his ecclesiastical *entourage*, to the modern villa in which Garibaldi—the persistent enemy of the temporal power of the Holy Father—sat in his well-known 'red shirt,' surrounded by many of the rough soldiers who had been with him throughout those wonderful expeditions that had proved so fatal alike to thrones and altars. It need scarcely be said that the visitor neither told the Pope that he was going from him to Garibaldi, nor Garibaldi that he had come to him from the Pope. He was received with the habitually simple yet dignified courtesy of Garibaldi, who thanked him for his kindness at Melbourne to his son Ricciotti, who had married an English-woman and emigrated to Australia. He mentioned that in 1852 he had himself visited the Australian waters in an Italian merchant-ship, and that he had ever since taken a warm interest in the progress of the British Colonies in Australia.

Six years later, Sir George Bowen, while Governor of Mauritius, was again in Rome ; and as we shall not have occasion to revert to the affairs of Italy, some letters written during this visit may here be quoted. They illustrate very clearly the views of the Vatican on the Irish question.

To an English Statesman.

Rome : January 24, 1881.

My dear Lord, . . .

Writing from Rome, I may perhaps be expected to say something about the affairs of Italy, in which I believe you are much interested. I have always taken a warm interest in the progress of Italy, and my long service at Corfu made me master of Italian, without a thorough knowledge of which language no stranger can really understand the Italians. I have also the advantage of having entertained at Melbourne, while I was Governor of Victoria, the Duke of Genoa, the 'sailor prince' of Italy, and brother to the reigning Queen. Consequently I have received the most gratifying attentions and hospitality at the Quirinal, and from the court generally; while through our ambassador, Sir Augustus Paget (my old friend and former schoolfellow), I am personally acquainted with the leading statesmen of all parties. On the other hand, I used frequently to ask the Roman Catholic Bishop of Mauritius to dinner, and from what I hope is more than the proverbial 'lively sense of future favours,' he has represented me to the Vatican as a sort of colonial Charlemagne ! So the Pope will give me a private audience next week, and has directed that every facility shall be granted me at the Vatican. I have already had interviews, and most interesting conversations, with Cardinal Nina, the late, and Cardinal Jacobini, the present, Secretary of State (i.e. Prime Minister of the

Pope), who spoke to me in a very frank and friendly way on many subjects. In particular, they both asked earnestly what I thought of the Pope's letter of January 3rd ult. to the Roman Catholic Bishops in Ireland. Of course I told them that I thought it excellent. The Vatican probably has gone quite as far as it could safely go in discouraging the present agitation in Ireland. Cardinal Jacobini remarked that the Fenians were regarded at the Vatican as a kind of Communists—a feeling which I encouraged, adding that it was everywhere hoped that the Vatican would continue to support the cause of law and order in Ireland. There was one point in Cardinal Jacobini's remarks which will, I think, specially interest you. Mr. Gladstone is regarded by the overwhelming majority of Italians as the chief foreign founder of Italian nationality, and with almost the same sort of affectionate veneration as that with which the Americans regard Lafayette. But I am free to confess that I was not prepared, after certain papers which he published some years back, to find that Mr. Gladstone's name appears to stand so well also at the Vatican. And yet Cardinal Jacobini spoke to me of the sense entertained there of the conduct of the party now again in power in England in removing all religious inequalities and Roman Catholic disabilities in Ireland, and in allowing full liberty in the British dominions to the Jesuits and other religious corporations recently expelled from France. He gave me the impression that the Vatican feels that it owes a practical return for this conduct on the part of the English Government.

I was very much struck with the statesmanlike views of Cardinal Jacobini. He is said to have more than the ability, without the equivocal personal character and political unscrupulousness, of Cardinal Antonelli. Indeed I have heard him described here as the 'ablest and best Papal Minister since Consalvi.' He was for many years Nuncio in Germany, and is said to be the only ecclesiastic who ever measured swords with any success with Bismarck. Moreover, he is a younger man than most papal functionaries, being only forty-nine, which (as you will recollect) Aristotle declared to be the prime of the intellect, as thirty-five is of the body.

I have also established friendly relations with Cardinal Howard and other prominent ecclesiastics. Indeed my 'officious' and personal relations with the Vatican are almost as cordial as with the Quirinal.

There can, I think, be no doubt of the successful consolidation of the Italian kingdom and dynasty. Of course, there are some *codini*, or reactionists, especially among that portion of the Roman nobility which sprang from the papal families. I met also at Lady Holland's charming parties at Naples some members of the old Neapolitan *noblesse*, who not unnaturally regret, but more, I fancied, in a social than in a political view, the loss of the local court and *corps diplomatique*. There is a similar feeling among a small *clique* also at Florence, Turin, and the other disestablished capitals ; but the best judges, native and foreign, believe that these feelings will pass away with the present generation.

On the other hand, Garibaldi's extravagancies have destroyed his influence except with a section of the people. I have heard several even of the advanced Liberals express their regret that he had not been, like Victor Emmanuel, *felix opportunitate mortis*, when his great work in the unification of Italy had been accomplished.

To the Same.

Rome, February 21, 1881.

My dear Lord,

Since I wrote to you on the 24th ultimo, I have had another most interesting interview with Cardinal Jacobini, and I have also been favoured with a private audience by the Pope, who received me in the most gratifying manner. His Holiness began by saying that he had given me a special audience because he wished to tell me that there were on record at the Vatican letters from the Catholic Bishops in the several Colonies that I had governed, and that they all expressed a high sense of the good offices which they had received from me; and that he (the Pope) desired to convey to me the expression of his entire satisfaction and thanks (*piena soddisfazione e ringraziamenti*). I replied (in Italian) that anything I had been able to do in the matter of which his Holiness had been pleased to speak in such gratifying terms was simply my duty, and in the execution of the instructions, and in carrying out the general policy of the English Government. The Pope rejoined that he had every reason to be satisfied with the instructions issued by the English Government to the authorities in the British Colonies with respect to their conduct towards the Catholic ecclesiastics, Bishops, Vicars Apostolic, and others; and that he was confident that these instructions would always be faithfully carried out by all the Viceroys and Governors as they had been by me. He added that he had especial reason to be satisfied with what had been done in this way recently ' at Calcutta and Malta.' I now thought that, after these compliments to myself and my Government, the time had arrived for me to say in my turn something pleasant, so I spoke to the following effect: ' *Santissimo Padre*, it must be very gratifying to every Englishman to learn that your Holiness has been pleased to express yourself in terms of satisfaction with the acts of the English Government, and of its servants, who, I repeat, have simply discharged their duty by carrying out their instructions. On the other hand, though I have no special authority to speak on behalf of the English Government, I feel confident that every Englishman is deeply sensible of the valuable support afforded by your Holiness to the cause of law and order in addressing to the Catholic Bishops in Ireland the excellent letter of January 3rd ult., which cannot fail to produce results favourable to public tranquillity.' I observed that the Pope 'pricked up his ears' (if one may use so familiar a phrase with regard to so great and sacred a personage) when I mentioned the word 'Ireland,' and that he listened to my remarks with profound attention, keeping his eyes fixed on mine. After a moment's pause, he replied, in very measured and decisive language and tone, nearly as follows:

'Yes, I addressed the Irish Bishops in support of the cause of order. Let the people of Ireland bring forward their grievances and complaints by way of petition and by legal and constitutional means (*per via di petizione e con mezzi legali e costituzionali*), but the Holy See will always support public order and discourage all revolutionary measures (*ogni misura rivoluzionaria*).'

The Pope then spoke of other matters;—of the Vatican Library, of which, as a learned theologian and accomplished scholar, he is a munificent supporter; and of my family, for he had kindly allowed me to bring my daughters with me to the audience. While speaking to me, he held in his hand, in a most gracious and paternal manner, the hand of my youngest daughter, a girl of twelve. He finally dismissed us with his blessing, laying his hand on the head of each of us; and he added that he would send the Apostolic Benediction 'to the faithful in your island of Mauritius (*a' fedeli nella vostra Isola di Maurizio*).'

I have had long conversations, to the same effect with that sketched above, with Cardinal Jacobini, Cardinal Howard, and other leading functionaries of

the Vatican.   All that I see and hear in Rome fully
confirms the belief that the Vatican would help us as
far as it can in our Irish difficulties; but the Irish
priests are nearly all taken from, and dependent upon,
the mass of the people; and, while they can do a
good deal to swell the cry against England, they have
little power if they try to stem the tide of popular
enmity to us.

I did not think it right to speak to the Pope on
a subject which is ' exercising ' the Vatican consi-
derably, and on which His Holiness recently spoke
strongly to a friend of mine—an English Roman
Catholic.   I refer to the re-establishment of at least
the former ' officious ' diplomatic relations, as carried
on with the Holy See by Lord Odo Russell, Lord Lyons,
and other members of our *corps diplomatique*.   The
Pope complained to the friend to whom I allude, that
he was often pressed indirectly to do good offices for
England with respect to Ireland, the Colonies, and
otherwise, and yet that the Holy See was not recognised by the English Government even in the modified
way of former years.   I should much have liked to
have spoken to the Pope on this point, to which
Cardinals Jacobini' and Howard had directed my
attention, but I abstained from doing so, partly on
account of my official position as an English Governor,
and partly because I have reason to know that my
friend Sir Augustus Paget is not favourable to the resumption of any diplomatic relations with the Vatican.
He can, and does, get things done sometimes, chiefly

through Cardinal Howard; but Cardinal Howard told me, in the strongest language, that he was thus placed in a most invidious position; that the Irish Bishops and clergy had come to suspect him, as an Englishman, of prejudicing the Vatican against Ireland; and that he was subjected to many slights and attacks in consequence. I may mention *en passant* that I frequently see here on friendly terms not only Cardinal Howard, but also Bishop Clifford (of Clifton), Bishop Vaughan (of Salford), Algernon Stanley (a brother of Lord Stanley of Alderley and a recent convert), and other English Roman Catholics of good family; and that they all scarcely conceal their dislike for some of the Irish clergy. However, this feeling evidently arises, in great part, from the want of sympathy of polished English gentlemen for persons whose manners often betray the peasant class from which they sprang. One of the most prominent of the Irish Prelates is Dr. Croke, now Roman Catholic Archbishop of Cashel, but who was Bishop of Auckland while I was Governor of New Zealand. He dined with me in 1871 while the Duke of Edinburgh was my guest in that Colony; when a naval officer said of him: 'By Jove, Sir George, this Irish Bishop has got a brogue on which you might hang your hat!'

There is undoubtedly a strong feeling at the Vatican in favour of the resumption of some kind of diplomatic relations with England; and this feeling is shared by the English here who have given attention

to the subject; and in particular, by Sir Henry
Layard, who is spending the winter at Rome, and
with whom I am carefully studying Roman art and
antiquities. Of course I am aware of the practical
difficulties in the way of either establishing 'official'
or renewing 'officious' relations.[1]

You will smile to hear that the King appointed for
his private interview with me the day appointed also
for my private interview with the Pope. Cardinal
Jacobini had given me an order for admission that
morning to the Pope's chapel at the Vatican, where
a solemn service, with the *Dies Iræ*, was performed
on the anniversary of the death of the late Pope,
in the presence of his successor and of the College
of Cardinals. I had some difficulty in hurrying
from the Vatican in time to present myself at the
Quirinal at the hour appointed by his Majesty. I
had a most interesting conversation with the King, who
spoke much of the progress of Italy, and of his recent
triumphal tour in Sicily and in the south. '*Non ci
manca altro che il danaro* (Nothing but money is
wanting to us),' was his summary of the position of
his Kingdom. You are aware that the Government
and Parliament are about to abolish inconvertible
paper, and to return to what the Americans call
'hard money.'

[1] On a visit to a country house in Ireland in the autumn of 1887,
Sir George Bowen met Monsignor Persico, whom Pope Leo XIII.
had sent to inquire and report on Irish affairs, and had much conversation with him; saying 'I am confident, Monsignor, that your
Report to the Vatican will be such that no Englishman will have to
say with Horace, "*Persicos odi, puer, apparatus.*" ' (*Carm.* I. 38.)

His Majesty proceeded to refer to English affairs, and spoke of Mr. Gladstone. He said that he had carefully studied the course of recent parliamentary proceedings in England, and that he felt certain that Gladstone and his Ministry would triumph over Irish disaffection and obstruction.[1] There is evidently even less sympathy for the Irish agitators at the Quirinal than at the Vatican. I was sorry to see the King look worn and weary. He is known to work much harder than most constitutional sovereigns. He observed that I must have sometimes felt tired of my exile of above twenty years from Europe as a Colonial Governor, but that he supposed that, like himself, I found consolation in the diligent discharge of my duty. He added that the day was often too short for all he had to do in his cabinet, in visiting public institutions, &c., and that his only recreation was an occasional day's shooting or hunting. King Humbert is generally regarded, like his father, as a thoroughly *honest* man—*re galantuomo*; while *la Perla d'Italia*, as the Italians delight to call Queen Margaret, is beloved for her grace and goodness, like our Princess of Wales.

As you are doubtless aware, Roman society is divided into *Bianchi* and *Neri*, i.e. adherents of the King and of the Pope, respectively; divisions somewhat analogous to those of the Guelphs and Ghibe-

[1] It will be recollected that this letter was written in 1881, and that Mr. Gladstone did not change his policy concerning Irish affairs till 1886.

lines in Italy in the Middle Ages, and of the Jacobites and Hanoverians in England during the first half of the eighteenth century. I need scarcely assure you that we are strictly neutral, and go one night to a Court ball among the *Bianchi*, and the next night to a ball of the *Neri*, among Princes Borghese, Altieri, and the other great papal families, and the ambassadors accredited to the Pope. It is believed that the *Jacobite* feeling will die out gradually in Italy, as in England. The younger Roman princes are gradually succumbing to the smiles of the Queen and the brilliancy of the Quirinal. What a revolution it is! When I was first at Rome in 1845, how little I dreamed that I should live to dine with a King of Italy in the old palace of the Popes!

There can, I think, be no question of the success of constitutional government in Italy. I attend frequently the debates in both Houses of the Italian Parliament (in which, by the way, I am always given a place of honour, as an English Governor—a distinction not accorded at home to English Ambassadors and Governors). The proceedings of the Italian Senate are as decorous as those of the English House of Lords. As an Italian Statesman remarked to me yesterday, *Non abbiamo una Irlanda nel nostro regno.*' The speeches of the leading members of both sides are practical and businesslike; without, I think, much pretension to eloquence. A fortnight ago there was a meeting at Rome of delegates of the Radical party from all parts of Italy; avowedly in favour of universal

suffrage, but really with republican objects. The
Government prohibited the meeting taking place on
the Capitol, as the promoters wished, and the whole
thing was a ludicrous *fiasco*, the Romans treating the
entire movement with contemptuous indifference.
The Italians are very proud of their showing themselves so much more capable of steady Parliamentary
self-government than the other chief nations of the
Latin race—the French and the Spaniards. I have
asked several Italian Statesmen to what they ascribe
this unquestionable superiority. They ascribe it partly
to their historical traditions of the old Roman constitution, and still more to their long training under
their municipalities in modern times. I fancy that
they are more indebted than they would like to
admit to the strong admixture of Teutonic blood in
modern Italy, through the Lombards, Normans, and
other northern invaders, and through the vast number
of northern captives imported by the old Romans.
The modern French are more Gauls, i.e. Celts (like
the Irish) than Franks; and the modern Spaniards
more Iberians (i.e. probably Basques) than Visigoths.
I was at a ball last night at the German embassy on
the Capitol (the house inhabited by Niebuhr and
Bunsen when Prussian ministers at Rome), and it was
interesting to hear this *Teutonic* theory strongly advocated in the old Roman fortress and sanctuary on
the top of the Tarpeian Rock.

CHAPTER IV.

ON LEAVE IN ENGLAND AND AMERICA—ENTERTAINED AT A PUBLIC
DINNER IN LONDON WITH THE DUKE OF EDINBURGH IN THE
CHAIR — VARIETIES OF LIFE IN ENGLAND, CANADA, AND
THE UNITED STATES—LORD DUFFERIN—PRESIDENT GRANT—
AMERICAN POLITICS—THE MORMONS—BRIGHAM YOUNG—SAN
FRANCISCO—' THE STARS AND BARS '—MISS LEE OF VIRGINIA
—RETURN TO MELBOURNE.

To return to 1875. Sir George Bowen travelled
from Rome direct to London, stopping only for a day
or two at Paris, to see the British Ambassador, Lord
Lyons, whom he had known twenty years before at
Athens, where he began his distinguished career as
Attaché to his father, then British Minister in Greece,
but afterwards the Admiral commanding our fleet
during the Crimean War. On his arrival in London,
Sir George Bowen was entertained at a public dinner
attended by nearly three hundred leading Statesmen
and politicians of all parties, and prominent Colonists
from all quarters of the Empire, with the Duke of
Edinburgh in the chair. We believe that this was the
first occasion on which any one of the Queen's sons
presided at an entertainment given to an individual.[1]

Lockhart, in his Life of Scott,[2] remarks that
the range of the society in which Sir Walter mixed

[1] In the chapters on Victoria and Mauritius will be found a full
report of this banquet, and also of that given to Sir George Bowen at
Paris in 1881 by the French planters of Mauritius. See Vol. II. chaps.
23 and 31.   [2] Vol. VI. (*first Edition*) chap. 11.

on his visits to London is strikingly exemplified
in the record of one day, when we find him break-
fasting at the Royal Lodge in Windsor Park, and
supping in ' honest Dan Terry's house like a squirrel-
cage' above the Adelphi Theatre.   A single day of
Sir George Bowen's social life puts even this versa-
tility into the shade.   It began with a reception by
the Queen, and luncheon at Windsor Castle.   The
same evening he was present at a dinner given in
London by the members of Trinity College, Oxford,
of which he had been a Scholar.   Lord Selborne, the
late Lord Chancellor, who had also been a Scholar of
Trinity, was in the chair.   Later on the same night,
Sir G. Bowen had accepted an invitation from Mr.
Henry Irving to attend the representation of ' Faust '
at the Lyceum Theatre, and afterwards to a supper
on the stage.   He got back from Windsor just in
time for the Trinity dinner, and he effected his retreat
from the dinner just in time to see the last act of
' Faust,' and to be received on the stage by Mr. Irving
in the costume worn as Mephistopheles.   On his explaining why he had to leave the dinner before the
company dispersed, a prominent politician present
said : ' You certainly have had an eventful day.   You
lunch with the *Queen*, you dine with the *Trinity*, and
you sup with the *Devil*! '

This was in 1886; but similar crowded days
occurred during his visit to England in 1875.   On one
day he was invited to dinner by the Archbishop of
Canterbury (Tait) and by the Prime Minister (Disraeli).
The ecclesiastical invitation came first and was accepted, so the bidding of the Premier had to be declined.   Mentioning this to Mr. Robert Lowe (now

Lord Sherbrooke), who supposed that the Archbishop would of course be thrown over for the Prime Minister, Sir George declared that he should stick to the prior engagement. 'How unwise!' said his friend. 'What possible good can an Archbishop be to a Governor? Oh! I see how it is. You are tired of being a Colonial *Governor* and wish to become a Colonial *Bishop*!'

In September 1875, Sir George Bowen, attended by his A.D.C. Major Pitt, R.A., left England to return to Victoria by way of America; his family proceeding shortly after by the less fatiguing Suez route, and rejoining him at Melbourne. At New York he remained a week and saw some of the best American society; thence he proceeded up the Hudson and by railway to Stockbridge in Massachusetts, a beautiful village with an ivy-covered church—like a country village and church in England—where he was the guest of Mr. Dudley Field, the eminent New York lawyer; thence to Boston, where he had letters of introduction to Longfellow, Oliver Wendell Holmes, Russell Lowell, and other eminent men; and where, as an Oxford scholar, he was entertained by the President of Harvard University. A letter written from Washington gives some further account of this tour in Canada and the United States.

To the Earl of Carnarvon.

Washington, November 22, 1875.

My dear Lord,

Mr. Herbert may probably have laid before you the letter which I wrote to him last month, while I

was staying with Lord Dufferin in Canada. I had
then seen New York, Boston (where I found the
literary society very brilliant, the talk at Harvard
University being better, but the dinners worse, than
at Oxford); Quebec, which quite deserves its reputation for beauty and interest; Montreal; and Ottawa,
that wintry Washington of Canada. I have since
seen Toronto, Niagara, Philadelphia, Baltimore, Richmond, and Washington. To-morrow I shall start on
my way across the continent, *via* Chicago, the Salt
Lake City, and San Francisco, and reach my post at
Melbourne at the expiration of the twelve months'
leave granted me after my sixteen years' continuous
service as a Colonial Governor.

Lord Dufferin and I have compared opinions on
many subjects of colonial interest, not, as he·said,
without mutual advantage. I have seen all the leading public men of Canada and the United States, and
I have collected a mass of information and precedents
of all kinds, which cannot fail to be of practical use
to me hereafter. Public men in Canada are of much
the same calibre as in Australia, but Canada is a poor
and cold country when compared with Australia. A
Canadian politician remarked to me, 'We spend
half of our short summer in providing for the
subsistence of ourselves and of our cattle during
our long winter.' The revenue of the single Colony
of Victoria is equal to that of the entire Dominion
of Canada.

At Toronto I frequently saw my old Oxford friend

Goldwin Smith. He has married a rich Canadian lady, and they make their very pleasant home a sort of Holland House for America. The newspaper edited by him is the oracle of the American *doctrinaires*. His idea would seem to be to make Canada independent of England, and to form it into a sort of American Belgium, a small Parliamentary State, near the great American Republic or Empire. A man must have visited the United States and conversed with all classes to understand how right Lord Dufferin was in showing that there is much more real and practical democracy (in the classical sense) under British institutions; and how well justified Louis Napoleon was in stating in one of his last speeches to the French legislature, that the institutions of France under the Empire and of the American Republic were somewhat similar, with the exception that in France there is an hereditary President. Americans are rather fond of boasting that their President and the Emperor of Russia are now the only two *personal* rulers among Christian potentates. As Kinglake (in his ' History of the Crimean War ') puts it : ' They alone can ring a bell and tell an aide-de-camp to order an army to march.' All American Presidents and State Governors, as incarnations of the popular will, and dictators *ne quid detrimenti capiat respublica*, are expected to *veto*, according to their personal discretion, all acts of the Federal and State legislatures to which they may personally object. Many Americans now rather distrust some of their legislatures owing to the corruption which they believe to be as prevalent as in the English Parliament in the days of Walpole. I may mention one illustration. I have seen a great deal of General Bristow, the Secretary to the Treasury (that is, the Finance Minister) of the United States. I asked him if he thought the United States Government would return to 'hard money.' He replied: 'Our Congress is not your House of Commons: the Executive here does not care ten cents for its acts, and the President will go on as he has done, steadily *vetoing* all " soft money " Bills.' An English friend said, 'Only fancy our Chancellor of the Exchequer boasting that the Queen would go on steadily vetoing all *money bills.*' The late Attorney-General (Mr. Evarts) told me that he dared not advise what he thought would be the best course with regard to the proposed trial of Jefferson Davis, for the late President, Andrew Johnson, would have turned him out, and replaced him by a more compliant lawyer. The Cabinet of the President, of course, are not responsible advisers, and constitutionally hold a *status* little higher than that of Permanent Under-Secretary in England.

I found that the great majority of Canadians are averse to Goldwin Smith's idea of a Canadian Belgium. They are loyal to the Crown, but say that if their connexion with England should be severed, they will prefer incorporation with the United States. They feel that the age of small States is past, and they are determined to be either Britons or Americans. Lord

Dufferin is generally, and most deservedly, popular in Canada, and his speeches have made a great impression in the United States.

Lord Houghton and I, and the English Minister, Sir Edward Thornton, were invited last week to a very interesting dinner at Mr. Hamilton Fish's (the Secretary of State's). There were present, President Grant and his Cabinet, with the principal heads of the public departments; the Chief Justice of the United States (Mr. Waite); Mr. Bancroft (the historian); indeed most of the principal official men of this country. There was excellent *badinage*. Lord Houghton humorously talked so much in favour of polygamy, that the President said, with a grim smile, that he really thought he must make him the next Governor of Utah. At this dinner at Mr. Fish's, I suggested, as I frequently do in conversing with Americans, that Lord Stanhope is right in the opinion stated in his History, that if England had not pursued so insane a policy towards the British Colonies a hundred years ago, the revolution would never have taken place. The President and his Cabinet, like most other Americans, agreed that if England had adopted in the eighteenth century her present colonial policy, and, as a high functionary present politely remarked, ' sent out such good Governors as Lord Dufferin and Sir George Bowen,' we should possibly still be all members of one United Empire; only, as the Attorney General added : ' Now that the great majority of the Anglo-Saxon race is on the west

side of the Atlantic, we Americans would claim that
the Queen should reside, at least partly, on our side.'
All agreed also that if the Queen were to visit the
Centennial Exhibition of 1876 at Philadelphia, she
would receive such a triumph as the world has
never seen. All Americans will be greatly disap-
pointed if one of our Princes does not come over on
this grand occasion. There is already a picture of
George IV. in the Independence Hall at Philadelphia,
where the famous Declaration was adopted on July
4, 1776 ; and the President of the Exhibition Commission told Lord Houghton and me that he is trying
to get a statue of George III. to put up in the place
of honour in the central hall of the Exhibition.

I sat next President Grant at the dinner to which
I have referred, and had much interesting conversation with him. He is a modest and unassuming man,
and told me many curious anecdotes of his early
career, as well as of his great campaigns. Alluding
to the luxurious habits of the young men of the
present time, he observed : 'My son often does not
get up before ten o'clock ; and I told him the
other day that when I was at his age I had to
rise before daylight to milk a cow and clean a
horse.' 'May I ask, sir, what your son answered ?'
'Oh ! he said that "*your* father was not so good to
you as *you* are to me."' 'He might have replied,' I
rejoined, 'that your father was not President of the
United States.' It was very interesting to hear simple
anecdotes of this kind from one of the great soldiers

of the century, and who now is also one of the greatest potentates in the world.

Turning to American politics, he told me that his own opinion inclined to agree with those who think that the President ought to be elected for six years, and to be afterwards ineligible. However, most Americans think that General Grant would be probably elected for a third term if it were not for their almost superstitious reverence for the unwritten law of the protest of Washington against any such prolongation, which he declined to accept for himself. There is a general feeling that Grant saved the Union in the late war; that he is a man of deeds, not words, and that he will also steadily veto any measure adverse to 'hard money' and to the secular system of public instruction, which is a favourite article in the political creed of the majority of Americans. I asked the President and other American Statesmen what they thought of the idea of a future alliance or confederation of the Anglo-Saxon race, such as Mr. W. E. Forster has often shadowed forth, and especially in his recent speech at Edinburgh. They all say that they like the idea, though of course they do not pledge themselves to any details; and looking to the recent utterances of some of our English politicians and journalists, they doubt if England at present really desires anything of the kind.

Lord Houghton and I were much interested in our visit to Richmond and the battlefields near it, the bloodiest in all history. The chief men in the South

still speak of the Union Government much as the Irish
Home Rulers speak of the English Government, while
the Southern ladies are all as fierce rebels [1] as the Jacobite ladies in Scotland a hundred and fifty years ago.
All however agree that there is no chance of another
attempt being made to break up the Union, at least
in the present generation. The Americans now feel
themselves a nation and not a bundle of States. The
war of Secession has done for their nationality what
the war with France has done for German nationality.
They are now less sensitive, while we are more respectful; they are like a successful young man who
is no longer bumptious when he feels his position in
the world to be secure. The statue of the Confederate
General, Stonewall Jackson, was lately set up at
Richmond with much ceremony, and a great parade
of English flags, and of sympathy with England. No
doubt, as the 'Times' said, it was very indiscreet in
any body of Englishmen to send it over; and their
indiscretion, some years ago, might have led to grave
consequences. But the Americans have now out-
grown the sensitiveness of their national youth; they
know that they have waged a war in which they had,
from first to last, and on both sides, more than two
millions of men under arms; they feel the great
position which they now hold in the eyes of the world;

---

[1] Sir G. Bowen was told at Washington that General Lee once met
with a flag of truce some Northern Generals to arrange for a cartel for
the exchange of prisoners; and that alluding to the term 'rebels' as
applied to the Confederates, he said, 'Gentlemen, I propose a toast
which we can all accept: "*The first* REBEL, *George Washington!*"'

they are almost as proud of their victory in law and diplomacy at Geneva in the 'Alabama' case, as of their warlike triumphs at Richmond and Charleston; in short, they are in good humour with themselves, and consequently with us. They really seem to care as little about a rich Englishman sending over a statue of Jackson to Richmond, as we should care if some rich American were to set up a statue of Cromwell at Worcester or Naseby.

According to my observation, the typical Yankee is now as nearly extinct as the typical John Bull. The overflowing kindness and courtesy everywhere accorded this year to Lord Houghton and myself, are meant as demonstrations of national good will to our country. In Lord Houghton they had one who combined two capacities which they like and admire, that of an English peer, and an English man of letters; and when I have remonstrated against some of the flattering attentions showered upon myself, I have been told that I am the first Colonial Governor they have had amongst them for a long time, and that they desire to show their respect and sympathy for one who represents alike the Queen and also that British Colonial Empire to which their fathers belonged. Colonel Scott, the 'Railway King' of America, insisted on sending me and my aide-de-camp across America from Philadelphia to San Francisco in a most comfortable 'President's car,' containing drawing-room, dining-room, bedrooms, and excellent kitchen and attendants. In fact, it was an hotel on wheels.

It was very interesting in the course of this tour
in Virginia to see the many traces of the Civil War
in the capital of the Confederate States and its
immediate neighbourhood. The Mayor drove Lord
Houghton and Sir George Bowen over the battlefields
near Richmond, many of which then resembled an
Australian goldfield, for they presented a surface of
crumbling earthworks, which had been pushed on
by the contending armies so close to each other that
in many cases the Northern and Southern soldiers
fought with their bayonets over the ridges of their
trenches. The drivers of the Mayor's carriages and
all the hack drivers of Richmond were liberated slaves
—cheery, laughing negroes, who seemed often to look
back with sympathy to their old masters and former
homes. In a letter which Sir George Bowen afterwards received from Lord Houghton, it was said : ' I
shall never forget the party to which we were invited
at Richmond by the Governor of Virginia, a former
Confederate general, who had been wounded in
battle; how much I was touched by a charming
American lady suddenly striking up my own song,
Strangers yet; and how, when the Governor apolo-
gised to us for retiring early, *because he had a ball
in his back,* you remarked to me that " such an *arrière-
pensée* was a sufficient excuse ; " a *mot* which I often
repeat in England as one of the most amusing I ever
heard.'

On their return to Washington, the travellers
visited together Washington's old home at Mount
Vernon, which resembles some of the early settlers'
houses in Australia. On crossing the Potomac, a
question was raised about the story related in some

of the popular biographies of Washington, viz. that he was so strong that he could throw a dollar across the Potomac, which is there far wider than the Thames at Westminster; for legends have already grown up about him as if he had been an early Christian saint. Lord Chief Justice Coleridge, on his tour in America some years later, was escorted to Mount Vernon by the Attorney-General of the United States, who when asked if this legend was true, replied : ' Well, my Lord, if you have read that story, I suppose it must have some foundation. At all events, it is not for me to belittle the Father of my country ; but your Lordship will please to recollect that a hundred years ago the dollar went much further than it goes now ! '

From Washington Sir G. Bowen returned to Philadelphia, and thence crossed the continent to San Francisco in the ' President's car ' attached to the express train. He stopped for one day at Chicago, and for four days at Salt Lake City.

To an English Statesman.

Salt Lake City : December 3, 1875.

This is a glorious place in point of scenery—as fine as anything in Switzerland. Moreover, when I say that the Great Salt Lake, surrounded by its amphitheatre of snowy mountains, varying in height from 8,000 to 12,000 ft., reminds me of Lake Wakatipu in New Zealand, and of the mountains of Otago, I mean that it reminds me of some of the most magnificent scenery in the whole world. But after all, ' the proper study of mankind is man ' ; and I have just returned from an interview with Brigham Young, who received me cordially, and with an evident desire to make a favourable impression on a British Governor. 'Oh, I do hope,' he said, 'that the time will come when England, whence we receive so many of our brethren and sisters, will do us the justice which America withholds.' And speaking of the next contest for the Presidency, he remarked: 'What we really want for President of the United States is a man like one of your stout old English admirals, who has no theories, and will stand no nonsense.' I had a letter of introduction to the Governor of the Territory of Utah, a sharp lawyer from Boston, and he took me a drive in the afternoon. I asked him what he supposed that Brigham Young meant in his remark about British admirals; when, after stroking his beard for some minutes in deep reflection, he replied: 'Well, Sir, I reckon that Brigham has read the life of your Lord Nelson, and believes that your "stout old British admirals" (as he calls them) would not object to a plurality of wives so much as does our General Grant.'

In appearance and manner Brigham Young resembles a cross between a Methodist parson and an American sea-captain. He has the white tie, the black clothes, and the unctuous manner of the first, and the clear cold eye, and look of habitual command of the other. All, however, admit that the Mormon prophet is a man of extraordinary personal influence and skill in organising labour and colonisation. His followers worship him much as the old Greek colonists worshipped their Œkists ;—as the Moses, who in 1846, after the assassination, or, as they call it, the 'martyrdom,' of Joseph Smith, led their Exodus across the American desert, through wild tribes of hostile Indians, over the Rocky Mountains, and through every species of danger and hardship, to their Canaan, or 'Sion,' which then formed part of Mexico, and lay beyond the jurisdiction of the United States. But the railroad, that Iron Horse more powerful than the American cavalry, has followed them up, and now there is a strong force of United States troops encamped on the hill above the city, whose guns (as the commanding officer said to me) 'could soon make it hot for the Mormons, if they should resist the law.'

The position of affairs here is very curious ; as you are aware, a 'Territory' is analogous in its constitution to a 'Crown Colony.' Although the population of Utah is now 150,000 (of which number 10,000 are 'Gentiles,' i.e. non-Mormons), and although Nevada, California, and other former Territories have been erected into States when their population was much smaller, the Congress steadily refuses to make Utah a State so long as the Mormon organisation continues ; for if the Mormons had full powers of self-government, they would of course have a Mormon Governor, and Mormon Executive Officers, Judges, &c., and would pass laws establishing polygamy, and rendering their country uninhabitable except by Mormons. While Utah remains a Territory, the Governor is appointed by the President from Washington ; and he has an absolute veto on all acts of the local legislature, which is entirely Mormon. All the Judges and chief public officers are also appointed by the President, and use the United States troops as a *posse comitatus* to execute their decrees ; nay more, the Governor is by law Commander-in-Chief, and he refuses to. allow the Mormons to parade or be drilled with their own rifles. Brigham bitterly complained to me, with the tone and air of a pious confessor or martyr, of the bondage in which his people are held, as 'worse than that of the Israelites in the Land of Goshen.' On the other hand the few 'Gentiles' in Utah say that their lives would not be safe if things were otherwise, and that in the country districts even now, apostate Mormons have 'disappeared' (ἠφανίσθησαν, in the phrase of Thucydides[1]), under the hands of the 'Avenging Angels,' or 'Danites,' as the secret police of the ruling priesthood is called. They are said to have perpetrated murders and massacres in the disguise of Indians.

Many people believe that this strange theocracy will break up on the death of Young; but that is not the opinion of the Missionary Bishop of the Anglican Church in the United States, who has a small congregation in Salt Lake City. He believes that the organisation has been so successful as a colonising power, that so many personal interests have grown up under it, and that it is worked by so many other able men besides Brigham Young, that it will not be easily de-

---

[1] Thucydides, III. 83. *Cf.* IV. 80.

stroyed. It is recruited every year by several thousand emigrants, chiefly from the labouring classes of Wales, Scotland, and Sweden, who find comfortable home- steads provided for them, while their women are (for peasant girls) luxuriously lodged in the houses of the rich Mormons. Polygamy in Utah, as in Turkey, is necessarily practised only by comparatively wealthy men. The Bishop told me, among many other curious facts and anecdotes, that Brigham Young often asks clergymen of various communions, who visit Utah, to preach in the 'Tabernacle,' as his large, theatre-like church is called ; warning them, however, that if they should say anything against the ' peculiar ' institution (polygamy), he reserved to himself the right of reply- ing at the end of the sermon. Mr. Newman Hall, the well-known Baptist Minister, was thus invited, and preached on the parable of the ' Rich Man and Laza- rus.' In the course of his sermon, he brought in an attack on polygamy, but wound up with the hope that all present, whether polygamists or monogamists, would meet at last in ' Abraham's bosom.' When he sat down, Brigham rose up, and merely said : ' My Mormon brethren, our reverend friend, Mr. Newman Hall, has forgotten in his eloquent sermon to remind us of one little fact, and that is that *Abraham himself was a polygamist.*'

San Francisco : December 8, 1875.

After crossing the Rocky Mountains by railway at a point higher than the convent of Mount St. Bernard, i.e. more than 8,000 ft. above the sea, and being whirled along for two days among snowy peaks, we descended to the soft Italian climate and perpetual summer of the Pacific coast, and reached San Francisco, the New York of the West. California closely resembles Australia in climate, products, and the general appearance of the country; while San Francisco has about the same population, though it is not so handsomely or solidly built, as Melbourne. A box at the principal theatre was this evening placed by the Mayor at my disposal, and, on my entrance, 'God save the Queen' was twice played by the orchestra, having been encored by the large audience, which received it with enthusiasm. But this is only a fresh proof of the respect and courtesy which the Americans are prepared to extend to every English official.

Nothing could be more gratifying personally, or more satisfactory on public grounds, than the reception accorded in the United States to Sir G. Bowen as a British Governor representing the Queen in one of the most important provinces of the Empire. This good feeling continued till the last moment of his stay on the soil of the Great Republic; for on embarking on board the mail steamer for Australia, the Directors of the Company gave a lunch in the cabin in his honour, inviting several of the chief residents of San Francisco to meet him. As he stepped on the deck, the American flag was hoisted, but by some mischance the rope gave way, and the flag falling enveloped in its folds a young lady standing near him. Sir George advanced to, as it were, unveil the lady, saying, 'I am sure it will do no harm to any American to be enveloped in the Stars and Stripes.' A voice came from under the flag : 'Sir, I perceive you are a Britisher. What have *I* to do with the Stars and Stripes ? *I* am for the Stars and Bars ' (the flag of the Confederate States). Her rescuer for a moment thought that in his last moments on American waters he might be a witness of what Americans call 'a difficulty,' that is, some sharp-shooting with revolvers. But a captain in the American navy, whose acquaintance he had recently made, stepped forward and said, 'Sir George Bowen, permit me to introduce you to Miss Lee of Virginia, the daughter of the famous Confederate General, Robert Lee ; and now you will understand why she prefers the old Confederate flag, though the country is now reunited under the National banner.' Such was his first acquaintance with Miss Lee, who afterwards became his guest in Australia, and whom he has since met at Rome, London, Paris, Hong Kong, and elsewhere.

The 'City of San Francisco' conveyed Sir George on a prosperous voyage back to his government of Victoria. There was but one stoppage, at Honolulu, before Sydney was reached. Here he found in the British Commissioner and Consul-General, an old Oxford friend, Mr. James Wodehouse. From Sydney he proceeded, after staying there for three days with the Governor, Sir Hercules Robinson, to Melbourne, where he was welcomed by his Ministers, and by the Mayor of Melbourne, who gave a banquet in his honour on his return, as he had done on his departure on leave of absence twelve months previously.

CHAPTER V.

MAURITIUS—HONG KONG—CHINA — JAPAN — INDIA — 'DUFFERIN
BURMANICUS ' — SIR EDWIN ARNOLD — PRIVY COUNCILLOR—
HON. D.C.L. OXFORD—HON. LL.D. CAMBRIDGE—RETIREMENT
—MALTA.

FROM 1879 to 1883 Sir George Bowen was Governor of
Mauritius, the beautiful island of ' Paul and Virginia,'
where, as in Canada, English is blended with French
colonisation; and where he succeeded in leaving all
races, creeds, and classes of the population in amity
and contentment.[1]

In 1883, after more than thirty years' continuous
service, he thought of asking permission to retire,
when it was proposed that he should undertake the
government of Hong Kong, 'the Malta of the Far
East,' where serious difficulties of various kinds
required the care of an experienced and conciliatory
ruler. We shall show in subsequent chapters how,
in two years, he had reconstructed the Colonial
Legislature, and established friendly relations with
the leading actors of all nations in the historical
drama then playing in that quarter of the globe. In
the beginning of 1885 he had reluctantly obtained
leave, on medical certificate, to visit England; but
the embarrassments consequent on the prolonged
Franco-Chinese hostilities and on the then threatened

[1] See Vol. II., Part V.

war with Russia convinced the Governor that it was
his duty to remain at his post, at whatever risk of
health. The Colonial Minister (Lord Derby) signified
in an official despatch his 'high appreciation of the
public spirit which led him to this decision.' When
peace was finally restored, his leave of absence was
renewed; and Lord Stanley of Preston, the Colonial
Minister who had succeeded Lord Derby, addressed
the Acting Governor in the following terms: 'I have
pleasure in availing myself of this opportunity of expressing my sense of the energy and ability with which
Sir George Bowen has devoted himself to the administration of the important government of Hong Kong.'[1]

Sir George Bowen returned from Hong Kong by
way of British India, and was the guest at Calcutta of
his friend from Oxford days, Lord Dufferin. He made
the acquaintance, while the guest of the Viceroy, of
many of the Indian Princes, and of the high functionaries of Government. Lord Dufferin, having
announced at an official dinner that the Imperial
Government had approved by telegraph his annexation of Burma, was saluted by his guest in the old
Roman fashion, as *Dufferin Burmanicus*;—an antici-
pation of the title of Marquis of Dufferin *and Ava*,
afterwards conferred on him by the Queen. Sir
George afterwards made a very interesting tour in
India, visiting Benares, Agra, Gwalior, Lucknow,
Cawnpore, and Delhi, where he was present with
the Viceroy at the grand review of January 1886,
when 40,000 troops marched past. He afterwards
proceeded through Jeypore and Rajpootana to Bombay, where he was the guest of the Governor, Lord

[1] See Vol. II., Part VI.

Reay, as he had been of the Lieutenant-Governor of the North-West Provinces, Sir Alfred Lyall, at Allahabad. He enjoyed, of course, special opportunities of personal observation, and of learning the views of many of the leading men of India, both English and native. He refers in his pamphlet on Imperial Federation (pages 13, 14) to the question as to how India should be treated in any general scheme of Federation. 'I said above that I did not, in this paper, reckon India with the Colonies. That great dependency might be treated as still (so to speak) *in statu pupillari* to the Imperial Crown and Legislature. Personally, however, I am inclined to believe that it should be regarded as a Crown Colony on a grand scale; and that former members of the Supreme Council at Calcutta, including a certain proportion of native princes, should hereafter be delegated by that body, or selected by the Crown, to represent India in any new Imperial Council at London. It should be borne in mind that, with regard to the gradual communication of the chief rights of British citizens to the natives of India, there is the example of Rome. Cicero considered the liberality of the Romans in admitting foreign nations to the rights of Roman citizenship as the main cause of the rapid extension and consolidation of the Roman Empire.[1] From what I myself saw and learned, I believe that we have a just right to apply

[1] '*Illud vero sine ullá dubitatione maximè nostrum fundavit imperium, et populi Romani nomen auxit, quod princeps ille creator hujus urbis Romulus fœdere Sabino docuit, etiam hostibus recipiendis augeri hanc civitatem oportere; cujus autoritate et exemplo nunquam est intermissa a majoribus nostris largitio et communicatio civitatis.*' (*Pro Balbo*, c. 13.) The liberality of the Romans in this respect was contrasted by Dionysius with the exclusiveness of the Greeks (*Ant. Rom.* II. 17.)

to the British Empire in India those noble verses in which the Roman poet Claudian described the Imperial policy of Rome:

Hæc est in gremium victos quæ sola recepit,
Humanumque genus communi nomine fovit,
Matris, non dominæ, ritu; civesque vocavit
Quos domuit, nexuque pio longinqua revinxit.' [1]

Sir George Bowen returned from Bombay to England by Suez, Cairo, Brindisi, Rome, and Florence. On the voyage to Suez there were in the P. & O. steamer a distinguished company of Anglo Indian Generals and Civilians; and also Sir Edwin Arnold, the accomplished author of the 'Light of Asia.' We subjoin the graceful verses addressed by him to Sir G. Bowen:

Lightly we talked, in our British way,
On the dancing deck, day after day,
Of times and peoples, and fair old sayings
From Grecian legend and Latin lay.

You, with the laurels of many a year
Nobly crowning your silvered hair,
Five times Consul, faithfully guarding
England's majesty, far and near.

King—for the Queen—in Queensland, long,
King—for the Queen—Victorians among;
Ruling New Zealand, ruling Mauritius,
Governing pig-tails in far Hong-Kong.

[1] *De Secundo Consulatu Stilichonis*, V. 150–153. Claudian (*ibidem*, V. 154–9) speaks of the facilities of intercourse introduced by the Romans into their vast empire, partly by the maintenance of peace, and partly by their roads—a passage which has been reduced to sober truth by railways and steamers in the British Empire:—

Hujus pacificis debemus moribus omnes
Quod veluti patriis regionibus utitur hospes;
Quod sedem mutare licet; quod cernere Thulen
Lusus, et horrendos quondam penetrare recessus;
Quod cuncti gens una sumus.————

I a poet, and scribe of the press,
Stealing a pause from its daily stress,
To wander once more in the Land of my boyhood,
India, wonderful,—measureless !

Swiftly those sea-leagues glided by,
Shortened by friendliest company ;
Fallentes iter—we cheated old Ocean
Of half his weary monotony.

But you—of five royal colonies chief,
What room is left for a myrtle leaf,
Vir nullâ non donande lauro!
In your wreath of honour ?　Yet here receive

One shipmate's word of the thanks and praise
Which England owes, and England pays
For great work wrought for the Commonwealth
In watchful midnights and burning days !

Nor deem you will come to the Mother-land
Unloved—unwelcomed, though placemen stand
Silent and foolish !　The nation knows !
Securus judicat populus !　And

History writes you in letters of gold
With those who have compassed the art to hold
Imperial mother and lordly children
In free affection ; their pride t'enfold

In bond of amity.　You, who see,
Teach us that large simplicity
Which voices of wisdom, and great dead heroes,
And kinship, enjoin, ' One Britain be ! '

So resting, Good Friend ! from toils sublime,
Rude donatus,—the latter time
Shall burnish the gold of your heaped-up honour,
And sunset be brighter than noon's broad prime.

　　　　　　　　　　　　　　EDWIN ARNOLD.

P. & O. Steamer ' Síam.'　In the Indian Ocean.　March 16, 1886.

Not long after his return to England in 1886, Sir
G. Bowen was sworn in before the Queen at Windsor
as a member of the Privy Council;—an emphatic

recognition of public services which has been granted
to very few other Colonial Governors. Annexed is the
letter addressed to him on this occasion by the Rt.
Hon. Edward Stanhope, then Colonial Minister.

Colonial Office, November 26, 1886.

My dear Sir George Bowen,

I saw with regret the premature announcement
in the Gazette, because I wished to be one of the very
first to write to you and express my deep sense of
satisfaction that your long and honoured services
should have been recognised by Her Majesty the
Queen. Speaking for myself, and for the Government with which I am connected, I should like to say
that our sense of the value of those services, and of
the example which you have set to the whole body of
men engaged in the work of Colonial Government, is
real and abiding ; and by enrolling you in the select
list of those Governors who have been summoned to
the Privy Council in recognition of their worth, the
Queen gives encouragement to your successors to
follow in your footsteps.

Thanking you for your personal kindness and
consideration towards myself, publicly and privately,
I hope you may be given long years of health to
enjoy the honours you have so justly earned.

Believe me, dear Sir George Bowen,

Yours very truly,

EDWARD STANHOPE.

It should be mentioned that, as Knights Grand
Cross of St. Michael and St. George are entitled to

supporters to their family arms, the Heralds' College assigned to Sir George Bowen two Maori Chiefs, in remembrance of his having engaged their aid to fight for the Crown; with the motto *Imperî Porrecta Majestas.* The lines of Horace from which this motto is taken,[1]

> *Per quas Latinum nomen et Italæ*
> *Crevere vires, famaque et Imperî*
> *Porrecta majestas ad ortum*
> *Solis ab Hesperio cubili,*

are still more applicable to the British than to the Roman Empire.

We must not omit to record that the Universities of Oxford and Cambridge respectively have conferred on Sir George Bowen their honorary degrees of D.C.L. and LL.D. The Latin speeches with which he was presented in the Sheldonian Theatre and in the Senate House both referred to his literary as well as to his official reputation; and he was received on both occasions with loud and general applause.

Towards the close of 1886, on account partly of ill-health in his family, and partly in consequence of a desire manifested in many quarters that his experience should be rendered available in Parliament, Sir George Bowen tendered the resignation of his office. Sir George Strahan, the Governor of Tasmania, was selected as his successor at Hong Kong; but on the sudden death of that officer, early in 1887, it was proposed to the former, in the most gratifying manner, by Her Majesty's Government, that he should resume his government; when he at once signified his readiness to place himself at their disposal. But the hope

[1] *Carm.* IV. 15.

of a seat in Parliament induced him finally to ask
permission to retire, unless his services should be
absolutely required by an early prospect of war or
other grave difficulties in the Far East. This permission was granted by Sir Henry Holland, now Lord
Knutsford, who had succeeded Mr. Stanhope at the
Colonial Office, and who wrote in the following terms
(June 24, 1887): 'I have read with interest the re-
capitulation of the important services which it has
been your good fortune to be enabled to render in the
Governments which you have successively filled; and
I fully concur in the expressions of appreciation and
approval with which my immediate predecessors in
this office have referred to those services. Those
communications are so recent that I need not now
repeat at length the sentiments which they contain.'

Sir George Bowen took a prominent part in the
public ceremonies which marked the Colonial and
Indian Exhibition of 1886, and the Colonial Conference and Jubilee celebrations of 1887. Having
such long and varied experience in the administration of both Crown and self-governing Colonies, he
has become a special authority on many questions
affecting the 'Greater Britain.'

Although he had formally retired from the permanent service of the Crown, the veteran Governor remained ready and eager to be employed in any mission
in which his experience might be useful. A few
months after his retirement such an occasion arose;
and he was appointed by the Queen, in December 1887,
to be the chief of a Royal Commission sent to Malta,
to inquire and report on the arrangements connected
with the new constitution granted to that island. The

principal parliamentary papers connected with this mission will be found in a subsequent chapter.[1] It will be seen that the two Commissioners, Sir George Bowen and Sir George Baden-Powell, received through the Secretary of State for the Colonies the thanks of the Queen for their 'care and ability'; and that all their recommendations were adopted by Her Majesty's Government.

Such, in brief, are the main features of the public life of Sir G. Bowen,—a life devoted to the service of his country. The fuller record of his work, to which the preceding sketch is introductory, has been compiled from the materials furnished by his public reports and addresses, and from a selection of his semi-official correspondence, and of his letters to his numerous friends among politicians and literary men of eminence. It will be easily understood that in so large a mass of documents, it has been found necessary to make many omissions and abridgments. In particular, care has been taken to avoid the reproduction of any part of his despatches which was of a confidential nature, or which could reasonably give pain or offence to any classes or individuals in the Colonies. The principal end which has been kept steadily in view has been to record in a permanent form, and to render more widely available for reference, the long and varied experience of his life, as a contribution to the history of the Colonies; and as a support to those statesmen who, rising above the strife of party politics, are labouring to establish on a firm and solid basis the unity of the British Empire.

[1] See Vol. II., Part VII.

PART II

THE FOUNDING OF QUEENSLAND

1859–1868

CHAPTER VI.

SIR G. BOWEN APPOINTED FIRST GOVERNOR OF QUEENSLAND—
LETTER FROM SIR E. BULWER LYTTON—ENTHUSIASTIC RECEP-
TION AT BRISBANE—ADDRESSES AND REPLIES—REPORT TO
THE SECRETARY OF STATE AND HIS REPLY.

FROM Corfu to Queensland is a gigantic leap, not in
space alone, but in habits of thought and traditions
of government. If political life in the Ionian Islands
was not all that might have been wished, at least
there was a settled system of administration, and
principles of government founded upon ancient precedents and not inglorious records. In Queensland
there was nothing of the sort ; and if ever a State was
entitled to the happiness which is said to belong to
the nation that has no history, that State was the
district of Moreton Bay, now, in 1859, on the petition
of its inhabitants, to be severed from the maternal
care of New South Wales, and to begin a separate life
of its own in the commonwealth of nations. As Chief
Secretary in the Ionian Islands, Sir G. Bowen had won
the approval of the Home Government in circumstances of no little difficulty ; and his appointment to
be the first Governor of the new Colony of Queensland was a proof of their confidence. But no one
knew better than himself how abrupt would be the
transition from the official guidance of a few small
islands to the government of a country half the size
of Western Europe ; and from the maintenance of a

constitution which had prevailed for over forty years, and was itself a survival of a far older system, to the inauguration of a State where the whole machinery of government and legislation had to be created.

Only the leading men resident in the Colonies really know how great and pervasive is the influence of a Governor who understands and performs his duty; how many—even in Colonies which have long enjoyed representative institutions—are the delicate crises to be smoothed away, and how serious the constitutional and imperial interests to be guarded—always, however, with the gloved hand and sheathed sword—by the Queen's representative. All such problems and difficulties naturally present themselves in the crudest shape in the first years of a new State, however well disposed towards its Governor, and desirous to learn those lessons of moderation and compromise which are of the essence of successful self-government. The responsibility of a first Governor is immense, but so is his reward. Few rulers enjoy so fully the high recompense of seeing their work shape itself beneath their touch as the Proconsuls of England's younger Colonies. As in a tropical climate the grain seems to stir and the fruit to ripen almost as soon as sown, and the husbandman has the happiness of speedily garnering the harvest which his own toil has prepared, so a generation in Australia effects more transformation than a century in Europe or a 'cycle in Cathay'; and the founder of a Colony may witness more national growth in a dozen years than the oldest Statesman in the old world can hope to survey; while, great as is the achievement of the present, the possibilities of the future are boundless.

The first Lord (then Sir Edward Bulwer) Lytton, as Minister for the Colonies, gave Sir George Bowen sound advice on the duties and bearing of a Colonial Governor in a characteristic letter which is here reprinted.[1] It comprises a code of public principles without which no Governor in a free Colony can hope for success; and is a proof of the practical statesmanship of the poet-philosopher.

The Rt. Hon. Sir E. B. Lytton to Sir G. F. Bowen.

Great Malvern : April 29, 1859.

Dear Sir George Bowen,

I have the pleasure to inform you that the Queen approves of your appointment to Moreton Bay, which will henceforth bear the appellation of Queensland. Accept my congratulations and my assurances of the gratification it gives me to have promoted you to a post in which your talents will find ample scope.

There is not much to learn beforehand for your guidance in this new Colony. The most anxious and difficult question connected with it will be the ' Squatters.' But in this, which is an irritating contest between rival interests, you will wisely abstain as much as possible from interference. Avoid taking part with one or the other. Ever be willing to lend aid to conciliatory settlement ; but, in order to secure that aid, you must be strictly impartial. Remember that the first care of a Governor in a free Colony is to shun the reproach of being a party man. Give all parties and all the Ministries formed the fairest play.

Mark and study the idiosyncrasies of the com-

---

[1] See *Speeches of Edward, Lord Lytton*, edited by his Son, Vol. I., page 121.

munity; every community has some peculiar to itself. Then, in your public addresses, appeal to those which are the noblest : the noblest are generally the most universal and the most durable.   They are peculiar to no party.

Let your thoughts never be distracted from the paramount object of finance.   All States thrive in proportion to the administration of revenue.

You will as soon as possible exert all energy and persuasion to induce the colonists to see to their self-defence internally.   Try to establish a good police ; if you can then get the superior class of colonists to assist in forming a militia or volunteer corps, spare no pains to do so.   It is at the commencement of Colonies that this object can be best effected.   A Colony that is once accustomed to depend on Imperial soldiers for aid against riots, &c., never grows up into vigorous manhood.   Witness the West Indian Colonies.

Education the Colonists will be sure to provide for.   So they will for religion.

Do your best always to keep up the pride in the mother-country.   Throughout all Australia there is a sympathy with the ideal of a gentleman.   This gives a moral aristocracy.   Sustain it by showing the store set on integrity, honour, and civilised manners ; not by preferences of birth, which belong to old countries.

Whenever any distinguished residents in your Colony come to England, give them letters of introduction, and a private one to the Secretary of State, whoever he may be.   This last is not sufficiently done in Colonies ; but all Secretaries of State who are fit for the office should desire it.   You may quote my opinion to this effect to my successors.

As regards despatches : Your experience in the Ionian Islands will tell you how much is avoided in despatches that may be made public, and done in private letters.   This practice is at present carried to inconvenience and abuse.   Questions affecting free Colonies may come before Parliament, of which no documents whatever afford the slightest explanation.

The communications from a Government should be fourfold :—

(1.) *Public* Despatches.

(2.) *Confidential* :—Intended for publication, if at all required.

(3.) *Confidential* :—Not to be published unless absolutely necessary for defence of measures of the Governor or of the Home Department.

(4.) Letters *strictly private* :—These, if frank to a Minister, or to an Under Secretary, like Mr. Merivale, should be guarded to *friends*; and should touch as little as possible upon names and parties in the Colony.   A Government may rely on the discretion of a Department, never on that of private correspondents.

As you will have a free press, you will have some papers that may be abusive.   Never be thin-skinned about these ; laugh them off.   Be pointedly courteous to all editors and writers—acknowledging socially their craft and its importance.   The more you treat people as gentlemen the more ' they will behave as such.' [1]

[1] The present Lord Lytton, in his Prefatory Memoir to his edition of his father's speeches (page 124), makes the following comment on this

G 2

After all, men are governed as much by the heart as by the head. Evident sympathy in the progress of the Colony; traits of kindness, generosity, devoted energy, where required for the public weal; a pure exercise of patronage; an utter absence of vindictiveness or spite; the fairness that belongs to magnanimity—these are the qualities that make Governors powerful, while men merely sharp and clever may be weak and detested.

But there is one rule that I find pretty universal in Colonies. The Governor who is the least *huffy*, and who is most careful not to over-govern, is the one who has the most authority. Enforce civility upon all minor officials. Courtesy is a duty which public servants owe to the humblest member of the public.

Pardon all these desultory hints; and, wishing you all health and enjoyment in the far land,

Believe me, yours very truly,

E. B. LYTTON.

P.S.—Get all the details of the Land Question from the Colonial Office; and master them thoroughly. Convert the jealousies now existing between Moreton Bay and Sydney into emulation. Your recollection of the old Greek States will tell you what strides States can take through emulation.

You are aware that since I have been the Secre-

text: ' This was the instinct of his nature; and in it is the explanation of all that was both Liberal and Conservative in his political aspirations. Not to pull down the highest, but to exalt the lowest class of the community; to elevate the soul of the whole nation; to induce every man, born the free citizen of a great empire, to feel that he is by birth a great gentleman.'

tary for the Colonies I have changed the old Colonial
uniform for the same as that worn in the Imperial
service.   I consider it a great point to assimilate the
two services in outward emblems of dignity.   The
Queen's servant is the Queen's servant, whether at
Westminster or at the antipodes.

E. B. L.

If their first Governor was deeply impressed with
the gravity and responsibility of the trust confided
to him, the people of Queensland were not less alive
to the importance of this epoch in their existence or
less sanguine in their anticipations of the golden age
which was to open before them.   What they thought
and hoped will be best understood from some passages
in the local press.   The work of a Governor, it must
be remembered, is not to be traced in his despatches
alone : it is largely made up of public ceremonies
and interviews, face to face with the Colonial Legislature and with all classes of the community ; and to
understand his influence one must not only see him at
his desk, but follow him to receptions and deputations,
hear his speeches and replies to addresses, and read
their effect in the public records and journals of the
time.   The feeling of the people of Queensland on the
arrival of their first Governor on December 10, 1859,
is faithfully represented in the following extracts from
the 'Moreton Bay Courier' :—

'The great event of our history stands recorded.
A new epoch in the annals of Australia has come to
pass ; " our era " has commenced ; and the delays
and disappointments of the past are amply com-
pensated for by the triumphant successes of the

present. We have, as a free and independent people, welcomed amongst us the first representative of royalty to whom the task of governing our young State has been allotted; and never was welcome given with heartier zest. . . .

'Yesterday week, the 5th instant, was the first day upon which the arrival of H.M.S. "Cordelia" was looked for, and upon that account a series of holidays, lasting over four days, was commenced. Steamers went down to the bay, visitors poured in from the country, and flags waving by day, and fireworks by night, gave a glimmering idea of the enthusiasm held in check until the actual landing. On Friday evening, about sunset, the troopers who had been upon the look-out at Sandgate rode with "hot haste" into the town, and announced that the "Cordelia" was coming across the bay. Flags were everywhere hoisted as the glad intelligence spread like wild-fire through the city, and other demonstrations of joy were also made.

'On Saturday morning the "Breadalbane" started for the bay, having on board Captain Wickham (Government Resident), Mr. Justice Lutwyche (of the Supreme Court), Colonel Gray, Mr. Pring (the Attorney-General elect), and several ladies and gentlemen. After we were moored alongside, Captain Wickham appeared at the gangway of the "Cordelia," and said that Captain Vernon Harcourt would be happy to see any one who wished to come on board. The invitation was no sooner given than accepted by the majority of the "Breadalbane's" passengers, and we had scarcely reached the deck of the "Cordelia' when we were informed that his Excellency was desirous of having everyone presented to him. It became evident in the course of this improvised levée that his Excellency had not failed to obtain informa‧ tion relative to the place previous to his arrival, for many of those who were introduced had already become known to him both by name and reputation. In the happy countenance of his Excellency were to be recognised the peaceful termination of all our struggles for independence, and the hope of a prosperous future.

' Various compliments were paid on the passage up the river, which were all noticed and acknowledged by his Excellency ; but it was not until the arrival of the steamer at the Botanical Gardens in Brisbane that the grand expression of feeling was evinced. Upwards of 4,000 persons were congregated on the banks, and the cheers that were given were worthy of any assembly of loyal Britons all the world over. His Excellency was received at the landing place by the Mayor and Corporation of the city of Brisbane ; and as he stepped on shore a salute of twenty-one guns was fired. At the same moment a party of twelve young ladies, uniformly dressed in white, presented to Lady Bowen a bouquet of choice flowers. Passing under the triumphal arch, his Excellency and Lady Bowen entered the viceregal carriage, and a procession was formed to escort them to Government House. Along the whole line of route his Excellency was cheered after the genuine English fashion, and the procession that followed was of very creditable length and appearance. The banners carried by the various bodies of working men were especially noticeable for their appropriateness to the occasion, and the flag adopted as the Queensland ensign was frequently to be seen along the line of the cortège. The Union Jack, blended (out of compliment to Lady Bowen) with the Greek flag, waved on every side, and all the windows and balconies were filled with enthusiastic spectators.'

'The administration of the customary oaths of office to the Governor, and the reading of the proclamation of the new Colony from the balcony of the Government House, concluded the formal proceedings of the day. Sir George then came forward and said :—" Gentlemen,—I thank you all for the warm and hearty welcome which you have this day given me. I shall not fail to represent to our gracious and beloved Sovereign the loyal greeting with which you have received Her Majesty's first representative among you. I shall have the pleasure of seeing you again at the pavilion at ten o'clock on Monday morning, and, till then, I bid you all good-bye." An enthusiastic outburst of cheers followed the delivery of these few words, and the large crowd quietly dispersed, leaving his Excellency to enjoy the peace and comfort of his new home, and the fine scenery of which Lady Bowen and he had already frequently expressed their admiration.' [1]

[1] A writer in the *Edinburgh Review* (October 1863) states that the city of Brisbane ' stands upon a scene of surpassing beauty. The noble river, which winds almost underfoot, and appears and disappears, and appears again, as it pursues its tortuous course to the sea, presents ever and anon points of view surpassingly beautiful; the thick brush on its banks, with the majestic Moreton Bay pine overtopping all the other giants of the forest, indicating the spots of extraordinary fertility, where the hand of man is erecting his future dwelling, and transforming the wilderness into smiling farms and fruitful fields.' It should be observed that very vivid sketches of the

The Governor's first reception at the Botanical Gardens on Monday, December 12, 1859, was attended by fully four thousand persons; and a large number of addresses of welcome were then presented to him. The first was from ' the people of Queensland ' :—

' May it please your Excellency.

' We, whose names are hereunto subscribed, have the honour to convey to your Excellency the congratulations of the inhabitants of Queensland on your arrival in the Colony, and to welcome your Excellency to your seat of Government.

' Suffering, as we have been, from the evils consequent upon a distant Legislature, which, however well disposed, could not, from the nature of the case, either understand or provide for our requirements with sufficient promptitude, we hail the advent of Separation and your Excellency's arrival with feelings of heartfelt gratitude to our beloved Queen.

' We desire to convey through you, her Representative, our love and devotion to our Sovereign. We see in your Excellency's presence amongst us another instance of Her Majesty's earnest desire to promote the welfare and happiness of her subjects; and keeping this steadily in view, it shall be our constant aim to prove ourselves worthy of the privileges ceded to us, and to render the Colony of Queensland not alone prosperous and happy in itself, but at the same time worthy of its Queen and mother-country.'

scenery of Queensland and of ' Life in the Bush ' will be found in some of the novels of Mrs. Campbell Praed, who was born in the Colony, being a daughter of Mr. Murray Prior, one of the earliest settlers, and afterwards a member of the Parliament and Ministry.

The Governor made the following reply :—

' Gentlemen,

'I have received with most sincere gratification your cordial welcome and your loyal address. I thank you with my whole heart for your good wishes, and for the assurance of your personal regard for myself and my family. Those good wishes and that personal regard we warmly return. Like myself, Lady Bowen contemplates with unalloyed satisfaction a residence of many years among you, in a country where the charm of the climate and the beauty of the scenery vividly recall the land of her birth.

' It will indeed be a pleasing and honourable duty for me to convey to the Queen, my august Mistress, your loyal expressions of heartfelt gratitude, love, and devotion. I know that our Sovereign will receive most graciously, and with cordial satisfaction, the many proofs which I shall be able to lay before her of your growing welfare and happiness. And here, gentlemen, let me announce a fact which I know you will all hear with delight. Queensland, the name selected for the new Colony, was entirely the happy thought and inspiration of Her Majesty herself. Other designations had been suggested to her, but the Queen spontaneously determined to confer her own royal title on this new province of her Empire. It should assuredly, then, be the constant aim of us all to show ourselves not undeserving of this signal mark of the favour and sympathy of our Sovereign, and (to quote your own well-chosen phrase), " to render the Colony of Queensland not only prosperous and happy in itself, but at the same time worthy of its Queen and mother-country."

'In your address (as in other addresses which have been presented on my arrival among you), your kindness has assigned to me many gifts and qualities that I only wish I could more confidently appropriate. But it is only simple justice to attribute to me the most lively sympathy and the most abiding interest in all that concerns the welfare of the great and rising Colony in which the Queen has been graciously pleased to name me Her Majesty's first representative.

'Supported and strengthened by the Legislature and population, as I am confident, from the warmth of your greeting, that I shall be, it would be unpardonable if I were ever to neglect the duties which I have undertaken to perform, or ever to spare the best exertions of which I am capable towards promoting your happiness and prosperity.

'I rejoice to witness around me the obvious progress alike of material industry, of mental activity, and of moral and physical well-being. Everything may be expected from such signs as these. They are strong proofs to our Queen and countrymen at home that the foundations of a mighty and flourishing province of the British Empire have already been laid in this part of Australia.'

In reply to the address of the Mayor and Corporation of Brisbane, the Governor said :—

' Mr. Mayor and Gentlemen,

'I request that you will accept my warmest thanks for the cordial and generous welcome to Brisbane which your address conveys to me. From my

reception here I have derived deep personal gratification, and the most favourable impressions of the
loyalty and good feeling that animate all classes of
the community.

‘ I esteem it no ordinary privilege to be permitted
to watch over the progress of this city and Colony, at
a period so full of promise as that of the inauguration of local self-government. My object here, as in
the other principal settlements of Queensland (all of
which I hope to visit within the next twelve months),
will be to see and judge for myself—to ascertain the
real wants and wishes of the inhabitants of all classes,
in order that the views and measures of the Governor
may harmonise with the voice of the people. Candid
expressions of opinion and full information on all
important topics of local interest, in the addresses
which may be presented to me, will materially conduce to this end. You may rest assured that all
suggestions emanating from public bodies—such as
the Municipality of Brisbane—will at all times command my attention.

‘ It has invariably been held by the highest
authorities, that the system of local government by
municipalities has been one of the main elements of
our national greatness, and of the stability of the
British Constitution. I rejoice, therefore, that the
city of Brisbane has set the example of applying for
incorporation—an example which I hope will be
extensively followed throughout Queensland. I am
anxious to draw general attention to the conclusions
on this subject, arrived at, after deliberate consideration, by the practical and experienced Statesmen who
form the Privy Council of Great Britain. In their

report on the political institutions to be granted to the Australian Colonies, which was presented to the Queen in 1849, I read as follows :—

'"We are of opinion that the existence in Australia of municipal bodies in a state of efficiency is scarcely less necessary to the public welfare than the existence there of representative legislatures. A large part of the benefit to be derived from such legislatures seems to us to depend on the simultaneous establishment and co-existence of incorporated municipalities. It is the only practical security against the danger of undue centralisation. It is the only security for the vigilant and habitual attention by the local legislature to the interests of the more remote localities. It is by such bodies alone that in those secluded societies public spirit is kept alive, and skill in the conduct of public affairs acquired and exercised. It is in such corporations that the colonists are trained to act as legislators in a larger sphere. By them and by them alone can any effectual resistance be made to the partial and undue dedications of the public resources to the advantage of districts peculiarly fortunate in the zeal and authority of their representatives in the legislature."

' These, gentlemen, are wise and weighty words. Still, this, like all other political questions, in a free country, must ultimately be decided by the people themselves. Far be it from me to attempt to press on the inhabitants of any portion of this Colony unwelcome duties under the name of municipal privileges. It has been rightly observed that "if such duties are not undertaken with alacrity, and performed with zeal, and controlled by public vigilance,

o

and rewarded by public applause, they would be undertaken to no good purpose."

'But, Mr. Mayor and Gentlemen, you may very probably consider that I have already said too much, while I myself am painfully conscious that I have said too little on a topic of such vital importance. I will, therefore, conclude by again thanking you, in the name of the Queen, for your loyal greeting to Her Majesty's first representative among you ; and by assuring you that you will at all times find in me a most willing coadjutor in all public works and measures that can conduce to the improvement and prosperity of the port and city of Brisbane.'

Other addresses from the Clergy and from several public bodies followed, and were duly acknowledged. Then came a numerous deputation of working men, whose foreman said :—

' May it please your Excellency,

'We, the representatives of the working-men of Brisbane, loyal subjects of the British Crown, would respectfully offer your Excellency our sincerest congratulations on your safe arrival on these shores as the first Governor of Queensland. We feel thankful that a gracious Providence has brought your Excellency and your family in safety to this the land of our adoption.

' We desire to record our gratitude to our illustrious Sovereign, Queen Victoria, who (with her Ministers) hath laid this young and rising community under the deepest and most lasting obligations. When we reflect on the calm and deliberate attention evinced by Her Majesty's Government, during this movement in the Northern district, which has eventually ended in separation from New South Wales : when we mark the unwearied assiduity, the strict and impartial justice, the total disregard of all the sinister influences brought to bear on the struggle by the neighbouring Colony, it affords another evidence of that liberal and enlightened policy which has characterised Her Majesty's reign, and under the shade of which the Anglo-Saxon in this southern hemisphere may dwell contented and happy.

'We now welcome your Excellency as the lawful representative of our Sovereign and the first Governor of Queensland. We hail your arrival on our shores with the utmost satisfaction. We look on this day as one of the brightest in the existence of the young Colony, and take it as an earnest of good things to follow. Starting into existence as another of that belt of Colonies, which at no distant day is yet destined to encircle this great island continent, there is much that necessarily remains to be done, in developing the various resources of the Colony, in opening up the interior, in working out the problem of responsible government; in cultivating literature, science, and the arts; in short, in everything calculated to raise a virtuous population—

——— A happy band,
To stand a wall of fire
Around our much-loved land.

These are works that require clear heads, strong hands, and above all, honest hearts; but if we speed onward, earnest and eager, though great the struggle, yet glorious will be the success.

'We now wish that your Excellency's connexion

with this new colony may be long and prosperous, with tranquillity in your Government and happiness in your personal and family relations.'

His Excellency replied:

'Gentlemen,—I have already received so many addresses since my arrival in this Colony that it is difficult for me to vary the expression of my thanks for the loyal spirit in which they are all conceived towards our gracious and beloved Queen, and for the kindly feeling which they all evince towards my family and myself.

'Gentlemen, this work of self-government by a free people is indeed, as you so well express it, "a work requiring clear heads, strong hands, and, above all, honest hearts." It is easy to see that you fully understand and appreciate the privileges, and I am confident that you will conscientiously perform the duties entrusted to you.

'I perceive, gentlemen, that you characterise your address as proceeding from "Working Men." I feel certain, however, that you do not mean by that phrase to imply that you belong to any separate class, whose feelings and interests are adverse to, or even distinct from, the feelings and interests of any other class of the inhabitants of this colony. In a new and free country, like that in which we are living, where there are no paid idlers or sinecurists, *every* man—Governor, Judges, Magistrates, Clergy, and *all—every* man, I repeat, is emphatically a "*Working* Man." Let us, then, all unite cordially in advancing our *common* interests. Capital is powerless without labour, and labour is unprofitable without the aid of capital. Without good government and good laws, impartially administered and cheerfully obeyed, neither capital nor labour is safe. These are old, but they are true and wise, maxims.

'The whole life of every active man in a free country is necessarily a life of labour and competition. It is a life of competition with those who are running the same race, of struggle with circumstances, often of fight against that adverse fortune which may now and then befall us all. But he who enters into the work with that dogged perseverance which is the peculiar characteristic of the Anglo-Saxon race, is sure to bring out successfully those talents with which nature may have endowed him. Whatever may be the amount of his abilities and opportunities, such a man will always be sure to improve those abilities and opportunities to the best advantage, and to apply them as successfully as circumstances will permit.

'Rest assured that I shall always remember with gratitude this flattering mark of your esteem and respect ; and that you will at all times find me your zealous *fellow workman*, in all that may tend to promote the happiness and welfare of the people of Queensland.'

Replying to the address of the inhabitants of one of the principal towns, Sir George laid special stress on the importance of maintaining amicable relations with the parent Colony of New South Wales :—

'You allude in your address to your recent struggle for separation from New South Wales. In that struggle you are now victorious. In gracious compliance with your own wishes, the Queen has

conferred upon you to the fullest extent, the privilege
of local self-government. Let all, then, forget henceforward any feeling of ill-will engendered by the
recent controversy, now happily terminated in your
favour. I wish these words to apply, not only to
those who now hear me, but throughout the length
and breadth of Queensland. If any inhabitant of
this Colony cherishes any lingering jealousy towards
the Colony of New South Wales, let him convert that
jealousy into emulation. Let us all unite in a generous rivalry with the neighbouring provinces. Let
us emulate them, in reverence for our religion, in
loyalty to our Queen, in obedience to the laws, in
energy, in enterprise—in a word, in all those qualities
which have made the British Empire what it is.
Such are the arts which have enabled us, the great
English nation, to overrun the earth from one end of
it to the other. It is thus that we have spread our
race and language over the North American Continent, from the Atlantic to the Pacific. It is thus
that we have annexed to Britain that India which
eluded the grasp of Alexander. It is thus, finally,
that we are now fast peopling our own Australia, that
" Great Southern Land " which lay beyond the ken
of the ancient world.'

The proceedings of December 12, 1859, are
memorable in many ways. To the people of Queensland the moment was of vital importance; and the
impression produced by their Governor's speeches
was very favourable. 'His welcome is no noisy
tribute of lip service, but a manifestation that comes

from the heart.'[1] The whole community accepted Sir George Bowen's advice in the friendly spirit in which it was obviously tendered. They realised that he ' thoroughly appreciated their position '; and they were willing to listen to the counsels of a Governor ' whose reputation must hereafter be estimated by the success or failure of his administration in Queensland ': that he would lay ' on broad foundations the happiness and prosperity of the colony ' was, they felt, ' guaranteed by the good sense of his language.'[2]

Sir George's own impressions of his reception are recorded in the subjoined despatch :

To the Duke of Newcastle, Secretary of State for the Colonies.

Government House, Brisbane, Queensland :
December 19, 1859.

My Lord Duke,

I have the honour to report, that on the 10th inst. I landed at Brisbane ; and that, after taking the usual oaths before Mr. Justice Lutwyche, Judge of the Supreme Court, I assumed, in obedience to the Queen's commands, the office of Captain-General and Governor-in-Chief of the Colony of Queensland and its dependencies. My reception was very gratifying to me personally, and eminently satisfactory on public grounds, as proving the excellent spirit with which all classes of the inhabitants of the new Colony are animated towards their Queen and mother-country. From a variety of motives, similar to those which

---

[1] *Moreton Bay Courier.*   [2] *North Australian*, Dec. 20, 1859.

actuated the people of the Colony of Victoria before
its separation from New South Wales, and which
it would be superfluous in me to recapitulate, the
inhabitants of Moreton Bay districts have, during
several years, petitioned the Queen to be formed into
a separate Colony.   My arrival as the first Governor
was a tangible proof that the prayer of their petitions had been granted and their long deferred hopes
fulfilled ; and the people of Queensland appear to have
determined, as one man, to evince their ' heartfelt
gratitude, love, and devotion towards their Sovereign,'
and ' their affectionate attachment to Her Majesty's
person and government,' by uniting in a hearty
welcome and loyal greeting to Her Majesty's first
representative among them.

The address from the people of Queensland (together with several other addresses from various
public bodies) was presented to me shortly after my
arrival, in a pavilion erected for that purpose in the
Botanical Gardens of this city, and in the presence of
(at the lowest estimate) 4,000 of the inhabitants of
Brisbane and its vicinity.   In my reply I took occasion to mention that ' Queensland, the name selected
for the new Colony, was entirely the happy thought
and inspiration of Her Majesty herself.   Other designations had been suggested to her, but the Queen
spontaneously determined to confer her own royal
title on this new Province of her Empire.'   The
announcement of this simple fact was received by
the 4,000 of Her Majesty's subjects who formed my

audience, with an emotion rarely witnessed in so large a concourse ; it was received with tears of joy, and shouts of ' God save the Queen ! '

These expressions of love and loyalty to the Queen, and the cordial welcome given to Her Majesty's first representative, are far from being mere phrases or empty compliments. The reception of a new Governor in other Colonies is, generally speaking, simply an affair of ordinary military display on the part of the garrison, and entails neither expense nor trouble on the inhabitants. But there is not a single soldier in Queensland. Here all preparations were made by a ' reception committee,' appointed at a public meeting of the inhabitants ; and the whole cost, including the hire of several steamers engaged to escort me up the river Brisbane from Moreton Bay to the seat of Government, and the purchase of cannon to fire salutes, was defrayed by public subscription.

It is an honourable duty for me to solicit your Grace to lay before the Queen not only the assurance of the devoted loyalty and gratitude of Her Majesty's subjects in this Colony, but also the manifold proofs which my official correspondence will afford of their growing welfare and happiness, and of the rapid progress here, alike of material industry, of mental activity. and of moral and physical well-being. ' Everything,' as I ventured to express my hope in one of my addresses, ' may be expected from such signs as these. They are strong proofs to our Queen and country-men at home that the foundations of a rich and flourishing province of the British Empire have been laid in this part of Australia.'

I enclose printed copies of the addresses presented to me on my assumption of office, and of my replies. It will be perceived that I have somewhat deviated from the set form of such compositions. · A Governor may be of much use here by explaining and adapting the social and political institutions, the feelings and habits, of the mother-country; in short, by looking at Australia with English and at England with Australian eyes. Accordingly, I seized the opportunity presented to me of offering observations and advice on some of the idiosyncrasies which distinguish this like all other communities. Thus, I reminded the people of Queensland in my reply to their address, that an arduous and responsible, but most important and interesting, task awaits them ; for the attainment of self-government is an epoch in the life of a State, resembling the attainment of his majority in the life of an individual. So again I pointed out to the Mayor and Corporation of the city of Brisbane the many direct and indirect advantages of municipal institutions, which have been somewhat neglected in Australia ; confirming my own views by a quotation from the report of the Privy Council on the Australian Colonies, presented to the Queen in 1849. So again, in addressing the 'representatives of the working men,' I deprecated the use of that phrase in any sense which could imply that it belongs exclusively to any separate class, whose feelings and interests

were adverse to, or even distinct from, the feelings
and interests of any other class of the inhabitants of
this Colony.   I reminded my hearers, moreover, that
in a new and free country, every man,—Governor,
Judges, Clergy, and all,—*every* man is emphatically a
working man. Let us, then, I continued, all unite
cordially in promoting our common interests.   I concluded by assuring my hearers that they will at all
times find me their zealous *fellow workman* in all that
may tend to promote the happiness and welfare of
the people of Queensland.   Finally, I took advantage
of some expressions of irritation made use of in one
of the addresses against the neighbouring Colony of
New South Wales, to exhort my audience to convert
such jealousies into emulation.

I trust that your Grace will approve the tone and
matter of my replies.   They certainly made a most
favourable impression in this country, as appears
partly from the applause with which they were received at the time of their delivery; partly from the
comments of the rival organs of the colonial press,
which have discovered a common ground of agree-
ment in their praise; and partly from the sensible
diminution which I am happy to believe is already
observable in the virulence of party spirit, and of
local and personal jealousies.

In his reply (April 11, 1860) the Duke of Newcastle wrote:

I have received your despatch of December 19,

accompanied by copies of several addresses presented to you on your assuming the Government of Queensland, and by copies of your answers. I have laid this despatch with its enclosures before the Queen.

The expressions of loyalty to our Sovereign and of goodwill to yourself, contained in the addresses presented by the inhabitants of Queensland on their reception of their first Governor, were highly satisfactory to Her Majesty. I cannot do otherwise than approve of the sentiments embodied in your replies.

I trust that the new Colony has before it a long career of internal prosperity and of friendly and advantageous relations with the other communities in Australia.

CHAPTER VII.

ORGANISATION OF THE PUBLIC DEPARTMENTS—LETTERS TO SIR
E. BULWER LYTTON—TO THE DUKE OF NEWCASTLE—TOUR
ON THE DARLING DOWNS—RAPID BUT SOLID PROGRESS OF
SETTLEMENT.

THE first three months after his arrival in Queensland
were devoted by Sir George Bowen to the task of
organising the various departments of the new
Government, studying the condition of the people
and the resources of the Colony, and generally
mastering the *carte du pays*. In consequence of
the wording of the Order in Council creating the
new province, the Parliament could not assemble
till May, and the interval was not a day too long
for the multitudinous administrative details to be
thought out and elaborated. As has been said,
every part of the machinery of government was only
in posse when the Governor arrived, and waited
to be formed and set in motion by his own hand.
Besides such constructive labour, he had the no
less difficult work to accomplish of learning the
needs and resources of the entire community.
Several burning questions had to be studied: the
land question foremost of all; then the improvement
of agriculture and the introduction of such new crops
as cotton and sugar; with many other matters of
serious moment. A close attention to these subjects

coupled with unremitting administrative toil kept the Governor closely engaged at Brisbane until March, when he was for the first time free to make a tour of visits among the inland districts of the Colony. His reflections upon the various problems lying before him are contained in the following letter to Sir Edward Bulwer Lytton, and in a despatch to the Secretary of State.

To the Rt. Hon. Sir E. Bulwer Lytton, Bart., M.P.

Brisbane, Queensland: March 6, 1860.

My dear Sir Edward Lytton,

When I was your guest at Knebworth shortly before I left England last year, you told me that you would always be glad to hear from me, though you were no longer in office.

I have now been nearly three months in Queensland. My official despatches to the Secretary of State contain a full account of what I have done; with proofs that my humble efforts to promote their well-being are satisfactory to the people of this Colony. My reward will be complete if I should be so fortunate as to deserve the approval of Her Majesty's Government; and, let me add (whether this letter finds you in office or out of it), of *yourself*, whose confidence placed me in my present position.

In congratulating me on my promotion to this Government, the Duke of Newcastle (who had formerly appointed me to the Chief Secretaryship at Corfu) wrote that ' the task of guiding the destinies of one of the Australian Colonies was worthy the ambition of *any* man whom duties at home do not prevent from undertaking it.' My position is, certainly, full of interest and encouragement. I have more of *creation* and *discovery* than falls to the lot of most Colonial Governors. Every department in this great and rising Colony may almost be said to be the work of my own hands.

A district within Queensland, covering about the area of the British Islands, is already studded with the stations of our 'shepherd kings'; and beyond those limits there are regions equal to the aggregate extent of two of the other principal monarchies of Europe. Fresh bands of pastoral settlers, driving their thousands of cattle, sheep, and horses before them, are fast pushing out into the wilderness; and it is confidently expected that, in the course of the next five years, there will be a chain of stations from Moreton Bay to the Gulf of Carpentaria; and thence a line of steamers to Singapore, opening up commerce with India and China, and with the Dutch and Spanish colonies in the Eastern Archipelago. The Queen might say of her loyal Queenslanders, as Jupiter said of the Romans of old:

> *His ego nec metas rerum nec tempora pono ;*
> *Imperium sine fine dedi.*[1]——

While zealously developing the resources of the districts already settled, I shall be able to do much

[1] Virgil, *Æn.* I. 278.

for geography and science in the vast and still unexplored regions comprised within Queensland. The
charm of the climate and the beauty of the scenery
in this part of Australia are hardly known in England.
At Brisbane, we have the climate of Naples, without
malaria or *scirocco*. We are also free from the ' hot
winds' blowing from the central desert which occasionally afflict Sydney, Melbourne, and Adelaide.
This district, too, is, in point of vegetation, a sort of
debatable land between the temperate and tropical
zones. The productions of both grow with equal
luxuriance. In the gardens, potatoes and pineapples,
cabbages and bananas, are flourishing side by side.
But I need not expatiate on these topics to the author
of ' The Caxtons.'

I will not trouble you with statistical figures. I
will only say that our English population is at present
calculated at about 25,000 souls. There are no
materials as yet for forming an accurate estimate of
the Chinamen, Aborigines, Indian coolies, &c., within
the limits of the colony. A regular census will be
taken in 1861, so that the periods may coincide with
those of the census in the United Kingdom. The
Treasurer estimates our revenue at about 180,000*l.*
for the current year; so that, if I mistake not,
Queensland, at her first start, takes the twelfth place
among the forty-eight British Colonies.

Your name as that of the creator of this Colony
enjoys the same sort of respect and popularity in
Queensland which was paid to the οἰκιστής of a

Greek settlement. The future port of Brisbane on
Moreton Bay has already been called *Lytton*; and I
have directed the Surveyor-General to call a rising
township *Knebworth*. This is only following the precedent of the Colonies now forming the United States
of America, where so many geographical names were
derived from English sovereigns and statesmen. I
am going to have a *Pakington* and a *Westwood*, in
honour of my friend Sir J. Pakington.[1] I find there
is already a *Gladstone*, a *Pelham*, and a *Clinton*.
When the native names are tolerably euphonious, I
shall preserve them.

After the general disaffection of the Ionian
Islands (a feeling exactly akin to the *sentimento
nazionale* which England fosters in Italy), it certainly is very pleasant to find one's self among so
loyal a population as that of Australia. Whatever
inconveniences may attend what is called 'responsible,' but should rather be called 'parliamentary'
government in our Colonies, it is certain that it has
had the effect of greatly tightening the bonds of
pride and affection which unite the Australians to
their mother-country. Since the full establishment
of local self-government, the colonists no longer 'feel
the collar,' to quote the phrase of a popular leader
here, who was formerly supposed to be disaffected,
but is now enthusiastic in his loyalty. If you grant
representative institutions without responsible government, you 'light the fire and stop the chimney,' as

---

[1] Afterwards Lord Hampton, G.C.B.

Charles Buller said. Witness the Ionian Islands. I question if there is any practical or logical *locus standi* between the form of government in Ceylon and Mauritius, and the form of government in Victoria and New South Wales.

My Parliament is to meet in May, on the 90th anniversary of the discovery of Moreton Bay by Captain Cook. That I may know something of the *carte du pays* before I convene the legislature, I am about to start on two tours, one of three hundred miles on horseback, and another of about one thousand miles by sea, touching at the settlements on the coast. I shall ride about thirty miles every day, and shall be comfortably lodged at night in the houses of the principal 'squatters,' or pastoral settlers, whose stations average that distance from each other. These gentlemen live in a patriarchal style among their immense flocks and herds, amusing themselves with hunting, shooting, fishing, and the exercise of a plentiful hospitality. I have often thought (especially in reading Thackeray's novel, 'The Virginians') that the Queensland gentlemen-squatters bear a similar relation to the other Australians that the Virginian planters of a hundred years back bore to the other Americans.

But there is a perfectly distinct class of people in the towns. Brisbane, my present capital, must resemble what Boston and the other Puritan towns of New England were at the close of the last century. In a population of 7,000,[1] we have fourteen Churches,

---

[1] Now, in 1880, the population of Brisbane is above 70,000.

thirteen public-houses, twelve policemen. The leading inhabitants of Brisbane are a hard-headed set
of English and Scotch merchants and mechanics ;
very orderly, industrious, and prosperous ; proud of
the mother-country ; loyal to the person of the
Queen ; and·convinced that the true federation for
these Colonies is the maintenance of the integrity of
the Empire, and that the true rallying point for
Australians is the Throne.

I hope that you will approve the tone and substance of my replies to the addresses presented to me.
You will perceive that I have attempted to look on
England with Australian and on Australia with English eyes ; and to tender some advice on the idiosyncrasies which distinguish this like all other societies.
In fact I have guided myself in this, as in all else, by
the precepts of the letter (wonderful for a Statesman who has never lived in a Colony) which you
wrote to me on the 29th April last.[1] One phrase
which I borrowed from you has become a household
word in Queensland : ' Let us convert our jealousies
into emulation.' There is another sentence of yours
in a published despatch to another Governor, which
is often on Australian lips : ' Wherever England extends her sceptre, there, as against the foreign enemy,
she pledges the defence of her sword.' We are
to have only one or two officers of the army in
Queensland to organise the volunteer force which I
have called into existence in compliance with your

[1] See above, page 81.

recommendation. We have splendid materials for yeomanry cavalry.

The great question to be settled when the Parliament meets is the land question. It threatens in all these Colonies to become an irritating contest between rival interests—between the towns and the country—like the corn laws in England, and the agrarian laws in ancient Rome. How exactly the squatter question resembles the strife between the patricians and plebeians about the *ager publicus*! We want an Australian Licinius Stolo. I think I remarked to you once before that it is also curious that ' runs ' (the colonial term for wide ranges of pasture) should seem a literal translation of the δρόμοι εὐρέες of Homer,[1] where Greek shepherd kings fed their cattle in a climate similar to that of Australia. How refreshing amid my daily cares are these classical parallels!

If I had not already exhausted your patience, there are many topics on which I might possibly interest you, and on which I have thought long and deeply myself. Such are—the division of the public debt between New South Wales and Queensland; the advantages and disadvantages of elective and nominated Upper Houses in these Colonies; the state of education; the best methods of promoting immigration, geographical discovery, and intercourse with India and China; and of ameliorating the condition of the aborigines.

[1] *Od.* IV. 605.

To the Duke of Newcastle.

Government House, Brisbane : January 6, 1860.

My Lord Duke,

Although I have been incessantly occupied since my assumption of office on the 10th ult. in creating and organising the several departments of government in this new Colony, I have not omitted to turn my attention to the vast, but as yet very partially developed, natural resources and productive capabilities of Queensland. In my despatch of November 28th ult., I alluded briefly to the valuable supplies of timber, and of minerals of various kinds, which await here the further introduction of labour and capital; and in a despatch of even date herewith, I have furnished some information as to the prospects of the cultivation of sugar within this Colony. I shall return to each of these subjects separately in future reports.

For the present there is no need that I should enlarge on the capabilities of this soil and climate for grazing purposes. It is a well-known fact that the wools exported from the Moreton Bay districts rank highest, and command the best prices in the European markets. A rich pasture land, extending in length from north to south about 120 miles, with an average width of 50 miles, was discovered so far back as in 1827 by that distinguished botanist and traveller, the late Mr. Allan Cunningham, and was named by him the 'Darling Downs,' in honour of General Darling, at that time Governor of New

South Wales. The description which its discoverer
wrote of this district is also, to some extent, applicable
to other pastoral regions which have since been
explored and occupied within the limits of the new
Colony :—

'These extensive tracts of clear pastoral country
commence about the parallel of twenty-eight degrees
south latitude. Deep ponds, supported by streams
from the highlands immediately to the eastward,
extend along their central lower flats. The lower
grounds thus permanently watered present flats which
furnish an almost inexhaustible range of cattle pasture
at all seasons of the year; the grass and herbage
generally exhibiting in the depth of winter an extreme
luxuriance of growth. From these central grounds rise
downs of a rich black and dry soil, and very ample surface, and as they furnish abundance of grass, and are
conveniently watered yet perfectly beyond the reach
of those floods which take place on the flats in a season of rain, they constitute a valuable and sound
sheep pasture with a most beautifully diversified landscape, made up of hill and dale, woodland and plain.'

Although the 'Darling Downs' had been discovered in 1827 by Mr. Cunningham, it was not until
1839 that the first sheepowners[1] drove their flocks
before them into that region, over the 'dividing
range' of hills which forms the watershed of Eastern

---

[1] One of these pioneers was Mr. Hodgson, now Sir Arthur Hodgson,
K.C.M.G., well-known by his exertions at the Colonial and Indian
Exhibition, who still holds the 'run' which he first occupied in 1839.

Australia, and separates the districts of the coast from those of the interior. The success of the early pioneers encouraged a host of followers. The history of this settlement relates how flock after flock and herd after herd came pouring in until the Downs were fully occupied, and the more adventurous and enterprising settlers found themselves constrained to push further out into the unexplored wilderness. Nearly two years ago it was computed that within the limits of the districts now comprised within the Colony of Queensland there were not less than 3,500,000 sheep, 450,000 horned cattle, and 20,000 horses; and the annual export of wool, tallow, hides and skins, was valued at above half a million of pounds sterling. It is probable that the census of the next year will show a notable increase; for already flocks feed within the tropics far to the northward of Port Curtis and Keppel Bay; and a region (all within the new Colony of Queensland), stretching nearly 600 miles from north to south, and about 300 miles from east to west, and enjoying a serene and salubrious climate, is studded with the stations of the pastoral settlers. Nor is, perhaps, the general expectation too sanguine which predicts the establishment within the next few years of a chain of settlements from Moreton Bay to the Gulf of Carpentaria, and the consequent opening of a rapid and easy communication with India and China by the way of Java and Singapore.[1]

[1] These anticipations have been far more than realised (1889); and the trade and general wealth of Queensland have increased even more rapidly than the population.

The subject of cotton engrosses at the present moment a large share of the attention of the press, and of the public generally in this Colony. It is felt that nothing more fortunate for the steady prosperity of Queensland could occur than that, while pastoral settlers spread over the highlands and downs of the interior, some enterprising capitalist, or association of capitalists, should introduce on an extensive scale the cultivation of cotton on the eastern seaboard and along the banks of the rivers. The peculiar adaptation of the climate and soil of this part of Australia for the growth of the most valuable description of this plant, the Sea-Island cotton, has long been a fact far removed from all doubt by frequent and successful experiments; and the demand in England, now chiefly supplied by the produce of American slave-labour, is practically insatiable. The whole of the low lands and alluvial plains near the mouths of the rivers of Queensland, as well as a seaboard of at least 600 miles along the shore of the Pacific, could be rendered almost immediately available for the production of this lucrative, because necessary, article of commerce. There is a succession of harbours at intervals along the coast, so that the cost of carriage to the port of shipment would be comparatively trifling. I will only allude to the advantage of rendering the English manufactures less dependent on foreigners for their supply of cotton and to the discouragement of slavery which would accrue from the successful cultivation of that plant by free labour.

It appears to me, that the cultivation of cotton might be carried on with success in Queensland on two different plans. In the first place, in the tropical districts of the Colony, where the climate is unfavourable to European fieldwork, on large plantations, and with Asiatic labour ; and, in the second place, in the temperate districts, on small farms occupied by English emigrants and their families.

With regard to the former plan. I presume, that the Government of British India would sanction the emigration of coolies to Queensland (should the Legislature of this Colony make proposals for that purpose), on conditions similar to those carried out with so much success at Mauritius. Why should not English capital and free Indian labour do for cotton in Northern Australia what English capital and free Indian labour have done for sugar, with so great advantages both to the employers and the employed, in the similar climate of Mauritius ? On this part of the subject, I beg to refer your Grace to ' A Letter to the Colonists of Queensland,' recently published in London by Mr. Marsh, M.P. for Salisbury, and a large proprietor in this Colony. That gentleman argues that the introduction of Asiatic labour would be to North Queensland what machinery has been to England, ' elevating the [European] labourer to the rank of a mechanic, and the mechanic to that of an employer, and contributing in a large degree to the well-being of every class of society.'

With regard to the second of the two plans proposed above, there appears no sufficient reason why, in the vicinity of Brisbane and Maryborough, and, generally, throughout the temperate districts of this Colony, cotton-growing should not be brought under the conditions of European labour, and made to form a part of the industry on small farms. This is done in Texas by German farmers, in a climate not less sultry, and infinitely less healthy, than that of Queensland. The whole subject, therefore, is as deserving of the attention of small farmers as of large capitalists; for it seems capable of proof, that cotton growing can not only be prosecuted with success on extensive plantations, and with Asiatic labour, but can also be made a profitable part of a yeomanry agriculture. In fact, the cultivation of cotton is one of the least expensive of all agricultural operations, especially in Australia, where, owing to the absence of severe winter frosts, the plant is perennial, and not as in North America, an annual. The women and children of English emigrant families could be employed in the light labour of picking the pods in harvest time.

As soon as the administrative machinery was fully organised, and the several departments were at work, the Governor set out upon a tour into the interior. So far, he had seen only the seaboard; he now

ascended to the magnificent stretches of undulating
table-lands and prairies, the southern portion of
which is famous in the annals of sheep-farming as
the 'Darling Downs.' These noble plains, extending within the tropics, but elevated some 2,000 feet
above the sea-level, spread from the southern limits
of Queensland, for a distance of over 1,000 miles,
to the Gulf of Carpentaria, and their breadth from
east to west is from 400 to 500 miles, giving a
total area of at least 400,000 square miles. 'The
whole of this area, with the exception of two partial
interruptions, may be described as a succession of
wide open downs, enclosed each within small sub-
sidiary basaltic ranges traversing the great plateau.
These downs are each of immense extent, and contain deep and most excellent agricultural soil, at present clothed with the richest grasses, growing in wonderful luxuriance. They are in a great measure
destitute of trees, but the bases of their enclosing
ranges are furnished with a very handsome and
stately description of pine, behind which, and retiring into their recesses, are found very valuable
cedars. These recesses are plentifully supplied with
numerous springs and rills, which trickling down the
slopes of the ranges, and traversing the enclosed
plains, unite and form the abundant network of
rivers by which this immense plateau is watered.
Travellers through these vast plains all concur in
their admiration of the luxuriance of the soil, the
coolness and salubrity of the climate, and the love-
liness of the entire landscape.' [1]

That Sir George Bowen was keenly appreciative

[1] *Edinburgh Review*, No. 243, Oct. 1863, art. 'Queensland.'

of the beauty of the Darling Downs is shown in the subjoined letter, in which he describes his first introduction to the homes of the pastoral Tenants of the Crown, commonly known by the American nickname of ' squatters.'

To Herman Merivale, Esq., C.B., Permanent Under-Secretary of State for the Colonies.

Government House, Brisbane : April 10, 1860.

My dear Merivale,

I have just returned from a very interesting and gratifying tour in the interior, during which I spent nearly a week in the ' County Merivale.' You should feel proud of being the ἐπώνυμος of one of the most picturesque and probably (putting gold out of the question) richest districts of all Australia.

I ascended from the *tierra caliente* of the coast to the table-land of the Darling Downs, of which your county comprises the southern portion, through Cunningham's Gap, a cleft between mountains of porphyry and basalt; which, though not equal, as some enthusiastic Queenslanders imagine, to ' anything in the Alps,' is certainly finer than anything that I ever saw in the British Isles. There is, however, a cascade falling three hundred feet into a chasm resembling the crater of a volcano, which would make the fortune of any valley in Switzerland.

Some of the squires, or ' squatters,' of Merivale had descended into the lowlands to meet and escort me to their houses; so we formed a very picturesque cavalcade as we wound up through the luxuriant forests of the Gap. On the summit I was greeted with loud cheers, which made the rocks re-echo as they probably had never sounded since the dawn of creation ; and there I found another batch of hospitable squatters, with a cold collation and plenty of champagne and hock, spread on the grass at the top of the pass, nearly 3,000 feet above the sea. The view from this point is most interesting and magnificent ; on one side the undulating hills and waving forests of the semi-tropical *littorale*, with the Pacific beyond ; on the other the broad downs, intersected by wooded ridges, of the table-land. The *Larissœ campus opimœ* of Horace [1] rose to my lips, for I assure you that the Darling Downs closely resemble the general aspect of Thessaly ; and the river Condamine is a good substitute for the Peneus. There are indeed no Pelion and Ossa ' flourishing side by side,' but the hills which encircle the basin-like plains vividly recall the lower ranges of Pindus and Olympus. Show what I say to Fortescue,[2] who has seen Thessaly ; he will recollect the splendid variety of birds and butterflies there. This is another point of similarity. The woods on the Darling Downs are full of birds of brilliant plumage and strange voices ; while stately bustards and emus stalk over the plains, and wildfowl of all kinds frequent the streams. The residences of the squatters, however, afford a striking

---

[1] *Carm.* I. 7.

[2] The Parliamentary Under-Secretary for the Colonies, afterwards Lord Carlingford.

contrast to the lodgings to be procured in Greece. I found carpets and curtains, plate and pianos, champagne and crinoline, in places where fifteen years before the face of a white man had never been seen.

If their country is like Thessaly, the squatters of Merivale are complete *Centaurs*. The cavalcade of well-mounted horsemen that everywhere came out to meet the first Representative of their Queen eclipsed anything of the kind that could be exhibited in ancient Greece, or indeed, in any part of the world, except in England or in Australia. I was escorted into your county town of Warwick by 400 horsemen. I rode one day, to the delight of the Centaurs—I mean of the Squatters,—and without the slightest fatigue, seventy miles in eight hours—of course, with a change of horses. You should never send a Governor here who cannot ride and shoot. His performances across country are one of the secrets of Sir W. Denison's success as Governor of Tasmania and of New South Wales successively.

In such a colony as Queensland was in 1860, before railways had penetrated into the interior, an active Governor, who was also a good horseman, was indispensable. Such official tours as those made by Sir George Bowen are among the greatest pleasures and also the most important duties of a Governor. It is only by such visits that he can see with his own eyes the needs of his people, and that the people can be brought into direct relations with the representative of their Sovereign. This tour in the south-eastern districts was eminently successful. On all sides the Governor was welcomed with enthusiasm; and even while confronting some of the keenest jealousies and prejudices of the time and place, his replies to the addresses presented to him at Warwick and the rival towns of Drayton and Toowoomba evoked none but golden opinions.

To the Duke of Newcastle.

Government House, Brisbane: April 7, 1860.

My Lord Duke,

I have the honour to enclose copies of the addresses presented to me at the three towns of Warwick, Drayton, and Toowoomba, which I visited during an official tour of inspection from which I have lately returned. It will be satisfactory to the Queen, and to Her Majesty's Government, to receive these further proofs of the affectionate loyalty of the people of this Colony to Her Majesty's throne and person; and (I may, perhaps, be permitted to add) of their confidence in the arrangement made, under Her Majesty's favour, for their government.

My recent journey extended through those districts of Queensland which have been longest settled and are most thickly inhabited. I was everywhere received with cordial hospitality by the principal settlers, and with loyal enthusiasm by all classes of the community.

As it was during your Grace's first administration of the Colonial Department that the wishes of the Australian colonists were crowned by the concession of responsible government, I will take leave to draw your attention to a paragraph in one of the enclosures, which expresses a sentiment generally entertained by this people. After stating that ' the journey of his Excellency has been one continued ovation from beginning to end '; that ' all classes have vied in doing honour to the representative of the Queen '; and that ' all little sectarian differences, petty jealou sies, and presumed rival interests have been merged in the laudable wish to give our first Governor a hearty welcome,' the ' Darling Downs Gazette ' proceeds as follows : ' Not the least pleasing reflection that suggests itself, when reviewing these demonstrations of general joy, is the confirmation of the fact, now so long and in so many lands established, that those descended from the old stock at home, to whom self-government has been a timely concession, not a charter wrung from the mother-country by the force of arms, still recognise and revere the grand old institutions which have made England the greatest power on earth.'

There cannot in my opinion be a greater mistake than the view which some public writers in England appear to hold, viz. that the Governor of a Colony, under the system of responsible government, should be merely a *roi fainéant*. So far as my observation extends, nothing can be more opposed than this theory to the wishes of the Anglo-Australians themselves. The Governor of each of the Colonies in this group is expected not only to act as the head of society; to encourage literature, science, and art; to keep alive by personal visits to every district under his jurisdiction the feelings of loyalty to the Queen, and of attachment to the mother-country, and so to cherish what may be termed the Imperial sentiment; but he is also expected, as head of the administration, to maintain, with the assistance of his Executive Council, a vigilant control and supervision over every department of the public service. In short, he is in a position in which he can exercise an influence over the whole course of affairs exactly proportionate to the strength of his character, the activity of his mind and body, the capacity of his understanding, and the extent of his knowledge.

In accordance with this view of the duties of my office, I took occasion, in my reply to the address of the town of Warwick, to explain the principal objects of my official tours. 'The chief motive,' I said, 'by which I am actuated, is an earnest desire to perform honestly and efficiently that portion of the work which the constitution has allotted to me in the advancement of this great Colony. All contribute to the revenue; all should benefit by its application. As it rests with the Governor to propose, with the advice of his Executive Council, the estimates which will be submitted for the decision of the Parliament of Queensland, it will be my constant endeavour to ascertain, by personal observation, the wants and wishes of the people of every district; and so to frame those estimates as to bring home to all an equitable share of the advantages which the rapid development of your almost inexhaustible resources, due to your own skill and industry, will each year enable the Government to extend.'

The warm coast land of this Colony is admirably adapted for the growth of cotton, of sugar, and of all semi-tropical fruits and productions. Queensland, like Mexico, has a *tierra caliente*, or hot region, near the sea, from which there is an ascent through fine mountain passes to the cool tableland of the interior, which is eminently fitted as well for pastoral settlement as for European agriculture. I have described in a former despatch that rich pastoral district of the table-land which is known as the 'Darling Downs.' Many large fortunes have been amassed there during the last fifteen years.[1] Some idea of the

---

[1] An extract from a letter of Sir G. Bowen to a friend in England illustrates this statement : ' Some of our larger squatters are owners of from 50,000 to 300,000 sheep ; and there are men in Australia who have above half-a-million. A successful Queenslander, who became a member of the House of Commons, where he supported Lord Palmerston, was invited to one of the political receptions of Lady Waldegrave at Strawberry Hill. That accomplished hostess prided herself on her information about her guests ; and on the arrival of the gentleman referred to, she is said to have greeted him with ' Oh, Mr. ——, I am very glad to see you. I hear that you have as many sheep and cattle as the Patriarchs, that, in short, you are a *second Job*.' Her guest replied : ' I hope, Lady Waldegrave, you do not mean to compare *me* to Job, who, as we learn from the Bible, had only 7,000 sheep, whereas I have 300,000. Job was a mere *stringy-barker*.' It should be explained that young settlers, on beginning sheep-farming in the interior, with only from 5,000 to 10,000 sheep, cannot generally afford to build at first houses of wood or stone ; and are obliged for some time to content themselves with comfortable huts made from the bark of the so-called ' stringy-bark ' eucalyptus. So they were often known to the great squatters by the *sobriquet* of ' stringy-barkers.' Many now wealthy

value set upon the stations on the Darling Downs may be gained from the fact that during the past year the leases of several of the tenants of the Crown in that quarter have been sold for prices ranging from 20,000*l*. to 50,000*l*. sterling, although these leases will expire in about six years from this time, and it is most improbable that they will be renewed on conditions equally favourable. While the impression created on my mind by my journey across the Darling Downs was still fresh, I stated in my reply to the Drayton address that 'it had filled me with surprise and admiration. Even before I left England I knew by report the rich natural resources and the picturesque beauty of this district. But I confess that I was not fully prepared for so wonderfully rapid an advance in all that can promote and adorn civilisation, an advance which has taken place during the fourth part of an average lifetime. Not only have I seen vast herds of horses and cattle and countless flocks of sheep overspreading the valleys and forests, which, within the memory of persons who have yet scarcely attained to the age of manhood, were tenanted only by wild animals and by a few wandering tribes of savages; not only have I travelled over roads beyond all comparison superior to the means of communication which existed less than a century ago in many parts of the United Kingdom;

'shepherd kings' look back with pleasure to the old days when they lived in huts, and, in the absence of ready money, used to play whist with each other for *Sheep points and a bullock on the rubber.*

not only have I beheld flourishing towns arising in spots where, hardly twenty years back, the foot of a white man had never yet trodden the primæval wilderness; not only have I admired these and other proofs of material progress, but I have also found in the houses of the long chain of settlers who have entertained me with such cordial hospitality all the comforts and most of the luxuries and refinements of the houses of country gentlemen in England. The wonderful advance of this portion of the Colony during the last ten years is due to no sudden and fortuitous discovery of the precious metals; it is derived wholly from the blessing of Providence on the skill and energy of its inhabitants in subduing and replenishing the earth. Assuredly I have observed during the past week very remarkable illustrations of the proverbial genius of the Anglo-Saxon race for the noble and truly Imperial art of colonisation.'

I will add in conclusion a striking proof of the singularly rapid progress of this district. A public banquet was given in my honour in the large and handsome ball-room attached to one of the three hotels which Toowoomba, itself the creation of the last ten years, already possesses. About 120 persons sat down to a dinner, very well appointed, and provided with as good music, wine, and viands as would be exhibited on a similar occasion in the majority of country towns in England. One of the principal gentlemen of the neighbourhood, who happens, moreover, to be a candidate for the representation of Toowoomba in the Queensland Parliament, reminded his hearers, in a speech delivered in the course of the evening, that he had himself been the first white man who had settled in that district, and that just fourteen years previously he had encamped in the then unexplored forest on the very site of the hall in which he was addressing them.

CHAPTER VIII.

THE FIRST PARLIAMENT—THE FIRST ELECTIONS—THE FRANCHISE
—RESULTS OF VOTE BY BALLOT AND MANHOOD SUFFRAGE—
MEETING OF THE PARLIAMENT—SPEECH OF THE GOVERNOR,
AND ADDRESSES OF BOTH HOUSES—ADDRESSES TO THE QUEEN
AND HER MAJESTY'S REPLY—THE 'TIMES' ON QUEENSLAND.

THE nearer the time for the elections for the first
Legislative Assembly of the new Colony approached,
the more sanguine grew Sir George Bowen's anticipations of the coming experiment in parliamentary
government. He had now seen enough of the
Queenslanders to be convinced of their loyalty,
good feeling, and public spirit.

'Pray tell the Duke of Newcastle,' he wrote to
Mr. Herman Merivale, in a letter (April 10), of which
part has already been quoted, 'that all our elections
will pass off with quiet and good-humour, in spite of
the disfranchisement of one-third of the men who
voted at the last general election, and that the Parliament will meet at Brisbane before the end of May.

'Doubtless we shall have our *crises ministérielles*,
like our elder colonial sisters ; but I have yet to
learn that they need cause any trouble or anxiety to
the Home Government. Nay, more, I have yet to
learn that the rapid succession of Ministries in New

South Wales and Victoria has materially retarded the progress of those Colonies. It is certain that the progress of Australia depends less on the skill and wisdom of its law-makers than on the energy and industry of the population. People who declaim against responsible government should recollect that, if it had not been conceded, these Colonies would soon have separated from the mother-country, or have been kept down only by force of arms in what you call in your book on the Colonies " unlovely and inglorious subjection." '

The partial disfranchisement alluded to in the above letter is explained in the following despatch. That it did not cause serious complications at the very outset of the representative organisation of Queensland speaks volumes for the good sense of the people.

To the Duke of Newcastle.

Government House, Brisbane: February 6, 1860.

My Lord Duke,

It has long been known that a large proportion of the animal and vegetable productions of Australia is distinguished by characteristics directly the reverse of what is familiar in Europe. It would almost appear that an anomaly of similar nature exists in the influences exercised at the antipodes by certain political institutions.

I find that it is a very general opinion among competent authorities that vote by ballot and man

K 2

hood suffrage, as compared with open voting and a low property qualification, are, in this community, institutions of a conservative character, and calculated to give increased influence to the landed proprietors and rich settlers in the country districts, as opposed to the mixed population of the towns.

In Australia, aristocratic influence cannot be said to exist, but the ballot protects the voter against the occasional violence and dictation of democratic opinion. Again, energy and industry, with the prosperity consequent on those qualities, are so common among the Australian settlers, that in the towns and villages of Queensland there is hardly a working man who does not possess at least the property qualification required by the New South Wales Constitution Act of 1853. In fact, the majority of our labouring classes live in their own houses, built on their own land. In the towns and villages therefore, manhood suffrage may almost be said to have practically existed before it was formally enacted (with slight modifications) by the Electoral Law of 1858.

If a general view be taken of the important question now under consideration, it will appear that vote by ballot and manhood suffrage are not likely to lead, in this Colony, to those dangers and inconveniences which have been apprehended from similar institutions in older, more thickly-peopled, and less universally prosperous communities.

In the first place, distress and pauperism, those

comprehensive terms so frequently used in European politics, are unknown in Queensland. All classes of this community appear to be thoroughly imbued with the love of law and order, and the other virtues which naturally grow up with the acquisition of property, however small, and with the enjoyment of that prosperity which is the legitimate reward of honourable industry.

Again, in an Australian Colony there exist none of those classes and institutions to which vote by ballot and manhood suffrage are supposed to be antagonistic. Here there are no paid idlers or sine-curists; every man, from the Governor downwards, is emphatically a working man. Nor have we a Church establishment, a House of Lords, or hereditary privi-leges of any kind to which democratic sentiments and prejudices are hostile.

But in this colony there is a numerous class of shepherds, stockmen, and agricultural labourers set-tled on the pastoral stations of the interior. Though equally trustworthy and prosperous, in most cases, with their fellow workmen in the towns, these men were excluded from the electoral roll by the pro-visions of the Constitution Act of 1853, because they are regarded, in some degree, as hired servants living in houses belonging to their employers. They ac-quired the franchise by the introduction, in 1858, of the principle of manhood suffrage, and are stated to have usually exercised their new privileges, when well treated by their employers, as those employers recommended. This class of men are now again disfranchised, in consequence of the construction put upon the Order in Council of June 6, 1859,[1] by Sir William Denison's legal advisers, and many of our great pastoral settlers ('squatters') consider that they have thereby lost a large amount of political influence.

The most important consideration of all yet remains to be stated. In several British dependencies, in the Ionian Islands, in parts of British India, and elsewhere, the full concession of political power to the people would have the unfortunate effect of arming alien and disaffected races against British supremacy. But next to an enlightened and reasonable attachment to the principles of local self-government, in analogy to the usage of the British constitution, the strongest political feelings of the overwhelming majority of the population of Queensland—let me say, of all the Australian Colonies—are undoubtedly at the present moment loyalty to the person of the Queen and pride in the mother-country. Speaking of Queensland in particular, I might say that the feelings to which I allude almost approach, in a large proportion of the inhabitants of this Colony,

---

[1] It was pointed out at the time by Mr. Justice Lutwyche that the drafting of this Order in Council by the Colonial Office was faulty. As the Law Officers of the Crown in England, when consulted by the Duke of Newcastle, confirmed this opinion, an Act of the Imperial Parliament was passed to correct the error of the department, and to place beyond doubt the legal validity of the Constitution of the new Colony. It was properly left entirely to the Queensland Parliament to settle what the electoral franchise should be in the future.

to that '*maladie du pays*, that passionate love of England,' which an acute writer of extensive colonial experience (Mr. Gibbon Wakefield) foretold thirty years ago would be the result of allowing the Australian Colonies to manage in their own way their own internal affairs. As Lord John Russell wrote in 1855, the avowed desire of the Australian colonists to assimilate their institutions as far as possible to those of the parent country is in itself a proof that their sympathy with that country is ' not merely the expression of a common sentiment arising from a common origin, but is connected with a deliberate attachment to the ancient laws of the community from which their own has sprung.'

The Governor's prediction was verified : the elections for the twenty-six seats in the Legislative Assembly passed off in perfect order and quiet, and his own Ministers were among the most popular candidates. No better proof could be given of the satisfaction with which the people of Queensland regarded the first steps taken by the Governor and his Executive Council, in ordering the affairs of the new State. At the same time the Legislative Council, consisting of fifteen leading settlers nominated by the Governor, was appointed, with Sir Charles Nicholson as its first President. On Sir Charles's departure for England, Sir Maurice O'Connell became his successor ; and the new Council derived much benefit from being presided over by two gentlemen of their position, experience, and high character.

To the Duke of Newcastle.

Government House, Brisbane: May 18, 1860.

My Lord Duke,

I have the honour to report that the elections for the first Legislative Assembly of Queensland began on the earliest day allowed by law, that is, on the 27th ult., and that they are now all over, having been everywhere conducted with perfect order, decorum, and good feeling. I am assured that the quiet of the elections was exceeded only by their purity, and that there is no complaint even of that species of political hospitality which is technically termed treating; and which, if it could be excusable anywhere, would be so in a country where voters often have to ride more than fifty miles to the poll.

This result of the elections will appear still more creditable to the inhabitants of Queensland when certain peculiarities of our position are called to mind. In the first place your Grace will recollect that most of our electorates are only just created, and that the majority of the electors therein had never previously exercised their privilege. They had, consequently, to control the excitement of novelty and inexperience. In the next place, in the electorates which existed before the separation of this Colony from New South Wales, manhood suffrage had been introduced in 1858; and a large proportion of the electors who had voted under that system at the last elections for the Parliament at Sydney, now find themselves disfranchised, through no fault on their part, but owing to a legal interpretation of the Order in Council of June 6, 1859, of which they find it difficult to understand the equity. Again, Queensland is the only Colony in the Australian group—indeed it is the only Colony of importance in any part of the Empire—where (not to speak of defence against external aggression) the dignity of the Crown and the authority of the law are entirely deprived of the support and *prestige* of a detachment of Her Majesty's troops. On my first assumption of office it could hardly be said that any public force whatsoever existed in Queensland. By dint of personal exertion and influence, I have now succeeded in organising a police corps, and also a body of rifle volunteers. Still, in the majority of the electorates, there was nothing but their own individual respect for the law, as authoritatively interpreted, to prevent a large number of the electors from insisting (if so disposed) on exercising the franchise of which they consider themselves unjustly deprived.

In the cases where the elections were contested, the choice of the constituencies has generally fallen on the candidates whom I am glad to see in the Assembly; so far indeed as I have any choice among gentlemen, who, however much they may differ on points of purely colonial interest, appear to vie with each other in loyalty to the Queen, in cordial respect for Her Majesty's representative, and in attachment to the mother-country.

It is, however, very gratifying to me to be enabled to report that all the three members of my Executive Council have been elected to the Assembly. Mr. Herbert, the Colonial Secretary (whom I brought with me from England),[1] received invitations from three separate constituencies, and has been returned without opposition for the Leichhardt district. Mr. Pring,[2] the Attorney-General, also received requisitions from two electorates, and his return for the Eastern Downs was unopposed.   Mr. Mackenzie,[3] the Colonial Treasurer, offered himself for the Burnett district, where there were already several candidates in the field, and came in at the head of the poll by a triumphant majority.   This result, I venture to submit, is an irrefragable proof that, on my first arrival here, I called to my councils men who already possessed, or who, while serving under my directions, have since acquired a large share of public confidence.   It would appear also an indirect testimony of approval, on the part of the people of this Colony, of the manner in which I have administered the Government during the last six months, while surrounded by many difficulties, and deprived, owing to the peculiarity of my position, of the advice and assistance of a constitutional Legislature.

[1] Now Sir Robert G. W. Herbert, K.C.B., Permanent Under-Secretary of State for the Colonies.

[2] Afterwards a judge of the Supreme Court of Queensland.

[3] He became afterwards (through the death of his elder brother) Sir Robert Mackenzie, Bart, of Coul, N.B.

To the Duke of Newcastle.

Government House, Brisbane: May 21, 1860.

My Lord Duke,

I have the honour to transmit herewith copies of the Proclamation summoning the first Legislative Council of Queensland. It will be composed of fifteen gentlemen, who have been carefully selected from among the leading colonists to represent in fair proportion the different districts and the chief interests of the Colony.

After full consideration I am inclined to the opinion that, looking to the number at present fixed for the Assembly, namely twenty-six, fifteen will be a fair proportion for the Legislative Council.[1] In fact, I have had some difficulty in properly filling up even that number, for all the more active and influential politicians desire seats in the Lower House. My own experience already tends to confirm in some degree an observation of Earl Grey,[2] to the effect that the attempts hitherto made to create in the Colonies a substitute for the House of Lords have been followed by very moderate success. 'Legislative Councils composed of members appointed by the Crown have, in general, had little real influence over public opinion, while they have been attended with the great disadvantage of rendering the Assembly less efficient, by withdrawing from the

---

[1] The number of members in both Houses was gradually increased with the progress of wealth and population.

[2] *Colonial Policy*, Vol. II., p. 98.

scene where their services might be most valuable, some of the persons best qualified, by the enjoyment of a certain degree of leisure, by their character and their ability, to be useful members of the popular branch of the Legislature. The number of such men in the circle of colonial society is necessarily limited ; hence it seems inexpedient that any of them should be taken away from the Assembly which must always exercise the largest share of power and influence.'

Two remedies have been ventilated rather than proposed in this Colony, for the inconveniences to which Earl Grey alludes in the above-quoted passage. In the first place, it is argued by some that under the present circumstances of Queensland the effect of dividing the Parliament into two separate chambers is to substitute two comparatively ineffective bodies for one of a superior character ; and that it would be well for us to revert, at all events for some years, to a single Council (like that which formerly existed in New South Wales), one-third of which should be composed of persons appointed by the Crown, and two-thirds of representatives elected by the people. But I greatly doubt if this system would work well now that responsible government has been introduced, and I feel certain that the Queensland Parliament will never be induced to take what would be represented as a retrograde step. On the other hand, there is in some quarters a popular cry in favour of making the Upper House here (as in Victoria and some other Colonies) elective equally

with the Lower, but by a different and more restricted constituency.   I again agree with Earl Grey
that 'if an Upper Chamber could be constituted in
such a manner as to have substantial weight and
authority, and to be thus capable of exercising a
salutary check upon the Representative Assembly,
while at the same time effectual provision were made
against the machine of government being brought to
a stand by differences between these two bodies, the
advantage of such a constitution of the Legislature
could not well be contested.   But to accomplish this
is a problem not yet solved by any colonial constitution of which I am aware.'   I will not trouble your
Grace with my own suggestions on this subject until
it shall have become of more practical interest.   In
the meantime, the Legislative Council, as at present
constituted, will prove an obstacle to any too hasty
legislation.   All the members have, individually, a
large stake in the welfare of this Colony, and I place
implicit reliance on their local knowledge and experience, as also on their patriotism and loyalty.

I have, moreover, the satisfaction of informing
your Grace that Sir Charles Nicholson has, at my
request, and entirely from a sense of public duty,
and a desire to render useful services to this Colony,
consented to undertake, during the first session,
the office of President of the Legislative Council
of Queensland.   On my arrival in Australia I soon
perceived (and my views were confirmed by Sir
William Denison), that it would be of great import-

ance to the best interests of the new Colony, if its first Parliament could be inaugurated under the presidency of a gentleman of the tried ability, long official experience, and high character of Sir Charles Nicholson; who had been created a baronet, as a mark of the Queen's approbation of the manner in which he had, during eleven years, and at an eventful period in colonial history, filled the office of Speaker of the first Legislative Council of New South Wales.

On May 22, 1860, the first Parliament of Queensland met at Brisbane. The Legislative Assembly unanimously elected as their Speaker Mr. Gilbert Eliott, the member for Maryborough, a gentleman of an old Scotch family, and formerly an officer of the Royal Artillery. All agreed that their choice could not have fallen on a man more generally esteemed and respected. On the following day the Assembly proceeded to Government House, and the Speaker Elect presented himself in the usual form for the approval of the Crown. I replied in the following words:

'Mr. Speaker, I approve, on behalf of the Queen, the choice which the Assembly has made in your person. It is with high satisfaction that I receive you as Speaker. I congratulate you cordially that your long and honourable career in the military and civil service of your country has been crowned by the distinguished position in which the confidence of the House has placed you.'

These formal proceedings on the English model, and the celebration of the Queen's birthday, when the society of the new Colony was gathered together for the first time at a Government House Ball, postponed serious business till May 29th; when the Governor, escorted by a troop of Volunteer Cavalry, and amid general demonstrations of respect, proceeded to the Parliament House and delivered his opening speech. It was deeply imbued with the solemn feeling inspired by an event of such moment as the inauguration of the first Legislature of so vast a country:

'Honourable Gentlemen of the Legislative Council and Gentlemen of the Legislative Assembly,—

'It is with feelings of no ordinary interest and satisfaction that I now, in the name and on behalf of the Queen, open the first session of the first Parliament of Queensland, and have recourse to your advice and assistance in the Government of this great Colony.

'It has been throughout my earnest desire to meet the Legislature at the earliest practicable period after my assumption of office in last December; but it was the unanimous opinion of the Law Officers of the Crown that, by reason of the lengthened periods fixed by the Constitution Act for the formation and revision of the electoral rolls, the elections could not legally begin before April 27. Consequently, it was impossible for the Parliament to assemble for the despatch of business sooner than the day for which you were summoned.

'This delay, however, has been accompanied with at least one advantage. It has afforded me time to make myself personally acquainted with our chief centres of population, with a large portion of our vast territory, and with the condition and requirements of its inhabitants.

'The genuine respect, the hearty welcome, the overflowing kindness with which I have been everywhere and on all occasions received, while deeply gratifying to me personally, are most satisfactory on public grounds as strong proofs of the loyalty to the Queen, and of the attachment to the mother-country, which animate all classes of this community.

'I now congratulate you on the full attainment of the object of your long-sustained efforts and aspirations in the establishment of this separate and independent Legislature ; and on the perfect order, decorum, and good feeling with which the people of Queensland universally exercised at the recent elections their privilege of self government. It is my firm hope and belief, founded on all that I have seen since my arrival here, that Her Majesty will have the high satisfaction of witnessing, as the result of her gracious boon to this Colony, its continued progress alike in material industry, in mental activity, and in moral and religious well-being ; its steady advance in wealth and social improvement, and the permanent happiness and welfare of her people.'

Some of the chief Bills to be laid before the Parliament were then enumerated ; Bills relating to education, police, finance, telegraphic communication, and the like ; and the Governor then turned to the main question of the hour :

'The land question is at once the most comprehensive and the most important with which you will have to deal. Queensland embraces a territory, blest with a salubrious climate and with a fertile soil, equivalent, at the lowest estimate, to nearly three times the area of France, and nearly ten times the area of England and Wales. Along our sea-coast and on the banks of our rivers we possess millions of acres, which bear the same relation to the cotton and sugar which the great pastoral districts of the interior hold to the wool manufactures of the mother-country. Of this gigantic patrimony the Crown has constituted this Legislature to be the guardians and administrators. The control and disposal of the whole are in your hands. I know that you are deeply impressed with the responsibility involved in such a trust ; for the mode in which you may acquit yourselves of the duties connected with it will, in all human probability, affect materially the interests of generations yet unborn. You will feel with me that hasty legislation is, above all things, to be deprecated.

.   .   .   .   .   .

' Next to a wise management of the public lands, a good system of immigration is, perhaps, the most essential element in the prosperity of a new country. Provision has been made by the Government, under the regulations now in force, for a supply of labour from the mother-country, adequate to the requirements of the present year.   I advise you to consider whether it would not be well materially to modify the existing system; and, in future, to grant, under certain conditions, remission certificates in the purchase of land to persons who reach our shores at their own cost, or who introduce labourers without expense to our Treasury.   A policy of this nature would soon have the effect of directing hither a permanent stream of immigration of the most desirable character.   It would thus prove a graceful method of communicating to our less prosperous fellow-subjects at home a share in the profits of that rich and magnificent estate with which our Sovereign has been graciously pleased to endow this Colony.

'I take this opportunity of informing you that I have felt much gratification in accepting, on behalf of the Queen, and in the terms of the existing laws, the services of several corps of Volunteers.   I trust that this movement here, as in the United Kingdom, will become permanent.   Communities which have entirely neglected to cherish the military spirit, or which have failed adequately to provide for their own external and internal defence, have seldom attained, and have still more seldom preserved, a vigorous manhood.   In this respect the British Colonies in North America afford us an example to be imitated, and the Spanish Colonies in South America a warning to be avoided. . . .

'The future destiny of this Colony will depend in no slight degree on the members of its first Legislature. You will feel with me that an arduous and responsible, but most important and interesting task awaits us, for the commencement of self-government is an epoch in the life of a State resembling the attainment of his majority in the life of an individual. For myself, I highly value the honour and privilege of having been selected by our Sovereign to inaugurate as first Governor of Queensland this new Province of the Empire. You may rest assured of my zealous and honest endeavours to carry out efficiently, as Head of the Executive, whatever measures you may have declared to be conducive to the public welfare, and to which I shall have signified my assent, as the representative of the Queen. But, I say it in all sincerity, it is on your prudence, knowledge, and experience that I depend. On these I implicitly rely, as also on your patriotism, and on that loyalty for which Australia is celebrated. This great portion of the earth—for Queensland embraces a territory far more than equal in extent to the aggregate of two of the principal monarchies of Europe,—this great portion of the earth, I say, begins its political life with noble principles of freedom, order, and prosperity. Let me conclude with the humble prayer that Almighty God may vouchsafe to direct our counsels, and that He may grant to all of us that

moderation, wisdom, and courage necessary to preserve and extend these inestimable blessings, and
to hand them down hereafter to our children's
children.'

Everything in the birth of a new State is instructive ; and a few paragraphs from the addresses of both
Houses of Parliament in reply to the Governor's
speech are therefore reprinted.

The Legislative Council said :

May it please your Excellency,
We, Her Majesty's most loyal and dutiful subjects,
the members of the Legislative Council of Queensland,
in Parliament assembled, desire to express through
your Excellency our feelings of loyalty and attachment to the throne and person of our most gracious
Sovereign, and to thank you for the speech with which
your Excellency has, in the name and on behalf of
the Queen, opened this the first session of the first
Parliament of Queensland.

We heartily reciprocate your Excellency's congratulations on the attainment of separate and independent government. We feel that as a branch of
the Legislature now called into existence we have
imposed upon us serious duties and grave responsi-
bilities, which we trust, under God's blessing, we may
be enabled to discharge in a measure conducive to
the well-being of this community.

The great questions involved in a right solution

of the difficulties surrounding our land policy are matters of the highest interest to all classes in the Colony of Queensland, and we will not shrink from adding our exertions to those of the other branches of the Legislature in endeavouring to establish that system which, on mature consideration, may seem most calculated to ensure the best results.

We rejoice to find that your Excellency appreciates the loyal spirit which has led many of the inhabitants of Queensland to volunteer their services for the defence of the country in case of need, and we trust the organisation given under existing laws to this body of Volunteers, may not only render them efficient in the hour of emergency, but also tend to foster that patriotic enthusiasm which alone gives life and spirit to the only warlike struggle likely to be known to the present generation of colonists, a war in defence of the country from attack.

Finally, we heartily join your Excellency in your aspirations for the future of this country; we pray that the blessing of Almighty God may rest upon the deliberations of the Legislature of this Colony; and we add our congratulations that on your Excellency has devolved that proud task you have so well begun, of guiding this young community in its first footsteps among nations.

The Legislative Assembly said:

May it please your Excellency,

We, Her Majesty's loyal and dutiful subjects, the members of the Legislative Assembly of Queensland, in Parliament assembled, desire to express to your Excellency our affection and loyalty to the person and government of our most gracious Sovereign, and to offer our respectful thanks for your Excellency's speech to this Assembly now for the first time convened.

We concur most cordially in your Excellency's estimation of the important influence that must be exercised upon the future of this territory by the inauguration within it of a separate Parliamentary Constitution, and while we reciprocate the hope and belief that this community may prove itself to have been not unworthy of Her Majesty's most gracious and considerate boon of self-government, we feel a deep satisfaction in learning from your Excellency that the inhabitants of all parts of the Colony have been successful in their earnest efforts to testify, by the reception of her first representative among them, that honest loyalty, that warm attachment, and that heartfelt gratitude which Queensland must ever feel towards her Queen.

Concurring cordially in the desirability of affording time for full and patient consideration before dealing comprehensively with questions of so varied and complicated a character as those concerning the disposal of the land, we will lend our ready attention to such special legislative action as your Excellency has recommended to us, with a view to the more immediate removal of obstructions to capital and enterprise.

In expressing your reliance upon the patriotism and loyalty of this Assembly, we trust that your Excellency will not have estimated too highly our earnest desire and purpose, under the blessing of Providence, to recommend and, through those who may from time to time be your Excellency's responsible advisers, to carry into execution, such measures as may have deserved your assent, and as may be conducive no less to the establishment of a sound system of independent government than to the enduring welfare and progress of all branches of this community.

The Addresses to the Queen voted by both Houses were a further proof of the loyalty of the youngest province of the British Empire. The Governor's covering despatch must here be quoted :

To the Duke of Newcastle.

Government House, Brisbane : June 30, 1860.

My Lord Duke,

The Parliament of Queensland has requested me to perform the honourable duty of transmitting to your Grace, for presentation to the Queen, the loyal and dutiful addresses to Her Majesty, unanimously

voted by both Houses of the Legislature, ' to express
their gratitude for the gracious and liberal concession
which has been made to this Colony in its establishment as a separate and independent province of the
British Empire.'

It will be perceived that both addresses breathe
the same spirit of fervent and grateful loyalty to the
Queen, of attachment to the British Empire, and of
well-founded confidence in the future prosperity of
the new Colony.

The Legislative Council says : ' By the establishment of this new Dependency, we believe that a
powerful impulse will be given towards the settlement and civilisation of portions of Australia at
present almost wholly unoccupied. We are persuaded
that these vast regions, so blessed by Providence
with all material resources, will at no distant period
be occupied by a numerous and thriving population,
enabled by their own prosperity to contribute to that
of the Empire at large, and cherishing and perpetuating
that spirit of loyalty and affection to your Majesty's
person and government which so happily animates
all classes of the inhabitants of Queensland.'

The Legislative Assembly expresses like sentiments
in different words :—' We approach your Majesty
with feelings of warm loyalty and affectionate attachment to your Majesty's person and government, de-
siring as the representatives of the people of Queensland to express to your Majesty our heartfelt
gratitude for your Majesty's gracious compliance with

the long-cherished wishes of the inhabitants of this portion of your Majesty's dominions by raising it to the rank of a British Colony, and by graciously conferring on it a designation which we believe will be found truly to express the relation of loyalty which will bind us and our posterity in duty and allegiance to your Majesty and your Majesty's successors.' And again : ' While expressing our humble thanks to your Majesty, we cannot refrain from expressing also our hopes regarding the future of the Colony, and giving an assurance that it will be our aim by a zealous and conscientious discharge of the high duties entrusted to us to promote the welfare, happiness, and progress of your Majesty's faithful subjects in Queensland ; and by avoiding all cause of offence, to promote a proper and friendly understanding between this and the adjoining Colony of New South Wales.'

The terms in which the Assembly refer, in the third paragraph of their address, to my own poor services afford me sincere gratification, as a proof of the confidence which the representatives of the people of Queensland repose in the representative of their Sovereign.

The Assembly conclude as follows : ' We humbly pray that Almighty God may continue to bless and long preserve your Majesty, and the mighty Empire to which we have the honour and happiness to belong, and that He may vouchsafe to direct our counsels, and make us worthy of our blessings and privileges '

From my own observation and experience, I can bear witness that in the addresses transmitted herewith, the Parliament of Queensland has simply given expression to the genuine feelings which animate all classes of this community.

I may mention, in conclusion, that your despatch, of April 11 ult.,[1] opportunely arrived at Brisbane on the day before that on which the address of the Assembly to the Queen was formally put into my hands by the Speaker, accompanied by the whole House. I seized the occasion to reply in the following terms : ' Mr. Speaker, and Gentlemen of the Legislative Assembly, it will be a pleasing and honourable duty for me to transmit to the Queen this loyal and dutiful address, which I am confident will prove a source of much gratification to our Sovereign. I will take this opportunity of reading (previously to laying it by message on the tables of both Houses) a despatch which arrived yesterday from the Secretary of State for the Colonies, and which informs me that the expressions of loyalty to our gracious Sovereign, and of goodwill towards myself, contained in the addresses presented to me by the inhabitants of Queensland on my reception as their first Governor, have been " highly satisfactory to Her Majesty." ' I then read your despatch, which was received with sincere gratification by my audience.

---

[1] See above. page 103.

We now give the reply of the Queen, through the Secretary of State, to the above-mentioned addresses. The Duke of Newcastle wrote as follows :—' I have to acknowledge the receipt of your despatch of the 30th June last, in which you forward addresses to the Queen from both Houses of the Parliament of Queensland, expressing to Her Majesty their gratitude for " the gracious and liberal concession " which she has made to the inhabitants of that portion of her dominions by raising it to the rank of a British Colony.

' Nothing can be more appropriate than the language and spirit of these addresses to an occasion which promises to be a memorable one in the history of the British Empire in Australia ; and I am commanded by the Queen to inform you, and, through you, the Parliament of Queensland, that she has received them with great satisfaction. Her Majesty does not doubt that the feelings of the Parliament and people of the young Colony towards herself and the mother-country are fitly symbolised by its name ; and she trusts that, under the Divine blessing, they may long continue to form a bond of union between the two countries, and so contribute to the honour and welfare of both.'

Having got his vessel of State under way, with every prospect of a prosperous voyage, Sir George Bowen confided his reflections to the Parliamentary Under-Secretary for the Colonies, who was an old Oxford friend.

To the Right Hon. Chichester Fortescue, M.P.

Government House, Brisbane : June 6, 1860.

My dear Fortescue,

I am sure that you will be glad that I have got so successfully over all the labours and anxieties of the last six months : and that my Parliament has made so calm and patriotic a commencement. I have made light of the difficulties with which I have had to contend, owing to the necessities of my peculiar position : for I hold that the Secretary of State should never help a Governor unless he has shown that he can help himself. But my position was (unavoidably on the part of the Home Government) without precedent. At the first start of all other Colonies, the Governor has been assisted by a nominated Council of experienced officials ; he has been supported by an armed force ; and he has been authorised to draw, at least at the beginning, on the Imperial Treasury for the expenses of the public service. But I was an autocrat ; the sole source of authority here, without a single soldier, and without a single shilling. There was no organised force of any kind at my arrival, though I have now, by dint of exertion and influence, got up a respectable police on the Irish model, and a very creditable corps of Volunteers. And as to money wherewith to carry on the Government, I started with just $7\frac{1}{2}d$. in the Treasury. A thief, supposing, I fancy, that I should have been furnished with some funds for the *outfit* —so to speak—of the new State, broke into the

Treasury a few nights after my arrival, and carried off the 7½d. mentioned. However, I borrowed money from the banks until our revenue came in, and our estimates already show (after paying back the sums borrowed) a considerable balance in excess of the proposed expenditure for the first year.[1]

The election by popular suffrage to the Assembly of *all* my Executive Councillors, and the addresses of both Houses in reply to my opening speech, show what the persons most interested—i.e. the people of this Colony—think of my administration. The enthusiasm with which I was received, as the first Governor, was in itself a source of danger, for it seemed too fervent to last long, and such outbursts are generally followed by a reaction. But I was as heartily cheered on my way to open Parliament last week as I was on my arrival six months ago. I can honestly say that there is scarcely any post in the Queen's service that I would willingly exchange for that which I held during the first half of this year, with all its difficulties and anxieties.

Will you tell the Duke that Robert Herbert (Fellow of All Souls), whom I appointed as my first Colonial Secretary, is leading the Assembly with ability and tact ?

The happy commencement of representative government in Queensland was hailed with admiration

---

[1] This historic sum of 7½d. has now (1889) risen to an annual revenue of above three millions sterling.

in the mother-country. The Secretary of State's despatches abound in eulogistic congratulations ; and the feeling of the public was eloquently expressed in the following leading article of the ' Times ' (August 20, 1860):

'Europe, Asia, and, we might add, America, present to us at this moment much movement with very little progress. Old faiths and traditions give way, and nothing rises up to supply their place. Barbarism has lost its energy, and civilisation seems arrested in its onward career. In Russia and Turkey we behold Governments. losing their hold on the affection and reverence of peoples without having created anything to supply the void which they are about to make. In France and Germany we see the energies of great nations frittered away by unworthy jealousies within, or in still more unworthy ambitions beyond the frontier. Italy is in the crisis of a revolution, to which many of the most sanguine do not venture to attribute a permanent success. Spain has wasted that strength in an abortive foreign war which she needs to consolidate and secure such liberty as she has saved out of so many revolutions and so many civil wars. It is refreshing to turn from this scene of blind and short-sighted ambition, from the doings of States that seem to know no other means of increasing their wealth and power except such as were known to Pagan Europe in the days of Macedon and of Rome, to the first efforts of young and prosperous communities developing, with the order and regularity of one of the vegetable products of nature, the elements of present freedom and future prosperity.

'In a remote corner of Australia, some six or seven

hundred miles to the north of the original settlement
of Sydney, is situated a vast territory, the very name
of which is scarcely known to a large number of our
readers.   The district of Moreton Bay appears, if we
may believe the accounts we receive of it, to be among
the most favoured regions of the world.   It is placed
at the commencement of that long barrier reef of coral
which, running parallel with the north-eastern coast
of the Australian continent, provides a smooth and
delightful passage to the navigator who would thread
the mazes of the Oriental Archipelago.   Unlike most
parts of Australia, the land adjacent to the coast is
watered by a succession of fine rivers, and is, within
a moderate distance of their course, exuberantly
fertile.   The climate is warm, but exceedingly healthy.
The woods are beautiful, and require only to be
known to become a valuable article of commerce.
At a moderate distance from the sea the land rises
for several thousand feet into a succession of beautiful
downs, enjoying all the freshness of a temperate
climate, and covered by innumerable flocks and herds.
This Colony, after a long and arduous struggle, has
obtained that which seems to be the great ambition
of all such communities—a separation from the
larger and older society to which it is attached.
With a territory three times the size of France, and
a population of some twenty or five-and-twenty
thousand souls, Moreton Bay—or Queensland, as it
is now to be called—has entered with the utmost
confidence and hope on the career of self-government.
This small and remote population supplies the materials for two Legislative Chambers, and bears into
the remote regions of the far East the feelings, the

habits, and the customs of our ancient monarchy.
With such simple pomp as the resources at his command can furnish, the first Governor, Sir George
Bowen, late Colonial Secretary of the Ionian Islands,
opens his first Parliament. We are favoured with a
copy of his Excellency's speech, similar in tone, and
by no means inferior in style, to the documents it
professes to imitate. Let us see what are the subjects
to which the attention of this new people is called by
their first Magistrate on that interesting and memorable day which places them for the first time in the
possession of the inestimable gift of self-government.
The Constitution Act seems to be a little clumsy and
unwieldy. The law officers of the Crown advise that
the elections cannot legally begin till April 27, and
it is not therefore surprising that the Parliament of
Queensland was unable to meet till the auspicious
anniversary of May 29, on the threshold of the first
winter month of those Antipodean regions. The
first business was to alter the Act giving the Constitution, so as to cut down the Upper House to a
number more consistent with the wants of the Colony
than the original instrument seems to have contemplated. Then we have the question of State assistance to public worship, which is broadly left to the
consideration of the Legislature, with the very sensible recommendation that it should be guided by no
abstract theories, but only by the wants and requirements of the country. Primary education follows
next, together with a recommendation, unique, as far
as we are aware, in the Colonies, for the foundation
of a High School with a number of exhibitions to
the Universities of the mother-country open to com-

petition among the students. That such a scheme should be considered feasible gives us a high idea of the wealth of the community; that it should be thought desirable is no inconsiderable proof of their good sense and attachment to the parent State. Then follows the appointment of Commissioners for the apportionment of the public debt between New South Wales and Queensland, an arrangement in which we may be permitted to hope that the parent will deal liberally with his sturdy offspring. The police are to be thoroughly organised, a system of annual statistics is to be formed, and an electric telegraph laid down for the purpose of uniting Queensland to the other Colonies of the Australian group; and to this is added a project for an electric line to Batavia, in Java, which would complete the telegraphic communication between Sydney and Melbourne and Singapore, and shortly with England. There is also a scheme for steam navigation in the Eastern Archipelago, which we cannot help feeling is, like the electric telegraph, destined to struggle with many obstacles before its final completion.[1] Of course the address of no Colonial Governor would be complete without the introduction of a Land Bill, and a measure for the purposes of immigration, in the course of which the Governor does not omit to suggest the grant of a remission of the purchase money of land to immigrants who pay for their own passages. The fact is noticed that Queensland already contains several corps of Volunteers; and after an address to the gentlemen of the Assembly and the gentlemen of the

[1] All these projects were successfully carried out within a few years after the delivery of the Governor's speech.

Legislative Council, quite in the English taste, the
speech concludes with a prayer framed exactly on
the model of that which ordinarily terminates the
address of our own gracious Sovereign.

'This speech and these incidents, trivial and commonplace as they may appear, have in our minds a
very high significance. After so many wars and
revolutions it still continues to be true, as it was in
the time of Burke, eighty years ago, that slavery can
be had anywhere, but that freedom is that pearl of
great price of which England alone has the monopoly.
With no other arms but our industry, our commercial
spirit, and the expansive freedom of our institutions,
while other countries barely maintain their position,
we are enabled to cover the world with communities
the faithful patterns of their mother-country, and
destined, we believe, not only to preserve our language, our arts, and our institutions, but to become in their turn the mothers of other Colonies,
and thus, in a circle gradually increasing, to spread
our language, manners, arts, and ideas to the remotest
corners of the earth. It is impossible to view, even
from this remote distance, scenes like that we have
endeavoured to describe without the liveliest emo-
tions of national pride. How vain and absurd is it
to attribute to England those vulgar schemes of
commonplace ambition which our neighbours so
ardently pursue, when, without a crime and without
a tear, without doing wrong to any one, and even
with the greatest advantage to herself, England is
able to give permanence and consistency to an
Empire more vast than the proudest conqueror ever
dreamt of, and stronger and more homogeneous than
was ever cemented by the action of the sword.'

CHAPTER IX.

WHAT the Parliament of Queensland accomplished in the four months of its first session may be read in the Governor's Prorogation speech of September 18, 1860:

' Honourable Gentlemen of the Legislative Council and Gentlemen of the House of Assembly,

' The advanced state of the public business, and the satisfactory conclusion to which you have carried no small amount of legislation, enable me to release you for a time from your attendance in Parliament, and to close the present session.

' During the recess, various measures of importance, to which your attention has in some cases been already directed, will be matured by my Government, and will be submitted for your consideration when you assemble again. As at present advised, I consider that the public convenience will be best provided for by my opening the next session of Parliament towards the close of the month of April in the ensuing year.

' It is a matter of deep satisfaction to myself, and of congratulation to you, that so much useful legisla-

M 2

tion should have been completed during your first session.   Questions difficult of settlement, and materially affecting the future prosperity of this Colony, have been approached and examined by you in a spirit of patient industry and of persevering inquiry ; and I entertain a confident hope that from legislation of such a character—based on no abstract theories but on practical experience, and neither impaired by haste, nor influenced by favour, nor impeded by faction —the results to be developed will prove both valuable and permanent.

'Looking to the solemn and most interesting duty in which we have been engaged, that, namely, of inaugurating this new and flourishing Colony, and of preparing it to assume that high position among the other provinces of the British Empire to which it has already attained ; looking also to those cordial relations, the existence of which between myself and the members of both Houses it is alike my pride and my happiness to acknowledge, I have deemed it natural and proper that my first addresses to the first Parliament of Queensland should not bear a merely formal character.   Further, as the speeches of Governors are laid before the Imperial Parliament, and are thus destined to authoritative circulation in the mother-country, it cannot but be desirable that my addresses should contain, to a certain extent, an official and authentic summary of the general condition and prospects of this Colony, and more especially of such recent legislation as may have at once enhanced its advantages and extended those advantages more freely to our fellow countrymen at home.

'With these views, I will now briefly pass in review the principal Acts which have received your sanction during the present session, and to which I have signified the assent of the Queen.

'The chief public bills which have already become law may be divided into the following classes:

'First in order stand those measures which were immediately necessary upon your meeting for the effective adaptation of the constitution of New South Wales to the altered circumstances of this Colony In addition to the Act whereby the number of members required to be present for the despatch of business is defined, and to the Act which limits the number of salaried officials capable of being elected to the Legislative Assembly, an important amendment has been made in the law under which voters are registered, ensuring greater accuracy in the electoral lists, and obviating a considerable expenditure of public money.

'The all-important interests of religion and education have received a full share of your careful consideration. The much-vexed question of grants in aid of public worship has been set at rest in accordance with the feelings of a large proportion of our population. Primary education has been provided for upon the general principles of that comprehensive system which experience has proved to be peculiarly adapted to meet the requirements of our colonial communities; at the same time, education of a more advanced order will shortly, under the provisions of the Grammar Schools Act, be placed within easy reach of the inhabitants of all the more populous districts.

' The necessary provision has been made for the collection of the census in this Colony on the same day of the ensuing year with that on which it will be taken in the United Kingdom and in many other portions of the Empire. The accurate statistical information which will thus be rendered available will prove of eminent interest and utility in your future labours.

' In taking the requisite steps for a settlement of the outstanding accounts between Queensland and New South Wales, your legislation has been based upon principles which can hardly fail to recommend themselves to the concurrence of the sister Colony, for they are identical with the principles originally adopted by the Executive, and sanctioned by the Parliament of New South Wales itself; and which have further received the approval of the Imperial Government. I am justified therefore in entertaining a well-founded hope that no long time will elapse before this, the last remaining difficulty of separation, shall be amicably adjusted, and the two great neighbouring Colonies, whose interests are so inseparably united, shall regard each other only with feelings of friendly emulation.

' Your adoption of an Act to regulate the exportation of warlike stores, proposed by my Government with a view to the lamentable outbreak in New Zealand,[1] affords me an opportunity of bearing my testimony to the sympathy existing here, as throughout Australia, with the troubles of our fellow countrymen in the aforesaid Colony. Queensland has hastened to offer an effective proof of that sympathy, by cheerfully contributing towards the augmentation of the forces at the seat of war that proportion of Her Majesty's troops which had been allotted for the defence of this Colony.

'The patriotic spirit with which the Volunteer movement has been supported by all classes of our community is a further and most valuable testimony to the undoubted loyalty of this portion of the Queen's dominions, and to the determination of our people, as they participate in the glory and prosperity, so also not to shrink from their share in the trials of the mother-country.

'I now come to those measures regulating the occupation and alienation of the Crown lands, on which you have bestowed so large a portion of your time and attention, with the full knowledge that the progress of Queensland will mainly depend upon the judicious discharge of the high trust involved in the control and administration of our vast territories.

'Having in the first instance adopted such means

[1] The reference here is to the second Maori War, which began in 1860, and lasted with little intermission till 1870, when it was brought to a final close, as will be seen in Part III., during Sir G. Bowen's government of New Zealand.

as were legally and equitably available for the purpose of checking that speculative monopoly of pastoral lands, under which wide tracts of country were
withheld from profitable occupation, you have thrown
open to real settlement those extensive districts, upon
conditions and with advantages such as will not fail
to secure a large and immediate accession to the
capital and producing power of the Colony.

' Again, that part of your legislation which is, perhaps, of paramount importance to the community
at large, by whom the proprietorship and occupation
of freehold properties upon favourable terms is so
urgently demanded, will also be regarded with satisfaction by those who are interested in promoting a
stream of emigration from England. The liberal
grants of land to immigrants arriving here without
cost to our Treasury; the facilities afforded to small
capitalists of extending their operations during the
first and more arduous years of their enterprise, by
leasing at a nominal rent the land adjacent to that
which they may have purchased ; the increased opportunities of settlement by a departure on the agricultural reserves from the system of auction, whereby
intending purchasers were often delayed or impeded
in the attainment of their object ; and the strong in-
ducements offered for the cultivation of cotton, to
which this soil and climate are so eminently adapted ;
these combined advantages will, I doubt not, prove
sufficiently attractive to draw to our shores that
immigration which we so much need, as the best in-

strument for the development of the rich and varied resources of this favoured country.

'In other matters not comprised within legislative enactments, I have observed with much satisfaction your earnest desire to look beyond the pressing requirements of the moment, and to devote a due proportion of the means under your control to objects less immediately, although not less closely, connected with the welfare of this Colony.

'From the reports furnished by the various select committees which have been occupied upon special subjects, an amount of practical information is to be collected which will prove not only of direct advantage to the Executive Administration here, but which, when made known in England, will be studied with keen interest by the many persons to whom this portion of the Island-Continent of Australia is an object of anxious attention.

'Again, by inquiries tending to facilitate the future settlement of the shores of the Gulf of Carpentaria, and the intercourse of Australia with India and China; by equipping an expedition of discovery in the direction of that system of rivers and tableland which holds forth the promise of the profitable occupation, at no distant day, of our northern districts; by procuring such scientific aid as may be available towards ascertaining the existence of the precious metals within our boundaries; and by making provision for an adequate representation of this Colony in the Industrial Exhibition of 1862, you have made no scanty contribution to the rapidly growing prosperity of Queensland, while adding new conquests to the domains of geography and science.'

'Gentlemen of the House of Assembly,

'I thank you, in the name of the Queen, for the liberal supplies which you have granted to Her Majesty. It will be the duty of the Government to exercise a watchful supervision over their expenditure, and in so doing to study such economy as may be consistent with an effective fulfilment of your expressed intentions.

'The steady and rapid increase of the revenue is a matter of no slight congratulation. It is most gratifying to observe that the second quarter of this year has produced nearly treble the amount of the first quarter; and I have every reason to hope and believe that this financial progress will continue on an equally satisfactory scale.

'You have devoted about one-fourth of the estimated revenue to the construction of roads, bridges, and public offices; to the extension of electric telegraphs and postal communication; to the improvement of our harbours; and to other works calculated to advance the material prosperity of our people. And it will not, I think, be forgotten in the future annals of this Colony that the first Assembly of Queensland was equally careful of the moral and social as of the material wants of the community; that, in its first session, it voted ample sums for the

formation and encouragement of hospitals, libraries,
botanical gardens, and schools of art ; and that it
appropriated for purposes of education alone, a sum
larger in proportion to our present numbers than is
devoted to that object in Great Britain itself—larger,
probably, than is devoted to it in any other country
of the world.'

' Honourable Gentlemen of the Legislative Council, and
    Gentlemen of the House of Assembly,
    ' The result of your labours fully justifies the hopes
expressed in the speech which I addressed to you at
the commencement of this session. You have left
little to be desired by the warmest friends of Queensland, except that future sessions may maintain the
high character which you have already earned for
this Legislature. I recently laid before you a despatch from the Secretary of State informing me that
the conduct of the inhabitants of this Colony on the
occasion of the first establishment of their new
Government was " highly satisfactory " to the Queen.
1 am confident that the happy initiation of Parliamentary institutions among you will afford additional
gratification to Her Majesty. It is my earnest hope
that those institutions, now so successfully inaugurated here, may be productive of all those blessings
which, when rightly administered, they cannot fail to
confer. This Colony has now, so far as human influences extend, its destinies in its own hands. I
humbly pray that, by the favour of the Supreme

Ruler, its onward career may be characterised by the same spirit of loyalty, moderation, and enlightened patriotism with which it has commenced the exercise of its rights and the performance of its duties as a separate and independent province of the British Empire.'

By far the most important of the Acts passed during the first session of the first Parliament of Queensland related to the tenure of land. In the early days of colonisation a vast proportion of the public land had fallen into the hands of the 'squatters' or pastoral tenants of the Crown, partly because grazing was the most rapidly profitable form of farming, partly because the earliest settlers were generally men of education and moderate capital, whose tastes and experience led them rather towards cattle and sheep-farming than towards agricultural labour. When a large element of lower social status and smaller capital, but at least equal physical energy, made its appearance in Queensland, a certain rivalry immediately arose with the squatters. Their square miles of territory were naturally coveted by men whose ambition aimed only at the successful cultivation of acres ; and there was for a time considerable fear that the agricultural interest, always a vital factor in every country, might seriously suffer from the prior claims of almost the monopoly of the public land by the great pastoral settlers. Above all, it was evident that a dangerous feature in land tenure existed in the possibilities of merely speculative investment in squatting rights which were secured only for temporary profit, to be

sold again as soon as a high bid should be made.
The first Government of Queensland was fully alive
to these dangers, and one of their earliest official steps
was to postpone all consideration of tenders for squatting 'runs' in the newly created pastoral districts
of Kennedy and Mitchell until August 1860; that is,
until the Queensland Parliament should have had an
opportunity of legislating upon the various difficulties
connected with the land tenure. The results of the
debates in the Council and Assembly on this subject
were contained in four Acts, viz. 'The Unoccupied
Crown Lands Act' (24 Vict. No. 11); 'The Land
Tenders Regulation Act' (24 Vict. No. 12); 'The
Alienation of Crown Lands Act' (24 Vict. No. 15),
and 'The Occupied Lands Leasing Act' (24 Vict.
No. 16); and these, wrote the Governor, 'form what
may be called the land code of Queensland.'   He
further remarked in a letter to a political friend in
England : 'The legislation of our first Parliament
has settled that long quarrel between the pastoral
and agricultural interests which has raged in all new
countries ever since the days of Abel, the " keeper of
sheep," and Cain, the " tiller of the ground." [1]   I may
observe that the proceedings of the pioneer settlers
in occupying fresh "runs" in Australia follow the
precedent of those ancient squatters, Abraham and
Lot, as described in the thirteenth chapter of Genesis.'

By these Acts, which were, at a later period, re-
vised and extended, not only were the conditions of
the occupation of pastoral land regulated and restricted, but a new departure in colonial land tenure
was begun. Provision was made for the increase

[1] *Genesis*, chap. II.

of agricultural holdings by conferring on the Governor
the power to mark out large areas of 'agricultural
reserves,' near the coasts and rivers, and in the neighbourhood of towns.   These reserves were destined
wholly for agricultural and not for pastoral settlers.
The land was to be sold at a fixed price of 1*l.* per acre,
and the purchaser of a certain number of acres enjoyed,
on easy conditions, the right of leasing a large adjoining area at a nominal rent with option of purchase at
the same price of 1*l.* at any period of his occupancy.
Immigration was encouraged by a provision for allot-
ting free land orders to immigrants paying their own
passages.   In this manner room was made for a
population of large and small agriculturists, and the
undue preponderance of the pastoral settlers was
restricted.

Commenting on these Acts in his despatch of
October 1, 1860, Sir George Bowen wrote:

'In an official letter written soon after my arrival
in this Colony, I made use of the following words:
"While maintaining, as the representative of the
Queen, a 'dignified neutrality' (to quote Lord Elgin's
happy phrase) between contending parties, I hope to
lend my aid to a conciliatory and permanent settlement of the land question, which otherwise threatens
to become in Australia an irritating and prolonged
contest between rival classes and interests, like the
Agrarian Laws at Rome, and the Corn Laws in
England."

'Earl Grey has remarked in his valuable book
on Colonial Policy that, even in the self-governing

Colonies, " an able Governor can do much by a judicious use of the influence rather than of the authority of his office." But the success attained in the first session of my first Parliament has exceeded my most sanguine hopes. Without pledging myself to absolute concurrence with every detail of the Land Acts now passed (which will be extended and enlarged in the future as the progress of colonisation may require), I regard them as a practical and satisfactory settlement of this much-vexed question, which is still embittering the social life and retarding the material advance of the neighbouring and elder Colonies.

'I confidently believe that the Acts, Reports, and other official papers already transmitted, will be found to contain ample justification of the favourable opinion which I expressed in my Prorogation Speech of the results of the first session of the first Parliament of Queensland. This Parliament may fairly boast of having passed, with due caution and foresight, a greater number of really useful measures, and of having achieved a larger amount of really practical legislation, than any other Parliament in any of the Australian Colonies since the introduction of parliamentary government. I will conclude by quoting the testimony borne on this point by the chief organ of public opinion in New South Wales, a journal which was at first by no means favourable to the creation and prospects of the new Colony of Queensland :—

' " Judging from the experience of the older
Colonies, it would have seemed safe to predict that
Queensland would not settle its land policy until two
or three parliamentary sessions had expired; until
half-a-dozen Ministries had climbed by its means
into power, and been baffled by the very tactics
by which they themselves succeeded; and until an
amount of social hatred had been engendered
which it would take years to extinguish. These
anticipations, however, would have been all false.
The Government of Queensland has been either very
fortunate or very judicious. The last to enter the
race, Queensland has shot ahead, and taken the first
place. While in Melbourne the popular rage has
been worked up by its guardians into riot, and while
in Sydney the tactics of the popular party have
succeeded in placing the land question in a position
of chronic blockade, in Queensland it has been
settled on a moderate and reasonable basis, and
without so much as a single ministerial crisis." ' [1]

In his reply to the above despatch, the Duke
of Newcastle congratulated Sir G. Bowen on the success of his government, and the general prosperity of
Queensland; adding that he perceived with great
pleasure the evidence afforded by the various Acts
of the first session ' of the industry, intelligence, and
good sense with which the Council and Assembly have

[1] *The Sydney Morning Herald*, September, 1860.

applied themselves to the practical duties of legislation.' Not less gratifying was the testimony of Sir
E. Bulwer Lytton, the Minister who had appointed
Sir G. Bowen to Queensland; and who now wrote to
him : 'You have managed admirably, and shown
great tact and ability. It is indeed a grand thing to
have been the Œkist, the founder of the social state of
so mighty a segment of the globe as Queensland, and
is, perhaps, more sure of fame a thousand years hence
than anything that we can do in the old world. It is
carving your name on the rind of a young tree, to
be found with enlarged letters as the trunk expands.'

CHAPTER X.

THE PROGRESS OF QUEENSLAND—OFFICIAL TOURS—SPEECH ON
EDUCATION—VISIT TO THE NORTHERN DISTRICTS—COLONIAL
FORCES—LETTERS TO THE DUKE OF NEWCASTLE, MR. COBDEN,
SIR G. CORNEWALL LEWIS, SIR ROUNDELL PALMER — MR.
GLADSTONE—AUSTRALIAN FEDERATION—PAX BRITANNICA.

To review in detail the legislation of the nine sessions of the two Parliaments which sat under Sir
George Bowen's rule in Queensland would be an
instructive but lengthy task. The beginnings of all
new States are interesting, and the wonderful progress
of Queensland in these early years of independent
existence is full of valuable lessons in the science of
self-government. Only a comparatively small portion
of the Colony was even partially settled when the
first Parliament met; but during the eight years of
the first Governor's tenure of office, the area of
civilisation was extended till the northernmost point
of Australia, Cape York, was occupied and incorporated in the organisation radiating from Brisbane.
So rapid and sweeping an expansion necessarily
created a vast amount of work for the Government
and Legislature; and many difficult problems had
to be solved. The sound sense and intelligence
displayed by the colonists in relation to the large
questions which thus fell under their purview were
remarkable ; and there is probably no other instance

on record of a similar peaceful and orderly assumption by an untrained legislature of so vast a responsibility, or of so wise and impartial an exercise of great power over so immense a dominion. and among so many conflicting interests.   The land question was, of course, the foremost difficulty, but the Acts passed in the first session were found to work so well that subsequent years saw little else but their expansion. With the rapid growth of the Colony other questions than the regulation of municipalities, schools, public works, and suchlike matters of local importance, came to the front.   One was the establishment of a comprehensive system of communication by railways and telegraphs.   Another was the question of the defences of the Colony.   What was done in all these and other matters will be seen in outline in the Governor's letters and despatches.   The details must be sought in the Parliamentary bluebooks and the colonial histories.

The Governor's duties, however, were by no means limited to the period of the parliamentary session, which generally lasted from April to September.   Much of his most important work was done in the annual recess.   It was then that he journeyed through all parts of the Colony in order to make himself thoroughly acquainted at first hand with the wants and wishes of all classes of the community.   It was the neglect of the Government of New South Wales to pay detailed attention to every part of its huge dominions that forced on the separation of one province after another, till Moreton Bay had followed the lead of Port Phillip, and Queensland had been separated in like manner as Victoria.   Sir

George Bowen was resolved that no such indifference
to the remoter parts of the Colony should be manifested during his rule; and he never permitted a
recess to pass without making a considerable official
circuit.   In his first year, as has been seen, even
before the Parliament met, he was able to make himself acquainted with the district of the Darling Downs.
In the following autumn he inspected the northern
districts as far as Rockhampton; in 1861, the central
districts; the next year he went north again to Port
Denison; and thus every recess found him encouraging the people to meet him and lay before him their
special wants and hopes.   It is worthy of notice that
in every one of these official tours he was throughout
welcomed with unbounded loyalty.   The addresses
which he received in each district that he visited
would fill a volume of respect, gratitude, and affection.   Addresses, however, are very similar in style
and matter, and the recital of one or two will give a
sufficient impression of the rest.   The Governor's
replies to the addresses presented to him were always
received with acclamation; and his advice, even when
trenching on deep-rooted prejudices, was heard with
attention.   His speeches were frequently occupied
with urgent counsels in favour of municipal organisation, of the raising of Volunteer forces for defence,
and the introduction of tropical crops, such as cotton
and sugar, into those regions where the cereals of the
cooler parts of Queensland were not suitable.   Thus
he told the people of Maryborough that 'The object
of my official tours, here as elsewhere, is to see and
judge for myself, to ascertain the requirements and
desires of all classes of the inhabitants of Queensland.

In this object I am confident that I shall derive valuable assistance from the members of your future municipality, for I rejoice to find that you have applied to be incorporated according to law. All political experience has proved that local municipal bodies are fully as necessary to the public welfare as central representative legislatures. It is in such corporations that men are trained to legislate on a wider stage. They are the best security against undue centralisation, and against the partial and unjust dedication of the public revenues to the advantage of favoured localities. It has been observed by a great statesman and philosopher, that "municipalities are to liberty what primary schools are to science; they bring it within the reach of the people. They teach men how to use and how to enjoy it." '

In reply to the address of the people of Rockhampton, Sir George again recommended municipal institutions, and added his advice that they should ' form in this district a corps of Volunteer riflemen, in imitation of the patriotic example set by the inhabitants of Brisbane and Ipswich, and generally by our fellow countrymen throughout the Empire. In addition to the obvious advantage of thus providing for your external and internal defence, such associations are eminently calculated to promote union and good feeling among a population thinly scattered over a wide extent of country ; and also to foster that spirit of independence and self-reliance, without which no people whose annals are recorded in history has ever attained to vigorous manhood.'

Nor did he ever fail to impress upon his audiences
the importance of education. As an Oxford first
class man and Fellow of his College, Sir George
was not likely to forget the uses of high training.
A University indeed would have been somewhat premature in Queensland, for ample facilities for the
higher education in all its branches existed in the
Universities of Sydney and Melbourne, but every
provision was promptly made for schools and col-
leges at the principal towns of the new Colony. Sir
George Bowen was always ready to do his part in
opening such institutions, giving away the prizes,
and encouraging the students. As an example of
his speeches on educational subjects, the following
address at the opening of the first Grammar School
may be cited :

' The Trustees of this institution having conveyed
to me a wish that I should take part in the interesting
proceedings of this day, I gladly accepted their invitation. Educated myself at an English public school
and university, my warmest sympathies are naturally
enlisted in the inauguration of the first public school
established in this new Colony, with the object of providing for our youth some of the higher branches of
a liberal education. And, as a public man engaged
during many years in the active business of life, I
desire to bring the living testimony of practical experience to confirm and enforce those precepts and
exhortations which the students will doubtless hear
from the learned head-master, and from the gentlemen associated with him.

'In the first place, I observe with great satisfaction that this institution will be carried out, so far
as circumstances may permit, on the well-tried plan
of the old public schools of England. So much, indeed, is implied in its name. This school professes
to teach *grammar* in its widest sense—that is, "the
science which has for its object the laws which regulate human language." Now it is, I imagine,
admitted on all sides that by education is meant not
a mere preparation for some specific trade or profession, but rather a preparation for the whole business of life—a preparation which shall fit the student
to fill his part well as a member of a family, of a
professional or commercial community, of society
generally, and of the State. Far be it from me to
say that no help should be furnished at school and
college towards the various pursuits of manhood.
Much *can* be done—and much, I hope, *will* be done
in this institution—towards that object, both directly
and indirectly : directly, by instruction in the principles and practice of law, commerce, and agriculture ;
and indirectly, by instruction in history, modern
languages, mathematics, chemistry, and physics.
Still the main end of a liberal education is so to discipline the understanding and the taste, and so to
strengthen the various powers of the mind, that when
the student proceeds, thus disciplined and strengthened, to learn the use of the weapons needful
for himself especially, he may acquire that use
most readily, and ever afterwards employ it most

worthily for himself and most beneficially for his country.

'Such, then, being the true aim of education, it follows that grammar, or the science of language, must hold an important place in it. Language is the medium of intercourse between man and man—the instrument, as it were, of thought. How can the processes of the mind be better understood than by a minute analysis of two of the most perfect languages that have ever been spoken? Or how can the young scholar learn more easily to think accurately for himself than by the study of the exact meaning of words and phrases? It has been asked indeed: "While the claims of language to form an essential part of education must be granted, why should the dead languages of Greece and Rome be chosen for this purpose?" To this plausible question convincing replies have often been given. It has been shown that while, on the one hand, the study of modern languages alone would prove an inferior discipline, so, on the other hand, the worth to all time of the stores of wisdom and learning contained in the classical languages of antiquity is almost incalculable. Greek and Latin are a better instrument for training the mind, because they are more elaborate in their etymology and syntax, expressing by copious inflexions what the languages of modern Europe express by mere juxtaposition of independent words. Moreover, the study of the ancient tongues from which the principal modern languages are derived, supplies a common standard and foundation for the philology, similar to that furnished in the elements of Euclid for the mathematics of all nations. Again, it has been truly said that we are hardly less closely connected with the people of Greece and Rome than with our own immediate ancestors. Not more truly do we owe most of our civil rights and social institutions to our Anglo-Saxon forefathers than we are indebted to the Greeks and Romans for most of our law, our literature, our science, and our philosophy.

'It has sometimes been objected, with all the audacity of ignorance, that classical studies are unfit for the present active age, and tend to make men "unpractical" and "mere dreamy scholars." But all experience refutes this superficial objection. Almost all the greatest English statesmen and lawyers in the last hundred years have been men pre-eminent for classical attainments. I need only mention in confirmation of this assertion, the names, on the judicial bench, of Lords Mansfield, Stowell, Ellenborough, and Tenterden; and, in political life, the names of Lord North, Mr. Pitt, Mr. Fox, Mr. Burke, Lord Grenville, Mr. Windham, Mr. Canning, Sir Robert Peel, Sir George Lewis, and Lord Palmerston. And who at the present day are the two foremost champions of the two great rival political parties, as consummate parliamentary orators and ready and acute debaters? Both these eminent Englishmen are not more proud of their success as statesmen than as scholars. They are rivals not only as political leaders but as trans-

lators of Horace.   Mr. Gladstone, the able and hard-
working Chancellor of the Exchequer and Minister
of Finance, a man of hard facts and dull figures, is
also the author of an elaborate treatise on the poetry
of Homer.   Lord Derby, as Chancellor of the University, recently welcomed the Prince of Wales to Oxford
in a Latin speech worthy to be compared with the
most renowned models of Roman eloquence.

‘ No doubt high distinction in public life has been
attained in some few instances by men not remarkable for classical acquirements ; but (to quote from a
speech of the late Sir Robert Peel) “ is there not strong
reason to believe that in their case success would have
been more easy and more complete, had such acquirements been superadded to their other qualifications? ”

‘ Having now spoken of some of the studies which
will be pursued in this institution, I shall conclude
by addressing a few plain and practical remarks to
the masters and to the scholars respectively.

‘ The true position of the instructors of youth has
been laid down for all time in those well-known and
beautiful verses of the Latin poet Juvenal : [1]

> *Di majorum umbris tenuem et sine pondere terram,*
> *Spirantesque crocos, et in urnâ perpetuum ver,*
> *Qui præceptorem sancti voluere parentis*
> *Esse loco.——*

I will only add that I am confident that the gentlemen whom I now address will not rest satisfied with
their present acquirements, but will ever day by day

[1] *Sat.* VII. 207.

seek to add to their stores of knowledge; so that, in the words of the late Dr. Arnold, one of the greatest teachers of any age, and who has done much to exalt the scholastic profession, "their pupils may drink not from a stagnant pond but from a fresh running stream."

'As for the scholars who will be educated here now and henceforward, I earnestly exhort them to prove by their diligence and good conduct, their appreciation of the many advantages procured for them by the wise liberality of the colonial legislature. It has been often said that in this happy land there is no barrier between classes, and that the highest positions can be attained by persons starting from the most humble origin. If a young man has only ability, energy, and perseverance, there is nothing within the range of the institutions of this Colony to which he may not aspire. I rejoice to learn that scholarships and other prizes will be provided as incentives and rewards for successful merit. I hope that the number of candidates at the examinations for these prizes will increase from year to year. Such examinations will produce among the rising generation a spirit of emulation, which is one of the noblest feelings of the human heart, and from which springs, in no slight degree, the greatness and prosperity both of individuals and of States. It is a spirit wholly distinct from that of envy or jealousy— a spirit compatible with the utmost kindness and goodwill towards those with respect to whom the

emulation is felt. I am aware that certain objections
have been made to the system of competitive examinations altogether. Some people say that it leads to
"cramming." Now it often happens, that when men
seize upon a word, they imagine that word to be an
argument, and go about repeating it till they persuade themselves that they have arrived at some
great and irresistible conclusion. So when they
pronounce the word "cramming," they flatter themselves that they have utterly discredited the system
to which that word is by them applied. But an excellent answer was once supplied to all loose reason-
ing of this sort by Lord Palmerston, in defending
competitive examinations. He said :—"Some people
seem to imagine that the human mind is like a bottle,
and that when you have filled it with anything, you
pour it out again, and it becomes as empty as it was
before. This is not the nature of the human mind."
The truth is that the boy who has been "crammed"
(to use the popular phrase), has, in point of fact,
learned a great deal, and that learning has accomplished two objects. In the first place the boy has
in the process of "cramming" been forced to exercise
the faculties of his mind; and in the next place, there
remains in his mind a great portion of this knowledge so acquired, and which probably forms the
basis of future attainments in different branches of
education. Again, it has been objected that competitive examinations make the young "vain and conceited." But this futile objection was also demolished

by Lord Palmerston in the admirable speech to which
I have already referred. "As to vanity and conceit,"
he said, "those are most vain and conceited who know
the least. The more a man knows the more he ac-
quires a conviction of the extent of that which he
does not know. A man must know a great deal to
understand the immensity of his own ignorance." You
will recollect the remark of Sir Isaac Newton, on his
death-bed, that he looked upon himself only as a
child picking up shells on the shore of the great
ocean of truth and knowledge.

'Finally, an old and familiar classical proverb de-
clares that "the beginning is half the whole":

  Dimidium facti qui bene cœpit habet.

There is some responsibility as well as honour in
being concerned with the opening of this institution
—the first of the kind in Queensland—but destined,
I hope, to be a model to many successors. I think I
may promise alike for the Government and for the
Trustees, that no care shall be wanting on their part
to secure a good beginning. I trust I may reckon
on finding in the whole body of the masters a conscientious zeal in the discharge of their duty. Still,
with whatever skill and attention their studies may
be chosen and directed, it must rest mainly with the
scholars themselves whether the result shall be successful. By every motive which can influence reflecting and responsible beings—by regard for their
own welfare and happiness in this world—by the fear

of future discredit—by the hope of lasting fame;
by motives yet more urgent—by nobler and purer
aspirations—by the duty of obedience to the will of
our Creator—by the awful account which we shall all
have to render of the talents entrusted to us for improvement;—by these high arguments, I affectionately
exhort all who now hear me, so " to number their days
that they may apply their hearts unto wisdom." '

The following despatch gives a brief account of the
Governor's tour in the spring [1] of 1860.

To the Duke of Newcastle.

Government House, Brisbane : December 4, 1860.

My Lord Duke,

In continuation of former despatches, I have the
honour herewith to transmit copies of the addresses
presented to me during my recent official tour of
inspection in the central and northern districts of
Queensland.

It will be seen that, according to my constant
habit, I took advantage of the customary replies to
afford useful information, and to tender practical
advice to the inhabitants of the several settlements
which I visited.

I was everywhere received during my recent tour,
by all classes of the community, with the same loyal
welcome as on my first arrival at Brisbane, now twelve

[1] It will be recollected that at the antipodes the spring months
are September, October, and November.

months ago, and as on my subsequent visits to the
southern and eastern districts of the Colony.

The first has been the most critical year of my
administration. I have now organised all the departments, and appointed all the officers of the
Government; I have, further, inaugurated the Parliament; and, what is also a delicate task in a new
country, I have (to a great extent) formed the society
which meets at the Government House. It is naturally
very gratifying to find that my conduct on all these
points has had a result the very reverse of impair-
ing the confidence and respect which the people of
Queensland were, from the beginning, inclined to feel
towards the first representative of their Sovereign.

The Colonial Architect, the Surveyor of Roads,
and others of the chief executive officers of the Government, accompanied me on my recent journey.
Arrangements were everywhere made in the several
districts for the immediate construction of the public
works, for which funds were voted in the late session
of Parliament. I am determined to leave no just
ground in this Colony for complaints of neglect on
the part of the central Executive, such as those which
led to the separation of Victoria and Queensland from
New South Wales.

A full description of Maryborough and its
vicinity will be found in a former despatch. On
the banks of the river Mary, as of all the other
rivers of Central and Northern Queensland, there
are vast tracts of country admirably adapted for the

growth of cotton, of sugar, and of all other tropical
and semi-tropical productions.

Port Curtis is probably the best harbour, after that
of Sydney, on the eastern coast of Australia. In
1854, the Government of New South Wales founded
on its shores a township, which has been named
Gladstone, and is the outlet of the adjacent pastoral
counties of Pelham and Clinton. The excellence
of the harbour, the salubrity of the climate, and the
beauty of the surrounding scenery, combine to render
Gladstone an eligible site for a flourishing town;
but the river Fitzroy, further north, affords a more
ready access to the interior of the Colony, and consequently the settlement of Rockhampton on its banks
has advanced more rapidly up to the present time.

The town of Rockhampton was founded in 1858,
and was then the extreme point of European settlement in this part of Australia. As the outlet of the
vast regions watered by the river Fitzroy and its
tributaries, it is even now a flourishing place, and
pastoral occupation has already extended to the Peak
Downs and to the shores of Broad Sound, fully
200 miles further inland and northward. As I have
reported elsewhere, the Queensland Government is
about to found a new settlement at Port Denison, as
the outlet of the recently proclaimed district of
Kennedy, which will reach to within about 300 miles
of the Gulf of Carpentaria.

Though Rockhampton is within the tropics, the
climate of the neighbouring districts, especially on the

upland downs and beautiful prairies of the interior, is in a high degree healthy and invigorating. Fresh settlers are fast arriving from New South Wales and Victoria, and bring their flocks and herds with them. Nor is the value of the wool of the merino sheep deteriorated, to any sensible extent, in these warm latitudes. What the fleece loses in weight, it gains in softness and delicacy.

It will afford some idea of the great space already covered by the settlements of this Colony, to mention that on my official tours during the past twelve months, I have myself visited two flourishing towns in Queensland (Warwick and Rockhampton), which are distant from each other by the nearest road at least 600 miles; that is, much further than Galway and Kirkwall respectively are distant from London. There is something almost sublime in the steady, silent flow of pastoral occupation over north-eastern Australia. It resembles the rise of the tide or some other operation of nature, rather than a work of man. Although it is difficult to ascertain exactly what progress may have been made at the end of each week and month, still, at the close of every year we find that the margin of Christianity and civilisation has been pushed forward by some 200 miles.

———————

A letter to Mr. Cobden records some of the Governor's impressions of the early beginnings of Queensland:

To Richard Cobden, Esq., M.P.

Government House, Brisbane: March 18, 1862.

My dear Sir,

I see it reported in the English newspapers that the state of your health will require you to take a long sea voyage, and to pass a short time in a more genial climate than that of England. Do not be startled if I urge you to pay me a visit at the Antipodes. Recollect that the journey from London to Sydney (whence there are weekly steamers in forty-eight hours to Brisbane, the capital of Queensland) is now a *voyage d'agrément* of about forty days. Your return would also require forty days; so that if you confine your absence to the parliamentary recess—say five months—you could spend about eight weeks with me at Brisbane. During these eight weeks you could learn more than in as many years in England of the real condition of Australia, and of that most interesting question, interesting alike to statesmen and philosophers, the working in these Colonies of the almost purely democratic institutions which have been conferred upon them.

You would find me living in a handsome and commodious Government House on the banks of the river Brisbane, here as broad as the Thames at Westminster. The climate of Brisbane resembles that of Madeira; and it is the resort of invalids from India and China, as well as from all the Australian Colonies. The summer (December to March) is rather warm, but very healthy. During the rest of the year our climate is delicious. The winter (May to September) reminds me of a succession of the finest days of a Neapolitan winter. The hot season is also the rainy season. Nothing can exceed the beauty of the indigenous vegetation of this part of Australia—especially of the flowering shrubs and ferns; while most of the European as well as semi-tropical productions grow with equal luxuriance.

Pray show this letter to Mr. Bright, whose acquaintance I first had the pleasure of making at your house in London in 1854. I wish I could persuade him also to pay me a visit in Australia, either alone, or in company with you. He will recollect that if he were to leave London by the overland mail at the end of July, he would reach Brisbane about the middle of September. He could stay with us for a couple of months till the November mail, which leaves us about the 20th. In this way he could be back in London by the middle of January with a good knowledge of the real state of things in Australia. In his political studies he could be assisted by an old schoolfellow and associate in the Anti-Corn Law League, Mr. T. B. Stephens, who is now the mayor of the city of Brisbane.

You are doubtless aware that vast tracts of this territory are admirably suited for the growth of cotton. Several local cotton companies are already in operation; but the great English manufacturers must embark some portion of their own skill, energy, and

capital in this enterprise, if cotton is to be grown on
an extensive scale here; for most of the local capital
is invested in wool. The Queensland Legislature has
done its utmost to aid the mother-country in the
present crisis of the cotton supply, by offering free
grants of land for cotton plantations, and premiums
(for several years) on the growth of that plant. And
there are no restrictions here, as in some of the other
Australian Colonies, on the importation of cheap
labour from India. But on this subject generally,
I would beg to refer you and Mr. Bright to Mr.
Bazley of Manchester, with whom I have had much
correspondence about it; and to the 'Cotton Supply
Reporter,' in which the Duke of Newcastle has
caused several of my despatches to be published.
Mr. Bazley wrote to me not long since, that he believed
that the best cotton in the world could be grown in
Queensland. He proceeds to say that 'he will endeavour to get up a company of English capitalists
to grow cotton on a large scale in Queensland.' I
beg to express my earnest hope that you will render
every assistance in your power to an enterprise so
important both for the parent State and for the Colony.
It appears that the cotton plantations of North
America cover in the aggregate little more than
4,000,000 acres—that is, about the area of Yorkshire.
Along the eastern seaboard of Queensland, which
extends for 1,200 miles, at least twenty Yorkshires
are open for selection by cotton planters—in a

salubrious climate, and under British laws and institutions (*tant soit peu* liberalised).

The people of Queensland paid me the compliment of electing to the first Assembly all the men whom, on my first arrival, I had appointed to the principal offices; and they then became my responsible ministers, and have now weathered the storms of three parliamentary campaigns; so that they have attained a patriarchal age for an Australian ministry. As you will see from the enclosed papers, we have already settled on a moderate and reasonable basis the land question, which, like the Corn Law question in England, has been the source of long and violent agitation in Australia. I submit that I have practically proved here the principle for which I have always contended, viz. that any imperfect success of parliamentary government in the older Australian Colonies does not arise from any defect in the system itself so much as from the errors of the naval and military governors who first inaugurated free institutions in this continent. Had I space, or you patience, I could give you numerous illustrations of my meaning. Suffice it to say that liberty began here at the wrong end. The professional habits and instincts of the soldier and sailor Governors led them to establish centralised bureaucracies, which have now, by a few rapid and inevitable steps, become centralised democracies. Ministries are upset in Australia, not so much on great principles of policy,

but rather on wrangles about the distribution of
the general revenue among the public works of the
various districts. Every member tries to get as
much as he can of the public money for his own
constituents. It is as if the fate of an English
Ministry depended on the erection of a bridge in
Wales, Scotland, or Ireland. *À propos*, the conduct of certain Irish members of the House of
Commons in 1861 respecting the Galway contract will
give you some faint idea of what takes place in Australia. To counteract this mischief I have laid great
stress here on the creation of local municipalities, as
being as necessary to well-ordered liberty as primary
schools to sound science. I have already succeeded
in persuading all our chief townships to apply to be
incorporated; and I hope soon to see established
in the rural districts a county system like that of
Canada.

But it is high time that I should relieve you from
these commentaries on Australian politics. Shall I
candidly confess that I am anxious to awaken your
curiosity, and that of Mr. Bright, so far as to induce
you to pay me a visit in this new and most flourishing
Colony—the youngest and most extensive dependency
of Great Britain? I have long been convinced, and
my conviction is fully shared by more experienced
politicians than myself, that if one or two of the
leading Radical statesmen of England were to meet
some of the Australian Radicals on their own ground
it would do a vast deal of good to both parties. And

what a contrast to the scene in {which I first had
the pleasure of making your acquaintance—the halls
of Oxford!

The importance of obtaining a good Chief Justice
from England led to the following letter:

To Sir Roundell Palmer, M.P., Solicitor-General.[1]

Government House: Brisbane, August 18, 1862.

My dear Sir Roundell Palmer,

When I used to dine with you at Lincoln's Inn,
and meet you at Lambeth in Archbishop Howley's
time, I always looked forward to your becoming
Lord Chancellor, but I did not anticipate that I
should one day address you on the selection of a
Chief Justice, and as the Governor of what is already
the most extensive in territory and the most favoured
in soil and climate, and is destined to become one of
the richest and most valuable to the parent State, of
all the dependencies of the British Crown.

I presume that before this letter reaches you my
despatches and the minutes of my Executive Council
respecting the selection of our Chief Justice will
have been forwarded to you from the Colonial Office.
From those documents and from Robert Herbert,
the Colonial Secretary of Queensland, you will learn
the whole state of the case.   He goes home on leave

[1] Afterwards Lord Chancellor and Earl of Selborne.

by this mail and will immediately put himself into communication with you.

In the Australian Colonies all appointments whatsoever, including the appointments of the Judges, are absolutely vested in the Governor, with the advice of the Executive Council; nor do they require any confirmation from the Queen or any other Imperial authority. Under the existing circumstances of this Colony, the Government and Legislature have determined to procure a Chief Justice direct from the English Bar, to be selected by some eminent legal functionary at home. As both Herbert and I are personally acquainted with you, we resolved to ask you to undertake this important trust, which I earnestly hope you will not decline. What we want is a *gentleman* rather than a mere lawyer. The principal officials in a Colony form a sort of social aristocracy. The Chief Justice ranks next to the Governor, and his influence extends far beyond the sphere of his judicial duties—indeed, whether for good or for evil, it is immense. The first Chief Justice of Queensland may set his mark for the future on this great and rising Colony. As I have told the Duke of Newcastle, the confidence of this new people can be easily and speedily won by a Judge of high personal character and impartiality, faithful in the discharge of his public duties, and animated with an honest and intelligent zeal for the public welfare. Whatever political party may be in power in the Colonial Legislature, there would be a strong desire on all

sides to defer to the opinion of such a man on all
questions affecting the administration of justice.   It is
hardly too much to say that he might become the
father of the jurisprudence of a future nation.[1]

People in England talk and write flippantly of
'Responsible,' that is, Parliamentary Government in
Australia, but they forget what great things it has
done and is doing for the English name.   What is
there in history to compare with the marvellous
growth of these Colonies?   Lord Palmerston was four
years old when the first settlers landed at Port Jackson, and already Sydney has a population of 80,000,
Melbourne of nigh 150,000, the latter city being the
growth of barely twenty-five years.[2]   Local self-government is simply indispensable if these great Colonies are
to remain what they now are, loyal provinces of the
Empire.   Englishmen in Australia will not submit to
be governed from Downing Street, 16,000 miles away.
I recollect pointing out to Mr. Gladstone, when he
was at Corfu, a passage in the twentieth chapter of
Macaulay's 'History of England,' showing that if you
grant representative institutions at all, you must grant
the logical sequence, a responsible Executive.   And
a Governor with a strong will, popular manners, and
sufficient political knowledge and official experience
to guide the deliberations of his council of ministers,
cannot fail to exercise a very commanding influence.

[1] Sir James Cockle, the Chief Justice appointed on the recommendation of Lord Selborne, proved to be all that was desired.

[2] Now, in 1889, Sydney has nearly 300,000, and Melbourne nearly
400,000 inhabitants.

The Governor of a Crown Colony is looked upon as the subordinate of the ' Downing Street ' department. The Governor of an Australian Colony, if he is worthy of his position, is regarded as the head of a people.

_____

The frequent references to Volunteer forces in the Governor's speeches pointed to a very important feature in colonial policy. The Imperial troops were withdrawn from all the self-governing Colonies, except so far as to form a nucleus for local organisations for defence; but Queensland was the only Colony ever founded ' without costing a soldier or a shilling ' to the British Treasury. The natural mode of supplying their place was by corps of Volunteers ; and Sir George Bowen lost no time, on his arrival in the Colony, in impressing upon the people the necessity of such provision. His first despatch on the subject is given below :

To the Duke of Newcastle.

Government House, Brisbane : April 10, 1860.

My Lord Duke,

On my assumption of office as Governor of Queensland, I found that Brisbane and Ipswich, the two principal towns of this Colony, each containing a large amount of British property in its banks and warehouses, could be easily sacked or laid under contribution by the boats of a single hostile ship of war. They were, in short, entirely defenceless ; the military detachment formerly stationed at Brisbane having been withdrawn several years ago, and there being absolutely no public force whatever in the two communities, except about twenty unarmed and undisciplined constables. Under these circumstances, I set myself forthwith to work to organise a Constabulary on the Irish model, and considerable progress has been made, with the assistance of an officer who had acquired much experience, and had shown great energy and resolution as commandant of the 'Native Mounted Police,' a corps of 100 black troopers stationed in detachments in the remote pastoral districts of the interior, for the protection of the outlying settlers from the attacks of the aborigines.

My next step was to encourage the formation of Volunteer Corps after the example of the mother-country. I omitted no favourable opportunity of impressing on the inhabitants of this Colony the necessity of providing for their own defence. An Act of the local Parliament enables the Governor 'to accept on behalf of the Queen the services of such of her Majesty's loyal subjects as may be willing to enrol themselves in Volunteer Corps, and to make provision for the regulation thereof.' Accordingly, in virtue of the powers thus vested in me, I issued a proclamation prescribing rules and regulations for the guidance of the Volunteer Corps which might be formed. This appeal has already been responded to. A corps entitled 'the Queensland Mounted Rifles,' and possessing an excellent *matériel* in both men and horses, has been enrolled at Brisbane. Companies of riflemen, to serve as infantry, are also in course of formation both here and in the neighbouring town of Ipswich.

My desire is not to rest content with enrolling a Volunteer force able to repel any external aggression on the seaboard. I wish to extend the movement to those inland districts where the settlers are still exposed to danger from the native tribes, which are far more numerous and more formidable in Queensland than in any other portion of Australia. This part of the question may need some explanation.

The life of the pioneers of colonisation on the distant prairies of the interior of this Colony presents several distinct phases when viewed in its connexion with the aborigines. The first sight of the horse and his rider appears to strike a tribe of blacks, as yet ignorant of the white man's existence, with supernatural terror, similar to the awe with which the American Indians contemplated the comrades of Columbus and of Cortez. But superstitious fear is soon succeeded by bitter hostility. Mutual provocations between the races lead to mutual reprisals. The fiercer spirits among the native warriors fall before the superior arms and skill of the European, or are driven still further backwards into the unexplored wilderness. The milder natures sink ere long into the condition of well-fed dependents of the colonists, and in the course of a few years no danger remains to be apprehended from them beyond some isolated acts of robbery or revenge.

In the early days of the occupation of each district, the colonists are frequently obliged to associate together, for self-defence against the blacks, in a somewhat irregular manner, and after the fashion, as I am informed, of the old Dutch *Commandos* in South Africa. For many obvious reasons, it seems highly desirable that this border warfare, when absolutely unavoidable, should be carried on under some control on the part of the Government. The establishment of the Native Police has contributed much towards this end; and I am inclined to believe that the enrolment of the principal settlers and their servants in several Corps of Yeomanry, or rather of Mounted Rifles, would contribute still more. Sir E. Bulwer Lytton wrote to the Lieutenant-Governor of British Columbia, that 'in a settlement which is surrounded by savage tribes, while sound policy will dictate every effort to conciliate the goodwill and confidence of such uncivilised neighbours, and while humanity will shrink from the application of armed force against the aborigines wherever it can be avoided, yet some military strength and disciplined organisation are essential preservatives to the settlers, and indeed will be attended with far less loss of life, with actions far less sanguinary, than when the white man is left to defend himself against the black without that decided superiority which is conferred by military skill over savages. In such conflicts the want of discipline is the want of mercy.'

In accordance with these views it is my intention to recommend the leading settlers in the remote pastoral districts of Queensland to form themselves into troops of Mounted Rifles ; and, in pursuance of the authority vested in me by law, to grant on behalf of the Queen, commissions as officers in these proposed Volunteer Corps to some of the local magistrates, and to other persons on whose courage and discretion equal reliance can be placed.

I am fully persuaded that I shall receive the support of the Colonial Legislature in carrying out the arrangements which I have shadowed forth in this despatch, and also in making all the provisions which an enlightened humanity may suggest for the interests of the aborigines ; and, whenever such a work may be commenced with a fair prospect of success, for their education and conversion to Christianity.

The response of the Queenslanders to the Governor's invitation was as prompt and hearty as could be desired.

To the Right Honourable Sir George Cornewall Lewis, Bart., M.P., Secretary of State for War.

Government House, Brisbane : August 18, 1862.

My dear Sir George Lewis,

I venture to ask you to cast your eye over the enclosed copy of a letter which I have addressed to the General Commanding in Australia, and which he will transmit by this mail to the Duke of Cambridge. A word from you would, of course, make certain the confirmation of the action taken by General Pratt, and I take the liberty of soliciting you, on the grounds of public policy stated in the enclosure, to say that word.   You will see that all I ask on behalf of the Government of Queensland is that the War Office and Horse Guards may approve of General Pratt sending an officer of the Royal Artillery to this Colony, with the special duty of organising our Volunteer Forces, and, in particular, of creating a corps of Volunteer Artillery here.   Without this aid, Queensland must remain defenceless against external attacks, and the guns recently sent out must continue useless.   Those gentlemen in England who are advocating the removal of all Imperial soldiers from Australia, and expect thereupon the sudden growth of efficient colonial regiments, would appear to forget that the old apologue of the dragon's teeth springing up armed men is not likely to repeat itself at the antipodes of Hellas.   As I told the Duke of Newcastle by the last mail, I cannot sow kangaroos' teeth under our gum trees, and then hope to see a crop of trained Volunteer gunners.   There must be a *nucleus* of military instructors.

All Queensland asks for is an Imperial contingent of one Captain of Artillery and an officer with a few soldiers of the line to drill and instruct our Volunteer forces ; that is, to enable the people of this Colony to defend themselves.   The Government of Queensland will find everything but the regimental pay of the officers and men, and will make any further contri-

bution towards the general defence of the Empire
which may be agreed upon by the Australian and
Imperial authorities.

It is, I believe, the general feeling of the Governors,
as well as of many of the principal colonists, that
adequate fixed contributions should have been reserved for Naval and Military Defence, when the
Crown Land revenues were absolutely surrendered in
1855 to the Australian Parliaments, which then represented little more than half a million of people.
Including the sale and lease of lands, and the royalties
levied in various shapes on the goldfields, the yearly
net Crown revenue of Australia cannot now be less
than two millions sterling. Why should not a fair proportion of this grand patrimony of the British nation
at large have been set apart for the general defence
and unity of the British Empire? I have told the
Duke of Newcastle that it is probably not too late
even now to rectify the grievous error which has
been committed. If the Secretary of State for the
Colonies were to make an appeal to the patriotism
and loyalty of the Australians, it would not be difficult to induce the several Legislatures to provide, by
permanent Acts, naval and military contributions proportionate to the revenue and population of each.[1]
You will recollect that this was the policy which
Benjamin Franklin suggested to George Grenville
instead of the fatal Stamp Act.

---

[1] This suggestion was practically carried out by the Colonial Conference of 1887.

So again, Sir George Bowen wrote to Mr. Gladstone on August 18, 1862 :

'As a Lancashire man yourself, you will be glad to hear that the news of the distress in Lancashire has evoked warm sympathy in all the Australian Colonies. I send you by this mail a Brisbane newspaper containing a report of a very enthusiastic public meeting held in this capital for the purpose of establishing a " Relief Fund." I was invited to take the chair, and I am glad to say that there will be sent home a sum of money, very considerable indeed in proportion to our existing population, for the succour of the distress " indistinctly heard of across half the globe," in that " dear mother-country," which our colonists regard with the proud sympathies and almost passionate love of a common allegiance and of a common nationality. It seems as strange to Englishmen in Queensland as it would appear to Englishmen in Devon or Yorkshire, to be told that they ought to be " emancipated " from the rule of Queen Victoria ; and strong denunciations are heaped on the head of my friend Goldwin Smith, for his proposals to that effect, by the Australian Press. Most colonists tell me that they delight in seeing a few soldiers among them, as reminding them of the " Old Country," on what Sidney Herbert aptly called " the British flag and redcoat principle." Besides, it is absolutely necessary for the effective defence of the Colonies against external attack, that there should be a few officers in each, to drill the Volunteers and other local forces.

'But I must now pass *per saltum* from the prairies of Northern Australia, and from the coral isles of the Pacific, to Downing Street and Carlton House Terrace. While you are reading this letter amid the fog, mud, and misery of a London autumn, we shall be (as Euripides[1] said of the Athenians)—

αἰεὶ διὰ λαμπροτάτου
ἀβρῶς βαίνοντες αἰθέρος,

enjoying the bright and exhilarating atmosphere and cloudless skies of an Australian spring, the most delicious climate in the world.'

The result of these appeals was so far successful that the colonial forces have improved year by year under trained supervision. But Sir G. Bowen never lost sight of this subject in any of the Colonies over which he successively presided. He pressed it in New Zealand, and afterwards in Victoria, where he advised (in 1877) the employment of the eminent Royal Engineer officer, Sir W. Jervois, who recommended the systematic scheme of fortification for all the Australasian Colonies which has now rendered their chief ports practically safe against foreign attack. And, as he had advised in 1862, the Colonial Conference of 1887 agreed that each Colony should provide a permanent contribution in aid of the common national defence.[2] In a recent letter, Sir G. Bowen writes:

[1] *Medea*, 830.   [2] See above, p. 208.

'What is now most urgently required is the Federation of the Australian Colonies in one Dominion, like that of Canada. Among the many practical advantages of such a Federation, not the least would be the consolidation of the local forces of each Colony into one general fleet and army, under one federal command and organisation. For this Federation I have always been a strenuous advocate ; as also for a future Imperial Federation which would preserve the unity of the British Empire. As Mr. W. E. Forster believed, a federated British Empire would probably form a friendly alliance with the great English-speaking Commonwealth across the Atlantic ; and the world would then see a *pax Britannica*, far transcending what Pliny [1] styled the *immensa Romanæ pacis majestas.*'

It has been well remarked by a writer in the 'Quarterly Review': 'We trust that the great interests of Australia will ere long become so identified with each other that its political amalgamation will be solid, enduring, and complete ; and that the mighty island-continent may never be aptly symbolised by the great composite image which the king of Babylon saw in his troubled dreams—the head of gold representing its riches and splendour, but the legs of iron and toes of clay, strength enfeebled by want of coherence, and power separated into democratic fragments by the violence of faction.'

[1] Pliny, XXVII. 1.

CHAPTER XI.

THE NORTHWARD EXPANSION OF QUEENSLAND—EXPLORING
EXPEDITIONS—GOVERNOR'S VOYAGE TO CAPE YORK AND
BACK—FOUNDATION OF A NEW SETTLEMENT—PUBLIC DINNER
AT ROCKHAMPTON—FOREIGNERS SETTLED IN QUEENSLAND—
LETTERS TO MR. CARDWELL.

IT was true, as Sir George Bowen often remarked
in his despatches and letters, that, owing to his
peculiar position as the first Governor of the vast
new Colony of Queensland, he had more of explora-
tion and discovery than had fallen to the lot of any
other Governor.   When he assumed the Government
in 1859, there was no settlement except in the south-
eastern corner of the great territory—altogether
more than five times the size of the United Kingdom.
Settlers (fewer than 25,000 in number) were then
thinly scattered over a space about as large as Great
Britain.   Rockhampton was the most northern settlement on the coast, and the pastoral stations hardly
extended beyond the Darling Downs on the west.   It
was, of course, one of the first duties of the new
Government to explore the remainder of their vast
dominion.   With this object, a number of exploring
expeditions were fitted out.   Mr. Augustus Gregory,
already well known for his successful journey through
a large portion of Northern and North-Eastern Australia, was appointed the first Surveyor-General of
Queensland.   One expedition was sent out under the

command of Mr. George Elphinstone Dalrymple, who explored the fine territory, larger than Great Britain, afterwards known as the Kennedy District, and founded as its shipping port the town of Bowen; another was led by Mr. Landsborough, who successfully crossed the continent from the head of the Gulf of Carpentaria to the southern boundary of Queensland, and afterwards to Melbourne; proving the existence in Queensland of great tracts of country hitherto unknown, but available for pastoral settlement; a third was under Messrs. A. and F. Jardine, who forced their way, driving their cattle before them, through the dense forests and hostile natives of the Cape York Peninsula, to the new settlement founded in 1862 in Torres Straits. These were the chief expeditions fitted out by the Government; but many adventurous men, in search of fresh country, followed them. Full reports of all these and of other similar expeditions were forwarded to the Royal Geographical Society, and were published in their Transactions. Sir Roderick Murchison, then the able and energetic President, often spoke at the meetings of the Society in high eulogy of the exertions of Sir G. Bowen in the cause of geographical discovery. In a letter of 1875, Sir George wrote : 'I was much pleased by my reception at a meeting of the Royal Geographical Society. In some remarks that I was called on to make, I related how when our Queensland explorer Landsborough was told that wool would not grow on sheep in hot latitudes, he exclaimed : "Sir, you are theorizing. *Does not wool grow on negroes in the Tropics?*" *A propos* of this, I reminded my audience of the story of the negro preacher in America, who,

in a sermon to his black congregation, said : "My
brethren, the Scriptures tell us that, at the last day,
the good Lord will divide the sheep from the goats.
Now, bless the Lord" (putting his hand on his own
woolly pate), " *we know who wears the wool!* "'

During the eight years of Sir G. Bowen's governorship, a line of new ports was opened all along the
eastern coast of Queensland, from Rockhampton to
Cape York, and also at the head of the Gulf of Carpentaria; and the pastoral settlers overspread the
entire interior, thus virtually adding to the British
Empire a territory four times larger than the British
Isles.   As the Governor remarked in one of his
speeches on this subject : 'Such are the triumphs of
peaceful progress ; they are victories without injustice
or bloodshed; they are conquests not over man, but
over Nature ; not for this generation only, but for all
posterity; not for England only, but for all mankind.'

Among the various exploring expeditions in
Queensland, that made by Sir George Bowen in
H.M.S. 'Pioneer' in 1862 was signally important,
for it led to the founding of the coaling station
and settlement near Cape York, the value of which
has been more highly appreciated every year since its
creation.   The various considerations which pointed
to the necessity of a station in the extreme north of
Queensland were summed up in a despatch from the
Governor dated December 9, 1861 :

'In a naval and military point of view, a post at
or near Cape York would be most valuable, and its
importance is daily increasing with the augmentation

of the commerce passing by this route, especially since the establishment of a French Colony and naval station at New Caledonia. It has been pointed out on high authority, that a small armed steamer with a light draught of water (such as one of the gunboats used in the Crimean and China wars), having a settlement at Cape York as her *point d'appui*, would command the whole of the commerce between the South Pacific and Indian Oceans. By establishing a signal post on one of the neighbouring hills, she might be warned of the approach of all ships, and of their number and character, while, " by making herself thoroughly acquainted with the neighbouring reefs and shoals, she might easily pick out tortuous and dangerous channels, which would afford her refuge and means of escape from a force superior in strength to herself." It is stated that the Admiralty intend shortly to increase the naval force on the Australian station. If so, it is hoped that a gunboat of light draught may be sent out for service at Cape York. In time of peace, she might keep up occasional communication between the proposed new settlement and the seat of Government at Brisbane, and might complete the surveys and charts of Torres Straits and of the Great Barrier Reef.

' In a political point of view, a station at Cape York could not fail to extend the influence and *prestige* of Great Britain over the Indian Archipelago, while it would form a link between our possessions in Australia, India, and China, assure us the possession of the north and north-east coasts of the Australian continent, "and, as it were, close the ring fence with which we have girt the fifth quarter of the globe." [1]

'The foregoing observations are eminently practical, and applicable to the present time. It has been remarked, however, that we may confidently augur for a settlement at Cape York a future destiny of a higher and more important character than would result from the above considerations alone. Fifty years ago the somewhat similar position of Singapore, then also a barren promontory, inhabited only by wandering savages, was chosen by the genius of Sir Stamford Raffles as the future site of a great emporium of commerce and navigation. Now it has been said, "the time must ultimately come when that great chain of islands, stretching from the east end of New Guinea to New Caledonia, shall be brought within the region of civilisation and commerce; and when the veil that rests upon New Guinea itself shall be raised. Torres Straits will then be the channel of the commerce between these regions, as well as between the more remote and mighty ones which lie beyond them. It will resemble the Straits of Malacca in this respect, and another Singapore may be expected to rise on its borders, just where the converging streams of commerce are compressed into the narrowest and closest channel. This must be somewhere about Cape York, or the entrance of Endeavour Strait. It is here, indeed, if anywhere, that the true analogy is

[1] *Voyage of H.M.S. 'Fly,'* p. 366.

to be sought for between Singapore and any point of
Australia—the narrowest strait, where, from physical
necessity the widespread commerce of neighbouring
seas must inevitably converge—the pass through
which one of the great highways of the world must
necessarily run." [1]

'Your Grace will perceive from the enclosed
Minute of Council, that the Government of Queensland will be willing, with the sanction of the Colonial
Legislature, to undertake the formation and management of a station at Cape York, and to support the
civil establishment there, on conditions which will
entail no trouble on the Imperial Government. Those
conditions cannot, I think, be considered as otherwise than liberal and reasonable, and as strong proofs
of the public spirit and of the attachment to the
parent State, with which I have ever found the members of the Queensland Parliament to be animated.
For this Colony, *as such*, has manifestly no direct
or immediate interest in the foundation of a settlement at Cape York, which is twelve hundred miles
from Brisbane, that is, further than Gibraltar is from
London.'

The Home Government was fully prepared to
entertain the proposals of the Queensland Government; and the Admiralty agreed that the Governor
and the Commodore in command of the Australian
Station should together proceed to Cape York. The
following despatch describes their successful voyage :

[1] *Ibid.* pp. 309–10.

To the Duke of Newcastle.

Government House, Brisbane : November 3, 1862.

My Lord Duke,

With reference to previous correspondence respecting the projected station at Cape York, I have
the honour to report that, in obedience to his instructions from the Admiralty, Commodore Burnett,
C.B., commanding the Queen's Naval Forces in
Australia, received me on board Her Majesty's ship
' Pioneer,' in Moreton Bay, on August 27th ult., for the
purpose of selecting, in conjunction with himself,
the most eligible site for the proposed settlement.

Falling in with the south-east trade, the prevailing
wind during the greater portion of the year on the
east coast of Australia, the ' Pioneer ' made a good
passage under canvas inside the Great Barrier Reef,
to Booby Island in Torres Straits, the furthest limit
to the north-west of the jurisdiction of Queensland ;
where we anchored on the evening of September 9th.
Here we deposited an iron case for the letters generally left on this rock by the passing ships of all
nations, to be conveyed to their respective addresses
by succeeding vessels.

On September 10th we commenced our return
voyage under steam, passing through Endeavour
Strait, having passed through the Prince of Wales
Channel on our outward track. From the 10th to
the 22nd September the ' Pioneer ' was at anchor near
Cape York, principally in Evans Bay and Port Albany.

During these twelve days Commodore Burnett and I
carefully examined, both by land and sea, the north-
eastern point of the Australian continent, and its
immediate vicinity.   After full consideration, we
both came to the conclusion that the proper site for
the projected settlement is at Port Albany, for the
nautical and other reasons so fully and clearly stated
in Commodore Burnett's report to the Admiralty, of
which I enclose a copy, with which he has furnished
·me.   I beg to take this opportunity of recording
my sense of Commodore Burnett's personal attention to myself while on board Her Majesty's ship
' Pioneer,' and also of the zeal and ability which he
devoted to the important objects of our expedition.
He has received the thanks of the Government of
Queensland, as will appear from the enclosed Minute
of the Executive Council, of which I beg that a copy
may be transmitted to the Lords Commissioners of
the Admiralty.   A piece of ground will, at the
request of Commodore Burnett, be reserved at Port
Albany as an arsenal and coal depôt for the use of
the Royal Navy.

It will be seen that Port Albany combines almost
all the advantages required for such a settlement as
that proposed.   Close to the landing-place there is
good and safe anchorage, sheltered from all winds,
for a limited number of vessels, while whole fleets
might ride safely at anchor, at no great distance, in
Evans Bay, during the south-east monsoon, or in
Newcastle Bay during the north-west monsoon.   On

Albany Island, and on the opposite mainland, from which it is separated by a deep channel only one-third of a mile broad, there is also abundant pasturage for sheep, cattle, and horses, large tracts of soil suitable for gardens and for general cultivation, especially of cotton, sugar, and other tropical productions, plenty of timber for building and firewood, as also of stone and of coral for lime. From the peninsular position of Cape York and its neighbourhood, the land receives the full influence of every breeze, hence the temperature is remarkably cool for the tropics, and healthy for Europeans. The thermometer was never above 85° during our expedition. Above all, we found, though our visit was at the close of an unusually dry season, a plentiful and evidently never-failing supply of fresh water, both on Albany Island and on the neighbouring mainland. Commodore Burnett's report will be found very minute on this vital point, respecting which preceding accounts had been vague and unsatisfactory. Near the north-east point of Albany Island, a rill of pure water, fringed with the flowering shrubs and grasses of Australia, trickles over the cliff into a small natural reservoir, which was named the 'Fountain of Arethusa,' from its close resemblance to the Homeric fountain in Ithaca.

It is proposed that the settlement shall be placed, in the first instance, near the anchorage at Port Albany. It will be named Somerset, in acknowledgment of the readiness with which the present

First Lord of the Admiralty, the Duke of Somerset, has lent his aid to an undertaking of such great importance to the interests of the British Empire in Australia. If a better site should be discovered hereafter in the same quarter, the Government establishment will be removed thither.[1]

Very friendly relations were established and maintained with the small tribe of aborigines frequenting the neighbourhood of Cape York. I had provided myself with a number of hatchets, knives, fish-hooks, and other useful presents for them. They daily came off to the ship in their own canoes, bartering fish, turtle, tortoise-shells, &c., for biscuits and tobacco, and were often visited by us in their camps on shore. We were enabled to communicate with them by the help of the excellent vocabulary of their dialect printed in the appendix to the ' Voyage of H.M. Surveying Ship " Rattlesnake." ' Commodore Burnett agrees with me in the opinion that a party of some twenty marines, or armed police, will be amply sufficient for the protection of the new settlement.

The physical characteristics of these aborigines at Cape York differ in no essential respect from those of the same race elsewhere; but their arms, canoes, and other implements are of a somewhat better description, owing, probably, to their occasional intercourse

---

[1] Several years afterwards, when regular steam communication had begun, the settlement was removed from Albany to Thursday Island; which latter is more directly in the track of vessels passing through Torres Strait, and is somewhat nearer the recently acquired British possessions in New Guinea.

with the inhabitants of the islands in Torres Straits, who belong for the most part to the Papuan or New Guinea race—a people of higher natural endowments.

During the voyage to and from Cape York, the 'Pioneer' was frequently anchored off various points of the north-east coast of Australia. We landed and examined the most remarkable sites, which will, probably, ere long be occupied by new settlements, since the tide of colonisation in Queensland is sweeping onward at the rate of about two hundred miles each year. One of the most important points which we visited is the plain at the mouth of the Endeavour River, up which we rowed for several miles. This is classic ground to every Englishman, and especially to every English seaman, and to every Australian settler, for it was here that Captain Cook, in 1770, careened and repaired his ship, after the damages sustained during his long and perilous navigation among the coral reefs and unknown shoals of the east coast of Australia, of which he was the first discoverer. It would have cheered the heart of the illustrious navigator, amid the cruel distresses and anxieties which he has so pathetically described, if he could have foretold that, within less than a century, in that 'Great Southern Land' on the shores of which he first suggested a settlement, a British Empire would have arisen, already far surpassing, in wealth, in trade, and in all the arts which promote and adorn civilisation, those American Colonies which in 1770 were on the eve of throwing off their allegiance to the mother-country.[1]

The 'Great Barrier Reef' of coral, and the chain of islands which fringe for nearly one thousand miles the north-eastern coast of Queensland, form a natural breakwater, securing a smooth and delightful navigation, by what is called the 'inner route,' for vessels passing through Torres Straits. The establishment of a line of steamers between Australia and Singapore by this route is clearly only a question of time, the solution of which will be accelerated by the establishment of a settlement and coal depôt near Cape York.[2]

The general aspect of the coast along which we sailed on our outward and homeward tracks, for nearly three thousand miles, resembles that of Southern Italy and Greece. The mountain ranges of Northern Queensland have much of the picturesque outline and rich colouring of the Apennines in Calabria, and of the hills of Eubœa and of the Peloponnesus, while the groups of islands through which we threaded our way often reminded Commodore Burnett and myself of the isles of the Ægean and Ionian

---

[1] The trade of the thirteen original American Colonies did not amount in 1770 to three millions sterling. In 1860, the trade of the single Australian Colony of Victoria exceeded twenty-five millions. In one of his Voyages, Captain Cook has recorded, with regret and pain, his witnessing the departure of one of the expeditions against the revolted American Colonies (*Third Voyage*, Vol. I. p. 9). A flourishing settlement, appropriately named Cooktown, and already, in 1889, containing several thousand inhabitants, has grown up near the mouth of the Endeavour River.

[2] This prediction was soon fulfilled, and a line of mail steamers has been running through Torres Straits for many years past (1889).

seas. If Queensland be without the classical and
historical associations of Greece, it enjoys a more
luxuriant vegetation and a more salubrious climate,
and possesses, of course, a territory more than forty
times larger than that of little Hellas.[1]

The happy results of the occupation of Cape
York have been since manifested in many ways, and
not least in the securing the possession of Thursday
Island, and thus holding the Torres Straits with a
commanding naval and military position in case of
war.

On his return voyage Sir George Bowen visited
some of the principal settlements in Northern Queensland.

To the Duke of Newcastle.

Government House, Brisbane: November 5, 1862.

My Lord Duke,

In continuation of former despatches, and with
reference especially to the report of my first tour
of inspection in the northern and central districts
of Queensland, I have now the honour to transmit
copies of the addresses presented to me on my recent
official visits to the four northern harbours of Port
Denison, Rockhampton, Gladstone, and Maryborough.
Subjoined are my replies.

My reception by all classes of the community was

[1] There are 678,000 square miles in Queensland, and 15,000 in the
kingdom of Greece.

everywhere very cordial, and nothing could be more gratifying than the marks which met my eye on all sides of rapid and solid progress during the two years which have elapsed since my former visit.

At that period, Rockhampton, founded on the river Fitzroy in 1858, was the farthest township towards the north. I reported at the close of the year 1860, that I was then about to open, in the recently discovered harbour of Port Denison, in Edgcumbe Bay, a shipping-place for the newly proclaimed pastoral district of Kennedy. Almost before my despatch could have reached the Colonial Office, the pioneer squatters were driving their flocks and herds before them into the interior; and a flourishing township, called by the first settlers after my name, was rising on the hitherto unexplored beach of Port Denison. Already, after the lapse of less than two years, the wave of pastoral settlement has overflowed the entire Kennedy District, and has even surmounted the dividing range or watershed of the York Peninsula ; for cattle already feed above four hundred miles due north of Rockhampton, in latitude 19° S., on the banks of the rivers which run, not into the Pacific, but into the Gulf of Carpentaria. In other words, during the short space of eighteen months, our pastoral settlers have practically added to the British Empire and pushed on the margin of Christianity and civilisation over a territory as extensive as Great Britain itself.

The first white men landed at Port Denison in

1860, fighting their way through a tribe of hostile savages.[1] A township has already sprung up there, as towns spring up in Australia, almost with the rapidity of the prophet's gourd. In its inns and private houses, Commodore Burnett and I found most of the comforts and many of the luxuries of England ; its inhabitants have, indeed, already imported our national games. Scarcely had H.M.S. ' Pioneer,' which conveyed me thither on my return from Cape York, cast anchor in the Bay, when friendly challenges were addressed to the officers and crew, from the ' Bowen Cricket Club,' to play a match on their ground on shore, and from the ' Bowen Boat Club ' to row a race on the waters of the harbour. The ' Pioneers ' were easily defeated in one innings at cricket, and had a tough struggle to gain the victory even on their own element over the amateur boatmen. I believe that your Grace will not deem too trivial any details which may enable you to form a picture in your own mind of the life of our countrymen in this remote corner of tropical Australia, sixteen thousand miles from the parent State, and eight hundred miles distant from the seat of the Colonial Government at Brisbane.

Most of the principal settlers in North-eastern Australia have been attracted from Victoria and New South Wales by the more liberal land legislation of Queensland. There is, however, a strong sprink-

[1] See the Report of Mr. G. E. Dalrymple transmitted with my despatch of December 8, 1860.

ling among them of retired officers of the army and
navy, weary of the routine of a mess-room or ward-
room, of Oxford and Cambridge men preferring an
adventurous life in the open air to the indoor labours
of a profession, and of other gentlemen of birth and
education recently arrived from England. I also found
among the most prosperous squatters and merchants
of Northern Queensland, numerous foreigners, several
of them political exiles from their native lands on
the continent of Europe, but all now naturalised
British subjects, and firm in their loyalty to the
Queen, and to their adopted country.   For example,
a Dane and a Dutchman are among the most successful squatters in the Kennedy district.   Again,
at the dinner given in my honour by the Mayor
and Corporation of Rockhampton, the chief town of
Northern Queensland, three of the toasts were proposed by foreigners.   One of these gentlemen was a
French Republican, a member of the ' Extreme Left '
in the National Assembly of 1848, who found it necessary to emigrate after the *Coup d'état* of 1851, feeling
(as he himself told me) that his only choice lay between Australia and French Guiana.   ' *M. le Gouver-
neur, cela vaut mieux que Cayenne,*' he remarked to
me, pointing to the arrangements of the tables, quite
as good as those of a public dinner at a country town
in England, and laid out in a handsome public hall,
erected almost on the very spot where in 1858, only
four years ago, the first white men who settled on the
banks of the river Fitzroy saw a tribe of aborigines

feasting on human flesh, and dancing their wild
' corobborees.' Another toast was proposed by a
German, formerly an officer in the Schleswig-Holstein
army, who fled into exile after the victory of the
Danes at Idstedt. A third toast was entrusted to the
cadet of a noble family at Corfu, whom I recollected
as by no means distinguished, when an Ionian citizen,
for his attachment to the British Protectorate, but
who now, as a naturalised British subject, is loud
in his loyalty to the Queen. When these gentlemen
were requested by the Chairman (the Mayor of Rockhampton) to entertain the company after dinner by
singing the national songs of their respective countries, the French Republican sang the ' Marseillaise '
with great vigour. The German officer gave the
revolutionary song of the Duchies; while the Ionian
noble poured forth Count Salomos' beautiful ' Hymn
to Liberty' (Σὲ γνωρίζω ἀπὸ τὴν κόψι), wherein are some
uncomplimentary allusions to the British Protectorate,
which in Northern Australia were intelligible (I need
scarcely say) to *my* ears alone. These songs appeared
to be sung with much the same sentiment with which
an Englishman of the present day repeats Scotch
Jacobite poetry. All the three foreigners afterwards
joined in a chant of ' God save the Queen,' declaring
that they now regard *that* as their only national
anthem, and that they yield in loyalty to no one
among their fellow colonists—the native-born British
subjects around them. I found, on inquiry, that almost all the foreigners to whom I have alluded have

married in the Colony, and that their children can
speak no language but English. Is not their position
a strong proof of what has been called the ' assimilat-
ing power of the Anglo-Saxon race ' ?

It appears to be the opinion of many persons in
England that the duties of an Australian Governor are
merely social and ornamental ; that he ' reigns ' but
should not ' govern.'   Certainly my experience here
would go far to show that such a theory is decidedly
opposed to the views and wishes of many of the Australians themselves.   I have often found it difficult
to confine myself strictly to the guardianship of Imperial interests, and to avoid that authoritative interference in the internal concerns of the Colony to
which bodies of the colonists have frequently urged
me.   It seems, indeed, probable that the Governor of
a Colony, in which all antagonism to the home authorities has been removed by the full concession of local
self-government, can generally, if he performs his
part well, exercise a more genuine and commanding
influence than the Governor of a Crown Colony.

Before concluding this sketch of the northward
expansion of Queensland, portions of two letters
written by Sir George Bowen a couple of years later
may be quoted in illustration of the progress of the
northern settlements :—

To the Right Honourable Edward Cardwell, M.P.,
Secretary of State for the Colonies.[1]

Government House, Brisbane : April 17, 1865.

My dear Sir,

In my letter to you by the last mail I mentioned that the first land sale at the new township named Cardwell was about to take place, and that speculators would be present from both Brisbane and Sydney. The upset price was 20*l*. per acre ; but the competition was so active that all the lots put up to auction were sold at an average price of 600*l*. per acre. In the same week took place also the first land sale at the new settlement at Cape York. Here again the upset price was 20*l*. per acre, but the price realised averaged only 150*l*. per acre. This result means that the speculators in land consider that Cardwell, from its central position and other advantages, has four times a better chance than Somerset of becoming one day the capital of a new Colony. The sums realised at the first land sales will fully repay my Government for the heavy expense of founding these two new settlements at so great a distance from Brisbane. It was certainly a grand invention of late years to *sell* instead of *giving away*, as formerly, the land in our Colonies, and thus to make colonisation pay for itself. I think the ' grant system ' alone was known to the ancients. Those who talk of the art of colonisation being one of the *artes perditæ* would

[1] Afterwards Viscount Cardwell. He succeeded the Duke of Newcastle at the Colonial Office.

seem to have forgotten that English colonisation in Australia alone has spread, during the last twenty years, over a far greater space than the aggregate of all the Greek and Roman colonies put together.

The patriotic and inspiriting remarks which you made about our Colonial Empire when your constituents at Oxford entertained you in last January, have been copied into the leading Queensland and other Australian journals. They have made a most favourable impression, and have done much good. A young and rising Colony feels the same pleasure and encouragement at praise from a leading statesman at home, as a young man of talent and ambition feels at any mark of approval from great and eminent personages. Such speeches as that which you recently delivered at Oxford are a ‘cheap defence’ of the Empire. At one of the Australian dinners in London, the Duke of Newcastle called Queensland ‘an infant in years, but a giant in strength, in efforts, and in aspirations.’ These words are often quoted here, and will probably (like some of the sayings of Burke and Chatham about the old North American Colonies) long survive.

To the Same.

Government House, Brisbane : November 18, 1865.
My dear Sir,

My despatch herewith gives a full account of my recent official visit to all our ports from Brisbane to Cardwell, a distance of one thousand miles, and

shows the remarkable progress of this Colony. I
was more than ever struck with the beauty of the
situation of *your* town. The mountain range behind
it, and the chain of hills which forms the backbone
of Hinchinbrook Island in front of it, average from
2,500 to 4,000 feet in height, and are clothed with
magnificent forests almost up to their peaks. They
vividly recall the picturesque outline and rich colouring of the mountains of Italy and Greece. The
channel which divides Hinchinbrook Island from
the mainland reminds me much of the Euripus between Eubœa and Bœotia. The town of Cardwell
is rising in a position analogous to that of Ther-
mopylæ, that is at the north end of this Australian
Euripus, where the mountains approach and slope
down into the sea.

On his discovery, in 1770, of the eastern part of
Australia, Captain Cook named the more prominent
features of the coast after the chief English statesmen of his day. Thus he named Rockingham Bay
after Lord Rockingham, the patron of Burke, and
Cape Sandwich and Hinchinbrook Island in honour
of Lord Sandwich, then the First Lord of the Admiralty. It will be seen that in the geographical
nomenclature of Queensland I have followed to some
extent the precedent set by the great navigator.
Thus the town called after you will perpetuate your
name in Australia :—

> —————————nomen
> *Hesperiá in magná, si qua ea est gloria, signat.*

So, too, I may say with Virgil,[1]

Et nunc servat honos sedem tuus.————

In reply to the above letter, Mr. Cardwell wrote: 'I am very proud to have *nomen Hesperiâ in magnâ*; and am much obliged to you for conferring on me a similar honour to that conferred in Virgil on Caieta, the *Nurse* of Æneas.   But I feel that your great and vigorous Colony stands in no need of *nursing*'!

[1] Virgil, *Æn*. VII. 3–5.

CHAPTER XII.

THE earlier years of Sir George Bowen's administration in Queensland were naturally the most momentous. In founding States, as in beginning everything else, *c'est le premier pas qui coûte*; and so successfully had the first step been made, that the subsequent progress was almost monotonously smooth and regular. The Home Government had shown its appreciation of the Governor's services by promoting him from the Commandership to the Grand Cross of St. Michael and St. George. The Queenslanders testified their satisfaction in numerous addresses, and by adopting the measures which the Governor and his Ministers recommended. Everything in the machinery of the State worked with singular ease; and such differences of opinion as must always arise among men of independent character in no degree impaired the general good feeling and practical efficiency of the Council and Assembly. The most praiseworthy of legislatures must die, however, sooner or later; and in 1863 the first Parliament of Queensland entered on its last session. It was dissolved rather before the expiration of its natural life, for reasons which are fully explained in the subjoined despatch.

To the Duke of Newcastle.

Government House, Brisbane : June 15, 1863.

My Lord Duke,

I have the honour to report that, on the 22nd ultimo, by the advice of my responsible Ministers, I dissolved the first Legislative Assembly of Queensland.

Soon after the commencement of the annual session of Parliament for 1863, it became evident that an appeal to the country would shortly become unavoidable. The Assembly had been elected on the first establishment of the Colony, and, according to the provisions of the Constitution Act, for five years. It was already in its fifth session, and it was argued, both in and out of Parliament, that a legislative body chosen in 1860, when our population was under twenty-five thousand, could scarcely be held to adequately represent the Colony in 1863, when our population exceeds fifty thousand souls. The statistical register, moreover, proved that during the same interval our trade and revenue, as well as our population, had more than doubled; and it was contended that, seeing the very rapid and solid progress of this young community, a triennial Parliament in Queensland was practically more than equivalent to even a decennial Parliament in England.

Matters were brought to a crisis owing to the introduction by the Government of a Bill to authorise the construction, by means of a loan, of a trunk railway leading from the head of the navigation of the river Brisbane towards the interior of the Colony. The incessant rains and heavy floods of the earlier part of this year had almost entirely suspended, during several months, all traffic between. the ports on the coast and the towns and pastoral stations in the inland districts. The existing tracks became impassable for bullock drays, and the squatters could neither send down their wool nor bring up their supplies. Under these circumstances, it was very generally felt that the improvement of the internal communication had become an object of urgent necessity. The Government, moreover, had received a proposal for the construction of a light railway on the American model, at a rate not exceeding four thousand pounds (4,000*l.*) per mile—that is, at a rate fully as cheap, if not cheaper, than that at which ordinary macadamised roads can be made in a country subject to be deluged by almost tropical rains, and where labour of all kinds is very dear.

The Ministry proposed to Parliament to sanction a loan of nearly a million sterling, chiefly for the purpose of constructing the trunk railway referred to above, and of extending the electric telegraph from Brisbane to the northern ports of the Colony, and thence to a point near the head of the Gulf of Carpentaria, where it would ultimately meet the projected international line connecting Australia with Asia and Europe. Many politicians of all parties, however, considered that the Legislature would not be justified in saddling the community at large with a debt of this amount until the public should have had an opportunity of pronouncing its opinion upon the new policy.   On this ground, strengthened, of course (as in all representative bodies), by a variety of party and personal feelings, several gentlemen, not usually found to act together, united in opposing the Railway Bill; which was carried, on its second reading in the Assembly, only by the casting vote of the Speaker. Mr. Herbert and his colleagues then advised me to dissolve ; and I felt, after mature reflection, that no other course was open to me.   Over and above the considerations already enumerated, it seemed not un-reasonable that the Ministers who had carried on the Government of the Colony ever since its first establishment, and during the most critical period of its history, should have an opportunity of appealing to the electors before surrendering their places to new men.   Moreover, such was the state of parties in the late Assembly, that it could hardly be said that there was any organised Opposition ready to assume office with any prospect of retaining it, even during the very brief term of ministerial life which is usual in most of the Australian Colonies.

The Parliament was accordingly prorogued with a view to an immediate appeal to the country ; but I was requested to delay for a few hours the formal dissolution, as both Houses were desirous to attend once more in a body the annual *levée* held by all Governors in honour of the Queen's birthday.   At the conclusion of that ceremony, I addressed the Legislature in the following words :

' Mr. President, Mr. Speaker, Gentlemen of both Houses,—In taking leave of the first Parliament of Queensland, I should not do justice to my own feelings if I were not to take this opportunity of expressing my deep sense of your cordial co-operation on all occasions with myself, as the representative of the Queen, and of the signal services which you have rendered to this Colony by much wise and moderate legislation.   It is easy to foresee that the first Parliament will fill an honourable place in the annals of Queensland, long after all party feelings of the present day shall have been forgotten.'

I submit that these brief remarks were natural in my position, and cannot fairly be accused of exaggeration.   For it will be remembered that Queensland is distinguished from all other British Colonies in two remarkable points.   In the first place, it has been established and organised without any cost to the mother-country; and, in the second place, this is the only Colony which was ever started in political life with full parliamentary and responsible government from the beginning, and with almost absolute powers of control and disposal over a territory more than three times as large as France. In all our other principal dependencies, parliamentary government was adopted only after the community had already reached a comparatively advanced stage, when the various departments of

the public service had been filled with experienced
officials, and when a body of public men, inured to
public life and fit to guide the deliberations of a
constitutional legislature, had been formed in the
old Councils and Assemblies. On the other hand, in
Queensland, on its separation from New South Wales,
there was scarcely a single man of practical experience in either official or political life. A population
of less than twenty-five thousand souls, dispersed over
an area far exceeding that of most of the States of
Europe, was suddenly called upon to provide materials, not only for a responsible Executive Government,
but for two Houses of Parliament. Most reflecting
men in Australia held this to be, if a highly interesting,
still a somewhat rash experiment. Yet it is now, I
believe, generally admitted that the small body of
graziers and merchants, of which two classes the first
Parliament of Queensland was mainly composed,
have falsified the predictions of their failure. Led
by several gentlemen of acknowledged ability, they
have shown much practical good sense, and an honest
and intelligent zeal for the public welfare ; while the
laws which they have enacted will certainly bear
comparison with the legislation of the other Australian Colonies.

The second Parliament, elected from a much
larger constituency, proved as practical as its predecessor, and being recruited from a wider area was
fully alive to the importance of the extension of rail-

way and telegraph communication.   The Main Trunk
Railway was immediately authorised, and the contract for its construction was undertaken by the great
firm of Brassey & Co., who entertained the Governor
and Parliament at a sumptuous luncheon to celebrate
the opening of the first section.   Many congratula-
tory speeches were then delivered; the Governor
remarking that 'the Brasseys might almost apply to
themselves what Æneas says in Virgil [1] :—

Quæ regio in terris nostri non plena laboris ? '

Subsequent sessions of Parliament approved the
extension of railways to the north and south, while
telegraph wires were soon stretching from one end of
Queensland to the other.   When Sir George Bowen
visited Rockhampton in September 1865 to turn the
first sod of the Northern Railway, which was to do for
the northern districts of Queensland what the Main
Trunk had already begun to effect for the southern
districts, he said in reply to the address of the Corporation :

'When I first saw Rockhampton, in 1860, it was
a small hamlet of wooden huts with scarcely five
hundred inhabitants, who had recently settled down
in the primeval wilderness.   I recollect well that
what Lord Macaulay has termed "a rude kind of
patriarchal justice, which was, however, better than
no justice at all," was then administered in a canvas
tent whenever a magistrate might happen to attend.
On my second visit, in 1862, your population had
trebled, and the hamlet had grown up into a thriv-

[1] *Æn.* I. 460.

ing township, with about fifteen hundred inhabitants.
Now, on this my third visit, I learn with much pleasure that your population has again more than
trebled during the brief interval that has elapsed
since my second visit. I see around me a flourishing
town of nearly five thousand inhabitants, with public
buildings of every kind—churches, schools, a mechanics' institute, a post office, a telegraph office, and
numerous banks and warehouses. I find a Judge of
the Supreme Court, surrounded by the leading members of the Colonial Bar, holding the assizes for
Northern Queensland in a commodious and substantial court-house; I am welcomed by a Mayor and
Aldermen; and I remark with great satisfaction in
the wharves which line your noble river, in the well-
ordered streets of your town, and in other signs of
material prosperity, the rapid progress of those advantages which municipal self-government, when
prudently and vigorously administered, is certain to
confer.

'I entirely agree with you, Mr. Mayor and gentlemen, in attaching high importance to the great public work which is to be initiated this day. It is
acknowledged in every quarter that the most pressing need of the entire Colony is the improvement of
our internal communications. With this object, the
Colonial Parliament has decided that two trunk lines
of railway shall be carried into the interior—one for
the southern districts, from the head of the navigation of Moreton Bay, and one for the northern dis-

tricts, from the head of the navigation of Keppel Bay.
It is well known that in 1862, in consequence of my
earnest representations, the Imperial Government
annexed to our northern territory an additional area,
larger than the United Kingdom, and that, during
several years, I have spared no exertion to push on
two enterprises calculated to be of great advantage to
the interests of the north. I mean the establishment of
steam communication through Torres Straits, and the
extension of the electric telegraph from Rockhampton to our north-western frontier, where it will meet
the international line which will ultimately connect
Australia with Asia and Europe. Both these projects
received the sanction of the Colonial Legislature in
its last session, and both will be carried into execution forthwith by my Ministers.'

A letter written immediately after this northern
tour, gives Sir George Bowen's further impressions of
what he saw :

To the Right Honourable W. E. Gladstone, M.P.

Government House, Brisbane : November 18, 1865.
My dear Sir,
    You will probably feel some interest in the con-
dition and progress of the beautifully situated town
in Queensland of which you are the godfather. I
venture, therefore, to enclose a copy of the addresses
presented to me on my recent official tour of inspection to the northern districts of this Colony, including

an address from the Mayor of Gladstone, and another from the miners on the neighbouring goldfields. You will see that in my reply to the Mayor of your town, I quoted from a speech recently delivered by you at Liverpool. The present Mayor of Gladstone is proud of being also a Lancashire man.

I have just returned from this cruise of 2,000 miles, all in the waters of Queensland. I was received with great cordiality at every seaport, especially by the Gladstonians, and also by the 'diggers' on the goldfields in the vicinity, who invited me to a public banquet given in a large tent in the centre of the 'diggings.' The dinner, wines, and speeches were all equally good. You are doubtless aware that Australian gold-mining has now become a regular pursuit, without the recklessness and turbulence of former years. The deputation of the mining body who had been elected by their fellows to act as my hosts were all evidently men of sense and education. I am confident that you will also learn with interest that the Queensland Parliament, on my recommendation, has adopted in this Colony those Acts which you have recently passed through the Imperial Parliament for the improvement and extension of the Government savings banks, and for the granting annuities and life assurances on the security of the public revenue, and for ameliorating in other ways the condition of the working classes. You will see from the enclosed copy of my prorogation speech that I alluded to this subject in closing

R 2

the session for 1865. From the concluding paragraph of the same speech you will learn the wonderfully rapid, but solid progress of Queensland during the six years of my administration.

At the close of this year's session, both Houses presented me with addresses, voted without a single dissentient voice, in which after thanking me in warm terms for the services which they are so indulgent as to believe that I have rendered to this Colony, they assure me that 'your Excellency's prudent zeal for the interests and welfare of Queensland have secured not only the respect due to the office which your Excellency fills, but also our personal regard and gratitude.' This is a gratifying testimonial from the representatives of the people whom I have governed for six years. I need scarcely remind you that Queensland is distinguished in two remarkable points from all other British Colonies. (1) It was started with parliamentary government full-blown from the beginning. (2) It has been founded and organised without the cost of a shilling to the mother-country. (3) The Queenslanders take annually at the rate of about 22*l*. per head (a far larger proportion than is taken in any other part of the world) of English manufactures and other produce of the British Isles. I submit that these facts ought to make this Colony popular in the House of Commons.

The conclusion of the prorogation speech referred to in the foregoing letter contains the following satisfactory statement:

'Since the establishment of Queensland in December 1859 our European population has increased from less than 25,000 to above 90,000; that is, it has been augmented nearly fourfold, while our revenue and our trade (including imports and exports) have been more than trebled. During the same short period, cotton, sugar, and tobacco have been added to our list of staple products; a line of new ports has been opened along our eastern seaboard from Keppel Bay to Cape York, a distance of a thousand miles; while pastoral occupation has spread over an additional area at least four times larger than that of the United Kingdom. In 1859 our settlers had hardly advanced beyond the Darling Downs to the west, or beyond Rockhampton to the north. Now, in 1865, there are stations 700 miles to the west of Brisbane and 800 miles to the north of Rockhampton. These facts, derived from the official statistics, cannot fail to be interesting and instructive to our fellow countrymen at home, while they must be to you, as they are to me, a subject of honest pride and of devout thankfulness.'

Commenting on this striking summary, the 'Times' remarked (December 1, 1865): 'In the earlier days of Australian colonisation it was supposed that the pastoral pursuits of the Colonies which lie within the

temperate zone could no longer be prosecuted with
success in latitudes lying within the Tropics, except in
the case of some tableland raised a great height above
the sea. This opinion continued to prevail until all
the southern country having been taken up, pastoral
enterprise must have ceased to extend itself unless
the warmer regions of the north were invaded. To
this happy necessity are due the rise and progress of
the Colony of Queensland, which has not only come
into existence under circumstances unforeseen and
exceptional, but may fairly claim to be at this
moment the model Colony among all our settlements.
The statements of the increase and progress of this
new settlement, as extracted from the speech of Sir
George Bowen to his Parliament, are really surprising,
accustomed as we are to the rapid developments of
new societies. . . . Singular and striking as they are,
they by no means exhaust the catalogue of the ex-
ploits of which Queensland has to boast. Although
possessed of responsible government, the Colony has
presented a remarkable instance of concord and
stability. While an Australian administration conveys to the mind the idea of a perpetual crisis,
Queensland has as yet known no change of Ministry.
The Colony obtained responsible government in the
same year as the Palmerston administration succeeded
to office, and its Ministry has been equally durable.
. . . Another circumstance, which an English tax-
payer will consider perhaps equally gratifying, is that
this fine Colony has been brought into its present
state of order, prosperity, and good government,
without the expenditure of a single shilling by the
mother-country.'

In similar terms the 'Edinburgh Review' concluded a very able statement of the progress of the
Colony up to 1863 : 'On every account, from its vast
extent, from its fertile soil, from its delicious climate,
from its extensive seaboard and abundant water-
courses, from its judicious institutions, and from the
wise and temperate spirit which has hitherto prevailed in its administration, Queensland deserves to
be regarded as one of the most interesting and
promising of those youthful States with which the
maritime and colonial genius of England has studded
the globe. Four years have not yet elapsed since
the province of Moreton Bay assumed the rank of an
independent Colony. The terms of service of its
first Governor, Sir George Bowen, and of its first
Minister, Mr. Herbert, have not yet expired : but
these accomplished and fortunate rulers have already
founded a State which cannot fail to rank amongst
the freest and most prosperous communities on the
face of the earth.'

When, in accordance with the usual rule, Sir
G. Bowen's term of office came to an end at the close
of his sixth year of government, there was a widespread feeling of regret at his expected loss, and anxiety
as to his successor. The following leading article
from one of the Queensland newspapers [1] expresses
no more than the general opinion of the colonists.
It reads like an indiscriminating panegyric; but
Australians are not given to speak so well of their
Governors without sufficient cause.

'Whoever may be appointed to succeed the present

[1] *Queensland Daily Guardian*, October 81, 1865.

Governor of Queensland will find the office no sine-
cure if he attempts to imitate Sir G. F. Bowen.   His
Excellency has managed to steer his way clear through
all the windings of local party politics, strong sectional
jealousies, and personal antipathies—has visited and
placed himself in direct contact with the people of
every important town in the colony—has heard all
sorts of complaints, mixed with all sorts of people,
listened and replied to all kinds of addresses,—yet
through all he has held his own, and is without
question the most popular man between Brisbane and
Cape York.   This would be no easy task to perform
under any circumstances.   In the case of Queensland,
however, the difficulties are more than ordinary.   His
Excellency found the Colony small in numbers, poor
in circumstances, and its inhabitants only unanimous
in their strong desire to have a Government and
a Governor of their own, and to manage their affairs
in their own way, coupled, moreover, with a high
notion of their capabilities as legislators, all the
stronger because unaccompanied by any practical
knowledge of legislative duties.   Out of this rather
unpromising material, " his Excellency, with the
advice of his Executive Council," has manufactured
a very respectable Legislature, has visited and re-
visited the different parts of the Colony, in order to
make himself practically acquainted with the localities
and the wants and wishes of their inhabitants, has
gradually reduced the discordant elements to something like order, and instead of becoming weary of
the work, he rather seems to like it, and becomes
more genial and good-tempered the more he has to
do.   In his late northern tour it is perfectly astonish-

ing how he could find the time to visit all the places he visited, talk to all the persons introduced to him, preside, or be the honoured guest, at so many public dinners, propose or respond to all the toasts, and write replies to all the addresses which were poured in upon him, conciliate everybody and commit himself to nobody—and yet he did it.   The whole secret of his success seems to be that he is every inch an Englishman, possessing a perfect reverence for English institutions, modes of thought, and courses of action—a lover of personal liberty and manly outspokenness, of fair play and straightforward dealing; and he is so well convinced of the existence of the same qualities among the bulk of the people he is placed over that he is quite content to look on, and only give an order now and then, or a word or two of advice when it seems necessary. These are the qualities he always appeals to when addressing the people, and he never appeals in vain.'

CHAPTER XIII.

THE GOVERNOR'S TERM OF OFFICE EXTENDED—FINANCIAL CRISIS
—THE GOVERNOR SUCCESSFULLY RESISTS THE PROPOSED ISSUE
OF INCONVERTIBLE LEGAL TENDER NOTES—APPROVAL OF HER
MAJESTY'S GOVERNMENT—OPINION OF LORD NORTON—PROMO-
TION TO NEW ZEALAND—FAREWELL ADDRESSES FROM THE
QUEENSLAND PARLIAMENT AND OTHER PUBLIC BODIES—
DEMONSTRATIONS OF RESPECT AND ESTEEM ON THE GO-
VERNOR'S DEPARTURE.

As a special mark of the Queen's favour, and in
appreciation of the success with which he had conducted the affairs of the young Colony in the difficult
position of its first Governor, Sir George Bowen's
term of office was prolonged from the customary six
to eight years.   Hardly, however, had this extension
become known when an event occurred which for
the moment threatened to undermine the popularity
which six years of hard work and unfailing good
humour had built up.   So far, there had never been
a clashing of rights and powers between the Governor and his Ministers.   But in 1866 there arose
one of those questions involving the prerogative of the
Crown, which every Governor is bound to take up,
ne quid detrimenti respublica capiat.   The constitutional reasons for his conduct are given in the following despatch ; other grounds for his action are explained in the subsequent letter to Mr. Robert
Lowe, M.P.

To the Right Hon. Edward Cardwell, M.P.

Government House, Brisbane : July 20, 1867.

Sir,

I have the honour to report that the recent monetary crisis and commercial panic in England have been the means of causing a financial and political crisis in Queensland.

The July mail is about to be closed; and I have time at present to submit to you only the outline of what has taken place. The negotiation of a fresh loan of about a million sterling, sanctioned by the Queensland Legislature in last May, was undertaken by the Sydney branch of the Agra and Masterman's Bank, which bound itself to furnish fifty thousand pounds (50,000*l.*) monthly for the prosecution of the railways and other reproductive works in this Colony. The heads of the intelligence which arrived from England by the July mail reached Brisbane by telegraph on the 11th instant; and among them was reported the stoppage of the Agra and Masterman's Bank. The Colonial Treasurer (Mr. Bell), on behalf of my responsible advisers, informed me on the following day that he proposed to issue 'inconvertible Government notes, and to make them a legal tender in this Colony.' After he had fully explained his project, I informed him that I regretted that I could not sanction it, and that, if a Bill authorising such issue were to pass the Colonial Parliament, I should feel obliged, in conformity with my instructions, to reserve it for the signification of Her Majesty's pleasure thereon. Nevertheless, the Colonial Treasurer, though in two separate interviews I pointed out the above facts, insisted on his project, and gave notice of his intention to introduce a Bill to authorise the issue of legal tender notes in the Assembly on the following day, and to move the suspension of the Standing Orders, so that it might pass forthwith.

Under these circumstances, the action taken by the Treasurer appeared to me to make it my imperative duty to address the Vice-President of the Executive Council (i.e. the Premier), to the following effect :—

'I need scarcely say that nothing can be further from my desire or intention than to interfere in the slightest degree with the freedom of debate, or with any of the other undoubted privileges of the Houses of Parliament. But (to omit other considerations), it appears to me that I should be justly liable to the charge of a want of due courtesy towards the two branches of the Colonial Legislature, from whom the Governor, as the Representative of the Crown, has invariably received the most loyal respect and support, if I were to approve the introduction by one of my Ministers, or if I were in any way whatsoever to become a party to the introduction, at the present crisis, of a Bill to which (as the Treasurer was made fully aware on Thursday morning last), I feel precluded by the Queen's Instructions from signifying the Royal Assent.

To engage the attention of the Parliament with a measure which cannot become law would seem to be equivalent to occupying unprofitably valuable time, which could be far better employed, during the existing emergency, in discussing and passing measures which can be brought into immediate operation.

'I earnestly hope that you and your colleagues will see your way to asking forthwith the sanction of the Legislature to the issue of Treasury Bills (like the Exchequer Bills of England), coupled with the imposition of that additional taxation which you have (as I understand) already determined to propose. This is the course which has been usually adopted with success in monetary difficulties, both in the mother-country and in the principal British Colonies. It appears that Queensland is as yet the most lightly taxed community in Australia.

'The measure proposed by the Treasurer, as explained to me by himself, is a Bill to empower the Government to issue inconvertible notes, and to make those notes a legal tender. It is obvious that I am required by the sixth section of my Instructions to reserve for the signification of Her Majesty's pleasure any Bill of the above-mentioned nature. For the fourth clause of that section prescribes the reservation of "any Bill whereby any paper or other currency may be made a legal tender, except the coin of the realm or other gold or silver coin." And the eleventh clause of the same section prescribes the reservation of "any Bill of any extraordinary nature and importance, whereby our prerogative, or the rights and property of our subjects not residing in the Colony, or the trade and shipping of the United Kingdom and its dependencies, may be prejudiced."

'Now, with regard to this latter clause, I must make the following remarks :

'(1) The measure proposed by the Treasurer is of an "extraordinary nature and importance"; for he admits that he knows of no precedent for it in any British community.

'(2) That measure may affect "the Queen's Prerogative"; for it is a well-known maxim that questions of coin and currency belong to the sovereign power in every State. We cannot legislate in our local Parliament on matters of this kind against the general policy established by the Crown and by the Imperial Parliament for the government of the whole British Empire.

'(3) That measure may prejudice the rights and property of British subjects not residing in this Colony, and the trade of the United Kingdom and its dependencies, for (as you truly observed in my presence to the Treasurer on Thursday last), a large proportion of the capital now in Queensland belongs to British subjects resident in the United Kingdom, and in other British Colonies, and their interests (as well as the credit of the Colony), may be gravely compromised by the proposed measure.'

In fact, the Managers of the Banks in Brisbane state that the proposed issue of 'inconvertible legal tender notes' would be equivalent to a forced loan on the British capital in the Colony.[1]

The Premier (Mr. Macalister) urged in reply, that it was necessary to prosecute the public works in Queensland, so as to give employment to the poorer classes, and that the only feasible way of raising money immediately would be to issue the proposed 'legal tender notes.' This conclusion was denied by almost all men in Queensland whose opinions are entitled to much respect on a financial question. A popular cry was, however, got up at Brisbane by the usual means of agitation through the press and otherwise, in favour of the Government proposal, just as violent and illegal methods of raising money for an immediate purpose were recently applauded by a section of the people of Victoria. My Ministers persisted in their project, and pressed me to engage to sanction it on the ground that this was one of the cases of ' urgent necessity' contemplated in the sixth section of my Instructions as dispensing the Governor from reserving Bills.

I reminded, however, my Responsible Advisers, that they had not furnished me with any *data* whatsoever proving the alleged necessity for setting the Queen's Instructions at naught, and that all the information within my reach pointed to less exceptionable schemes as far preferable. I added that there

[1] See 'Evidence given before the Select Committee on Financial Arrangements.' Ordered by the Legislative Assembly to be printed, July 17, 1866 (*Votes and Proceedings for* 1866, p. 949).

could hardly exist an 'urgent necessity' for the adoption of expedients of an extraordinary and questionable nature, until the financial position of the Colony should have been fully examined by the Legislature, and the simple, ordinary, and legitimate measures usually adopted during financial emergencies elsewhere had been tried here and proved to be failures.

I further added that, of course, my objections applied to the Bill proposed by the Treasurer, and as explained to me by himself. It would be my duty to examine it carefully when it should have passed the two Houses of Parliament, and had been presented to me for the Queen's assent; and I would signify that assent forthwith to any measures adopted by the wisdom of Parliament, provided that they be not repugnant to the letter and spirit of the Queen's Instructions. I concluded in the following terms:

'You are well aware, my dear Mr. Macalister, that in matters of purely colonial policy, I have always deferred to the advice of my Constitutional Ministers for the time being, although my own personal opinion has sometimes differed from theirs on practical questions of importance.

'But the present is a case in which Imperial interests are concerned, and I must do my duty to the Crown; which, as I believe, is in this as in most other instances identical with my duty to the Colony, and with the true interests of the people of Queensland.'

These arguments did not, however, seem to prove satisfactory to the Ministers, for soon afterwards they tendered their resignation in a body. At first I declined to accept it, stating that—

'It seems a most unusual course for Ministers to tender their resignation, practically because, in one single case, in which Imperial interests are concerned, the Governor felt it to be his duty (for reasons assigned) to inform his Ministers that he must act in conformity with the Queen's Instructions.

'The Governor fears that the motives of the Ministers will be liable to grave misapprehension if they resign their trust at the present crisis on a wrong issue, and in direct contradiction to the recent and public declaration of Mr. Macalister, viz. that they would retain their offices so long as they should appear to possess the confidence of the Parliament.

'The Governor cannot accept the resignation tendered to him on a ground of such nature.

'The Ministers will, of course, introduce such measures as they think proper; and the Governor will reserve all action until the proposed Bills shall have been passed by Parliament and presented to him for the Royal assent.

'The Governor has much pleasure in reciprocating towards the Ministers their expressions of personal good-will.'

The Ministers, nevertheless, again tendered their resignation on the following day, when I felt constrained, though reluctantly, to accept it.

It has been alleged, both in and out of the Legislature, that their real motive was to escape a parliamentary defeat which they knew to be imminent, and
to resign on a question which at the present moment
is so popular with a portion of the town electors as is
this question of 'legal tender notes,' or ' greenbacks,'
as they are usually called in the American phrase.
However this may be, my late Ministers and I parted
in mutual good humour, and I shall be prepared
to co-operate with them as cordially as before, should
the course of parliamentary proceedings again place
them in office.

I now entrusted Mr. Herbert [1] (who has not yet
left the Colony) with the task of forming a new
Administration. He will have many difficulties to
contend with; but he believes that he will be able
to arrange with the local banks for the advance of
sufficient sums of money for the public works on
the security of our debentures, which can be pledged
for that purpose under the provisions of a recent Act.

It will be seen that the point on which I have
taken my stand is, not the character of the policy of
my Ministers—in which I, of course, leave them quite
untrammelled; but that I must not, to enable them
to carry out a special object, act contrary to the
letter or spirit of my Instructions, which are, indeed, a part of the constitutional law of the Colony.

I trust that the course which I have steadily and

---

[1] Mr. Herbert had shortly before resigned office, urgent private
affairs requiring his presence in England. He was succeeded as
Premier by Mr. Macalister.

firmly pursued throughout these transactions, and in disregard of much pressure of various kinds, will meet with your approval. That course seems to be in accordance with the judgment and feeling of a majority of both Houses of the Colonial Parliament, and of the educated and dispassionate portion of the community, without distinction of political party or of social class.

July 21.

P.S.—Since this despatch was written, Mr. Herbert has formed a Ministry which seems to be supported by a large majority of both Houses of the Colonial Parliament. In the Legislative Council, there is hardly any opposition to it at all; and in the Assembly, it appears that Mr. Herbert has at present about eighteen votes out of thirty-two.. Both Houses passed last night a Bill authorising the issue of three hundred thousand pounds (300,000*l.*) in Treasury Bills (like the Exchequer Bills of England), which sum is estimated as sufficient to carry the Colony through the present financial crisis.

To the Right Honourable R. Lowe, M.P.[1]

Government House, Queensland: August 21, 1866.

My dear Lowe,

Knowing the interest which you take in Australian affairs, I venture to address you on the subject

---

[1] Afterwards Viscount Sherbrooke, G.C.B. He expressed his entire concurrence with Sir G. Bowen's action.

of the recent financial and political crisis in Queensland—now happily over—but which has caused much excitement throughout these Colonies.

The Agra and Masterman's Bank had engaged to negotiate the sale of the Queensland Debentures, and to advance upon them 50,000*l.* monthly for the prosecution of our railways and other reproductive works, which the Legislature had authorised to be constructed by loan. I may say, *en passant*, that I have diligently striven, so far as a Constitutional Governor can interfere in such matters, to check the extravagance arising out of the constant ' log-rolling ' of a Colonial Parliament, and to introduce the practice of local self-government by District or Provincial Councils and Municipalities. I have been able to do much in this direction, but not all that is wanted. The sudden failure of the Agra Bank during the commercial panic in London stopped our supplies, and threatened to stop our public works, and so to reduce to destitution a large number of workmen and their families, many of them skilled artizans, brought out from England with the prospect of constant employment. The obvious remedy for our temporary financial embarrassments was the issue of Treasury Bills bearing interest, like the Exchequer Bills of England. But the late Treasurer, at the instance of some irresponsible advisers, obstinately insisted on an issue of ' inconvertible legal tender notes,' like the *assignats* of the first French Revolution and the *greenbacks* of the recent Civil War in America. A still closer pre-

cedent may be found in the forced paper currency of
some of the original American Colonies, which was
so strongly condemned by Adam Smith ('Wealth of
Nations,' Book II. chapter 2) and prohibited by the
Act 4 George III. cap. 34. In Queensland it was de-
liberately proposed to make the new paper currency
a legal tender, and to force the banks, the public contractors, the members of the Civil Service, and all
public creditors whatsoever, to accept it in payment
of the Government obligations at *par*, though, of
course, it would have become enormously depreciated
in a short time. It was also proposed to accept the
' greenbacks ' at the Treasury in payment of all taxes
except customs. It would be superfluous to point out
the disastrous consequences, familiar to all political
economists, which would have resulted from the adoption of a policy of this nature. It appeared that this
was one of the extreme cases in which the Governor
of a Colony possessing parliamentary government
would be justified in interfering to save the Colony
from itself. On the other hand, it has been argued
that Colonial interests are the concern, not of the
Governor, but of the local Ministry and Parliament.
I felt desirous to avoid even the appearance of iden-
tifying the representative of the Queen with either
political party, or of obstructing in any way the proceedings of either ; and therefore I based my objections to the ' legal tender notes ' (as you will see from
my correspondence with my late Ministers, of which
I enclose a copy) mainly on the fact that I am re-

quired by the Royal Instructions to reserve any Bill of
the nature proposed for the signification of the Queen's
pleasure thereon—in short, I based my objections on
Imperial not Colonial grounds. The populace of Brisbane was told by a few stump orators that an issue of
unlimited 'greenbacks' would create unlimited funds
for their employment on public works, while at the
same time it would ruin the bankers, squatters, merchants, and other capitalists—those objects of the
jealous dislike of a democracy. A so-called 'indignation meeting' was held, at which the Governor and
the majority of the Legislature (which was also hostile
to 'greenbacks') were denounced in violent terms;
several leading members of Parliament were ill-treated
in the streets; and threats were even uttered of burning down Government House, and treating me 'as
Lord Elgin was treated at Montreal in 1849.'

I need scarcely say that I am not to be intimidated
in the discharge of my duty. Besides, all the education, property, and intelligence of the Colony were
on my side. In common with both Houses of the
Colonial Parliament I steadily and calmly held my
course, and in a few days, indeed in a few hours,
public confidence and tranquillity were restored. The
late Ministers made my refusal to sanction the issue
of 'greenbacks' a pretext for resigning in the midst
of the financial crisis, though their real object was
universally believed to have been a desire to make a
little political capital, and to avoid a parliamentary
defeat, which they knew to be certain. Mr. Herbert,

who had been Premier for the first six years of the political career of Queensland, resigned office some months back, as his private affairs required shortly his presence in England. As he had not yet left the Colony, I sent for him ; and he formed a new Ministry, and carried at once an Act authorising the issue of Exchequer Bills, which have found a ready sale in Australia, and will extricate us from our temporary embarrassment, when coupled with retrenchment, economy, and additional taxation.

As Mr. Herbert was obliged to leave for England by the August mail, it became very desirable to form a strong Government, by a fusion of parties, so as to be able to carry the new taxes and other measures urgently required. By inflexibly maintaining, with regard to the party conflicts of the Colony, that neutrality which belongs to the Sovereign whom I represent, I have been enabled on this, as on many other occasions, to intervene as mediator in controversies which would otherwise have become irreconcilable. After some negotiation, a coalition Ministry has been successfully formed, and the crisis is over.

I trust that the stand which I made, in spite of various kinds of pressure, in defence of the prerogatives of the Crown, and of the authority of the Royal Instructions, will be appreciated in England. The overwhelming majority of the education, intelligence, and property of all the Australian Colonies is on my side.

The Earl of Carnarvon, who had succeeded Mr. Cardwell at the Colonial Office, conveyed in the following despatch his entire approval of the conduct pursued by Sir George Bowen during the financial crisis.

Downing Street : September 26, 1866.

Sir,

I have the honour to acknowledge the receipt of your Despatch of the 20th of July, in which you inform me of the resignation of your advisers, and of the return of Mr. Herbert to office.

It seems that your late Ministers proposed to introduce into Parliament a Bill authorising the issue of inconvertible Government notes, and making such notes a legal tender; that you thereupon informed them that you would be precluded by your Instructions from assenting to such a law, except under circumstances of urgency such as had not yet been proved to you to exist; and that, after having in vain tried to alter your resolution, they tendered to you their resignation, which you ultimately found yourself constrained to accept.

Understanding these to be the circumstances of the case, I have no hesitation in approving entirely your refusal to adopt a course at variance with your Instructions; and I do not permit myself to doubt, that in the course you have adopted, you will receive that support which you appear to anticipate from the Colonial Legislature.

To an English Statesman.

Government House, Brisbane : November 20, 1866.

My dear Lord,

I am grateful to Lord Carnarvon for conveying to me so promptly and in such explicit terms his approval of my conduct in refusing to act at variance with the Queen's Instructions in the matter of the proposed issue of ' inconvertible legal tender notes.' I have already shown his despatch to my Ministers, including the Premier, who, like his colleagues, entirely acquiesces in the decision of Her Majesty's Government, and regrets that he ever allowed himself to be persuaded to take up the so-called ' green-backs' or *assignats*. The truth is that the leading politicians in Australia are generally ready to defer to the *ex cathedrâ* judgment of the Home Government on points connected with the legal and constitutional relations between the mother-country and her principal dependencies. And the overwhelming majority of the property, education, and intelligence of each of the Australian Colonies is ready to rally round the Queen's Representative in support of the authority of the law, provided that there be some assurance that the Governor will be upheld by the Home Government. All depends upon this point. A prominent and influential politician here lately remarked to me : ' If the trumpet of Downing Street give an uncertain sound, who shall prepare himself for the battle ? '

The little temporary excitement of two months

ago is now almost forgotten, and men of all parties
and classes generally applaud or acquiesce in the
action which I felt it to be my duty to take. Still,
no one who has not himself tried it, can know how
painful and embarrassing is the position of a Colonial
Governor if he is not sure of the approval and support of his official superior. I would hazard the
remark that the result of the late session proves
beyond doubt that I was not too sanguine when I
confidently anticipated the support of the Colonial
Legislature. Since the adjournment which took place
at the end of last July in consequence of the Ministerial crisis, not a single voice was raised in either
House of Parliament in favour of an issue of 'inconvertible legal tender notes,' or to question my
conduct. On the other hand, it will be seen from
my despatches by this mail that the additional taxation, and the other measures for securing the revenue
and credit of the Colony, which I suggested from
the beginning, were adopted almost without dissent.

Of course, no constitutional ruler can expect to
be able to carry out all his plans for the public good;
but I submit that I am far from being reduced to
that pathetic complaint of the Persian noble in
Herodotus, which Dr. Arnold was so fond of
quoting:—ἐχθίστη δὲ ὀδύνη ἐστὶ τῶν ἐν ἀνθρώποισι
αὕτη, πολλὰ φρονέοντα μηδενὸς κρατέειν.[1]

---

[1] Herodotus, ix. 16. Thus translated in Grote's *History of Greece*
(Vol. V. page 214): 'Truly this is the most hateful of all human sufferings—to be full of knowledge, and, at the same time, to have no power
over results.'

The crisis was soon over; and the good sense of
the majority of the Queenslanders soon recognised
that in exercising an undoubted Imperial right their
Governor had also saved them from a step fraught
with disastrous consequences. Had the legal tender
notes been issued, all debts, even Government loans
from England, loans received in gold, might have
been paid back in depreciated paper; with the inevitable result of the destruction of the credit of
the Colony and the impossibility of raising in future
the money necessary for the construction of the
railways, harbours, and other public works. That
Sir George Bowen firmly resisted this measure, at
the risk of his popularity, was one of the greatest
boons that he conferred upon the Colony; and it
is not too much to say that his example saved not
only Queensland but the other Australian Colonies
from jeopardising their credit by the issue of inconvertible paper money. What one Governor had successfully accomplished, another could do; and so
Australia heard no more of the legal tender note.
Sir George was able to assure Lord Carnarvon a year
later that 'almost everybody here now agrees with
my policy respecting the proposed issue last year of
" greenbacks," and that the support which your Lordship accorded to me in that affair has put a stop to all
schemes of meddling with the currency, both in this
and in the other Australian Colonies.'

We may here quote an extract from the book on
' Colonial Policy' published in 1869 by Mr. Adderley,
Parliamentary Under-Secretary for the Colonies (now
Lord Norton):

'Sir George Bowen, the first Governor of Queensland, is a man of such high public spirit, energy, and intelligence that he has kept the Colony always in active interest about its public questions, and this country in full information of its proceedings. . . . A ministerial crisis occurred in 1866 on the question of issuing inconvertible paper currency as legal tender, in a scheme for raising a million sterling to meet monetary difficulties; which proposition Sir G. Bowen firmly resisted as contrary to the Queen's Instructions, and indeed to the spirit of Imperial legislation, which from the first adopted Adam Smith's arguments against paper money being permitted as legal tender. . . . He soon outlived the popular resentment against this necessary and legitimate exercise of the prerogative. The chief danger of the democratic spirit of colonial constitutional freedom, is not that it chafes too violently against the barriers placed against it, so much as that it is always making sacrifices to local popularity in dispensing public resources.'

Towards the close of 1867, Sir George Bowen was promoted to the unusually difficult Government of New Zealand, as a mark of the Queen's appreciation of his eight years' service in Queensland. When his farewell Message was read to both Houses of Parliament, telling them of his 'deep sense of their constant, loyal, and cordial co-operation with him, as the representative of the Queen,' and declaring that he for his part had ' earnestly laboured, throughout the eight years of his administration, to perform his duty to the best of his judgment and ability,' and that in the future he would always 'regard with proud and grateful interest the progress of the Colony where he and his family had received so much sympathy and respect'; the two Chambers cordially joined in a reply reciprocating to the full the Governor's good wishes and expressions of esteem, and adding: 'Throughout the lengthened period of your Excellency's administration, you have exercised your judgment and ability to the utmost in furthering the interests of Queensland; and as we believe that the Colony has thereby been much benefited, we take this opportunity of tendering your Excellency our thanks. While your Excellency will continue to watch our future progress " with proud and grateful interest," it will be no less our privilege to watch, with equal regard, the future career in your Excellency's new sphere of action, of a public officer so long and so intimately associated with us.'

Other addresses were of a more personal nature, and spoke of the Governor's departure less as the change of a ruler than as the loss of a friend.

Early in January 1868, Sir George and Lady Bowen, with their children, three of whom had been born at Brisbane, embarked for New Zealand, amid a hearty public demonstration of respect and esteem. His name must remain for ever inseparably connected with the history of the great Colony of which he was the first Governor.

PART III.

NEW ZEALAND

1868-1873

CHAPTER XIV.

THE history of New Zealand has been often written.
First discovered and named in the seventeenth century
by the great Dutch navigator Tasman, its coast was
carefully examined towards the close of the eighteenth
century by the great English navigator Cook.   In the
early part of the nineteenth century, a few traders and
missionaries established themselves at various points,
but no attempt was made at systematic colonisation
until 1840, when an assembly of Maori chiefs ceded
to the British Crown the sovereignty of their country
by the Treaty of Waitangi.   There soon arose between
some of the native tribes and the colonists quarrels,
generally to be traced, directly or indirectly, to disputes
about land, which led to the two Maori wars—the first,
which lasted from 1845 to 1848, and the second, which
lasted, with little intermission, from 1860 to 1870.[1]

Of all British Colonies, New Zealand was assuredly
the most difficult to govern when Sir George Bowen
was appointed in 1868.   The second Maori war,

---

[1] It may here be observed, once for all, that the narrow limits of
these volumes will allow of the insertion of but a small part of the
despatches of Sir G. Bowen and of the other Governors of New Zealand.   The rest will be found in the great mass of papers respecting
that Colony which have been presented to the Imperial Parliament.

which had already lasted for eight years, was only slumbering, and the Maoris had not been really beaten. Nevertheless, the Home Government had withdrawn almost all the regular troops, and had resolved to remove the last British soldier, and to leave the colonists to carry out their own views, and to fight their own battles. Under such circumstances the obvious policy was one of conciliation; it was 'alike more politic and more humane,' as Sir George Bowen frequently urged, to outlive than to fight the Maori race, which was gradually dying out, while the colonists were fast increasing. 'Our race is gone like the Moa,' the Maoris pathetically exclaimed, referring to the gigantic ostrich of New Zealand, which is now extinct. The new Governor exerted himself earnestly to procure the adoption by his Ministers and Parliament of the friendly and bene-ficent measures, the chief elements of which are explained in the despatches and addresses printed below.

To the Duke of Buckingham and Chandos,
Secretary of State for the Colonies.

Government House, Wellington, New Zealand:
February 6, 1868.

My dear Duke of Buckingham,

I found your letter here on my arrival yesterday (February 5). My reception at Wellington by all classes of the community was very hearty. My predecessor, Sir George Grey (who remains at his beautiful island of Kawau,[1] near Auckland), has, moreover, written

[1] A good description of Kawau will be found in Mr. Froude's *Oceana* (chap. 18). Among its many attractions, not the least is the

to me in very friendly terms, and I need scarcely say that I have cordially reciprocated his courtesy.

My position here is necessarily one of extreme difficulty and delicacy; but the full explanation of your Grace's views in your letter will be of great assistance and support to me. Perhaps I may be pardoned if I say that I am one of those who believe it to be the clear duty of a Governor, whatever his personal opinions or feelings may be, to carry out loyally the instructions of the Secretary of State. But I am thoroughly convinced that the policy of 'mutual forbearance' which you intend to enforce both by precept and example, is the only policy which can terminate the present difficulties, or even, perhaps, permanently maintain the existing connexion between the mother-country and New Zealand. It is certain, at all events, that in your own words, ' continuing discussion would only keep alive the differences which have arisen between the Imperial and Colonial authorities, and which experience shows to be of a nature that correspondence is more likely to

collection of animals which Sir G. Grey has brought thither from the different Colonies which he has governed. There are zebras, antelopes, and ostriches from the Cape; kangaroos, wallabies, and emus from Australia, and so forth. We may here repeat the story, well known in New Zealand, of a conversation between an English statesman (A) and a distinguished colonist (B). A. said, 'What a pity it is that Sir G. Grey keeps wallabies in his island!' B. 'Why should he not? it is a very innocent amusement.' A. 'Sir, I am sorry to perceive that your Colonial morality is lax. I am informed that there is a whole seraglio of wallabies.' B. 'You do not seem to be aware that a wallaby is a small kind of kangaroo.' A. 'Oh! you have taken a weight off my mind. I thought that, as a mulatto is a half-caste between a white and a Negro, so a wallaby is a half-caste between a white and a Maori!'

T 2

intensify than to remove, especially when carried on at a distance of half round the world.'

I dare not conceal from you, moreover, that the leading men here object to the tone far more than to the substance of many of the despatches from home, during the last four or five years. All who have lived much in our dependencies know that English colonists in general, even more than other men, are governed by the heart rather than by the head. It is quite possible to lead them, but it is equally foolish and dangerous to attempt to drive them, or even to treat them with what seems to their sensitive *amour propre* a want of due consideration. I have already had several long conversations with my Ministers, and I am bound to say that nothing can be better than their demeanour towards me personally; and that they seem inclined to meet in a proper spirit my endeavours to throw oil on the troubled waters, by assuring them that there can be no intention on the part of the Imperial authorities to treat New Zealand with neglect; and that your desire is to disconnect yourself with all that is unpleasant in the past, and, looking forward, to lead the Home and Colonial Governments into a line of friendly co-operation.

To the same.

Government House, Wellington: March 5, 1868.

My Lord Duke,

Among the manifold and urgent questions which have necessarily pressed themselves on my attention during the month which has now elapsed since my assumption, on the 5th ult., of the Government of New Zealand, I have given much thought and care to that very complicated and difficult but highly interesting subject, the present condition and future prospects of the Maori race.

By my desire the Minister for the Native Department (Mr. J. C. Richmond) has addressed to the principal officers and agents of the Government throughout the Colony a circular directing each of them to furnish, for the information of the Governor. a detailed report on native affairs in his district. This report is to contain as full a history as possible of the last few years, and of the events that have come under the personal cognisance of each Government agent. Reliable information is called for as to the actual number of the Maoris; the causes and influences affecting their increase or decrease; their feelings towards Europeans generally; their physical and moral condition; the rise, objects, progress, and tendency of the 'Hau-hau'[1] movement; the opinions of the Maoris in respect of the recent war; of the removal of the Imperial troops; of the suppression of the late outbreaks of rebellion on the East Coast of the North Island, and elsewhere; and of the prospect of the permanent restoration of peace. Finally, the several agents of Government are re-

---

[1] This was the name of the wild and fanatical rites adopted by those Maoris who had fallen away from Christianity. It was the religious phase of the political and racial movement against the Colonial Government.

quired to notice the working of the recent Acts of the New Zealand Legislature, in reference to the lands, the education, and the parliamentary representation of the Maoris; and, generally, to supply such further information as may appear likely to be useful in forming an accurate opinion on the present state of native affairs.

Te Puni, the well-known chief of the Ngatiawa tribe (now in extreme old age, but to whose protection the early settlers in this part of New Zealand were formerly much indebted), and the other principal Maoris resident near Wellington, attended my first *levée*. I have also received, as the representative of the Queen, numerous addresses of respect and welcome from the loyal chiefs and tribes in all parts of both islands; from the powerful clan of the Ngapuhis, at the Bay of Islands, in the extreme north; from the small remnant of Maoris in Otago, in the extreme south; from various chiefs of Taranaki and Wanganui, and of the shores of the central lake of Taupo.

It would, of course, be as yet presumptuous in me to pronounce any judgment on native questions. It is obvious, however, that the old institutions and rites of the Maoris have crumbled away; and so, it is to be feared, has, to a deplorable extent, their recently adopted Christianity. When I visited Te Puni a fortnight ago at his own village, the old chief told me, in the presence of the Bishop of Wellington (Dr. Abraham), that he believed that he was now almost the only real Christian in his tribe, for most of his kinsmen had become either 'Hau-haus' or drunken profligates. It is, moreover, a significant fact that the so-called Maori King has lately re-nounced his baptismal name of Matutaera (Methu-selah), and openly adopted the heathen appellation of Tawhiao. He is stated to have taken no notice whatsoever of certain overtures that were made to him before my arrival, with the object of inducing him to give his submission to the 'Queen's Son' (the phrase by which the Duke of Edinburgh is known to the Maoris), during the approaching visit of His Royal Highness to New Zealand. With regard to this sullen and hostile isolation, a loyal chief, at a recent interview, addressed me in the following terms : 'O Governor! Tawhiao is now like a single tree left exposed in a clearing of our native forests. If you attack it with fire and steel, it will fall on you and crush you; but if left alone, it will ere long wither and die. My word to you, O Governor! is to leave Tawhiao alone.' This is, in fact, the policy of my present Government.

One or two examples of the many Maori addresses of welcome to the new Governor may here be given. They are translated literally.

The first is an address from the powerful chief of Taupo in the interior of the North Island: .

To Sir George Bowen, Governor of New Zealand.

'Tapuaeharuru, Taupo : December 18, 1867.

' Friend,

'Salutations. I have heard that you are coming to this island, to New Zealand, to be a parent to us, and to take care of us, that is, of the whole of this island.

' O father! salutations. Come on shore, come to your land, New Zealand, and to your people; come to see the evil and the good of this island.

' O friend ! salutations. My desire is this, that you should travel through your island, and also through our settlements.

'Enough. From your friend,

'TE POIHIPI TUKAIRANGI.'

Address from the chiefs of Otaki, in the South :

' Otaki: February 20, 1868.

' O father, Governor Bowen ! salutations. Here are we writing this our letter of love to you ; for you are to be the Governor for us all, for the Maoris, and for the Pakehas. That is why our hearts are glad at your coming to New Zealand.

' Welcome hither, O father ! to us your children ; although we be foolish children, do you teach us. We have received instruction at the hands of the other Governors, your predecessors; but we, this people, the Maoris, still abide in our ignorance. You are the sixth Governor.

' Welcome hither to us ; be kind to us with the great kindness of our gracious mother the Queen.

' O father ! we enclose herewith a copy of our letter to the Government for you to see; it depends on yourself whether you bring the son of the Queen here to see us.

'That is all we have to say.

'Your friends,

'TAMIHANA TE RAUPARAHA,[1] and others.'

To an Official Friend.

Wellington, New Zealand: March 8, 1868.

You speak in your last letter of the difficulties with which I shall have to contend in New Zealand. They are indeed great and manifold. As to the Maori question, you might say to me in the words of Horace:[2]

> Motum ex Metello [3] consule civicum,
> Bellique causas, et vitia, et modos,
> Ludumque Fortunæ, gravesque
> Principum[4] amicitias, et arma

[1] Tamihana te Rauparaha is the son of the famous chief of that name, who was long opposed to the English at the first settlement of New Zealand. Three generations of this family illustrate the progress of the Maoris. The grandfather of Tamihana had killed and eaten men, and was himself killed and eaten, 'like a fine old Maori gentleman, one of the olden time.' The father of Tamihana had killed and eaten men, but died in his bed, a convert to Christianity. Tamihana himself, while fighting for the Crown, has killed men, but has not eaten them, and is a zealous Christian and loyal friend of the English. He is the last of his race—of a long line of chieftains and warriors; and when the Duke of Edinburgh came to Wellington, he presented to 'the son of the Queen of England and of New Zealand,' with not ungraceful emotion, the *mere* of his ancestors, which they had borne for many centuries, and in many battles, but which there was no one to inherit. The *mere*, or jade sceptre, of a Maori chief is analogous to the hereditary σκῆπτρον of an Homeric king.

[2] *Carm.* II. 1.   [3] Governor Gore Browne.

[4] Sir G. Grey and General Cameron, who were at strong variance with each other.

Nondum expiatis [1] uncta cruoribus,
Periculosæ plenum opus aleæ,
Tractas, et incedis per ignes
Suppositos cineri doloso.

The fact is that the Maoris have not really been conquered, and *they know it.* The smouldering flame of discontent may at any moment burst into a conflagration. Again, the commercial depression and general poverty of the present period are very distressing. They have prevailed in Australia also ever since the monetary crisis of 1866, but they are aggravated here by the sudden cessation of the military expenditure; by the crushing weight of taxation to pay the interest of the war debt, and of the extravagances of former Governments; by the cruel disasters caused by the recent hurricanes and floods, and by several other causes. In fact, the financial state of the Colony gives me more anxiety than even the native question—which, indeed, is closely connected with it.

Among our other embarrassments, the Fenians have 'cropped up' among the Irish on our southern goldfields, and have started, I believe for the first time in this quarter of the globe, a rabid Fenian newspaper at Hokitika. The principal Government officers write in terms of great alarm about the impending outbreaks there. My Ministers will doubtless support me in acting with firmness in the event of any open breaches of the law; but there

[1] No full *utu* (as the Maoris say), or expiation, had yet been made for the blood shed in the war.

is no general police force in New Zealand, as in each
of the Australian Colonies. The 'Centralists,' as the
party akin to the 'Federalists' in America are called
here, scarcely disguise their hopes that the downfall
of the provincial system will be accelerated by riots
on the goldfields, which there is now no efficient
force to repress; just as some of the colonists hardly
conceal their wish that the remnant of the Maori race
should be allowed to accelerate their own extinction
by the Government permitting, if not encouraging,
the internecine strife to which they are prone, when
not banded against the English settlers.

There are, among our New Zealand politicians,
many men of ability and accomplishments, over whom
any English Statesman might be proud to preside;
and our social relations are very pleasant. I hope to
do much good by bringing the leading families of all
parties together on the neutral ground of the Government House.

To the Duke of Buckingham and Chandos.

Government House, Wellington: March 17, 1868.

My Lord Duke,

In continuation of my previous despatches respecting the present condition of the Maoris, I have
the honour to transmit herewith a map showing
the distribution of the several native tribes in New
Zealand. With few exceptions they are all resident in the Northern Island. I annex a nominal list
of these clans, and of the principal chiefs; together

with a statement of the estimated number of each tribe at the present time, and of its attitude, whether loyal or hostile to the Government, with other explanatory remarks. These documents have been carefully prepared at my request, in the department of the Native Minister, by officers of great experience in Maori affairs. On my arrival here, I found that no full or accurate documents of this kind were on record; and yet it is obvious that without such aid no accurate knowledge can be acquired, and no adequate opinion can be formed on the state of New Zealand, especially in England, at the distance of half the circumference of the globe.

It will be seen that the lands confiscated some years ago for rebellion are estimated in the aggregate at nearly three millions five hundred thousand acres; but that a large portion of this territory has been already restored to the former owners on their submission; while another large portion has been appropriated as compensation for the services of friendly natives. The titles to certain lands on the East Coast of the Northern Island have been long in dispute, and are now under investigation before the proper legal tribunal, in pursuance of Acts passed by the New Zealand Parliament in 1866 and 1867.[1] I am informed that it is probable that in a majority of cases the present holders will be confirmed in possession of the lands which they now occupy.

---

[1] *East Coast Land Titles Investigation Act*, No. 27 of 1866; partially amended in 1867.

The total Maori population is estimated now, in 1868, at about forty-five thousand ; of which number all, except from fifteen hundred to two thousand, reside in the Northern Island. Ten years ago, in 1858, a Government census returned the total Maori population at fifty-six thousand; twenty years ago, in 1848, the Maoris were estimated at about one hundred thousand.

The causes which have contributed to produce this rapid and deplorable decay have been discussed at length by several writers of ability and local experience. I would refer more particularly to the works of Mr. Fox,[1] formerly Prime Minister of this Colony; and of Dr. A. S. Thomson,[2] who was resi-dent in New Zealand for many years as surgeon to the 58th Regiment. Mr. Fox shows that the gradual disappearance of the Maoris is not to be attributed in any large degree to their intercourse with Euro-peans, for 'that, for the most part, has led to the adoption of better food, better dwellings, better general habits of life. The one great cause has been, and is, their utter disregard of all those social and sanitary conditions which are essential to the continuing vitality of the human race ; this cause was in existence long before there was an European in the islands ; and there is little doubt that the race was on the decrease when Cook first landed there.' Dr. Thomson observes : ' The extinction of aboriginal

---

[1] *War in New Zealand*, pp. 255–61, by Mr., now Sir W. Fox, K.C.M.G.
[2] *New Zealand, Past and Present*, Part III., chap. 1.

races has been often caused by evil treatment; the
hands of the early settlers in America, the West
Indies, Tasmania, Australia, and Africa, are not clean
from this imputation; but as far as the story of New
Zealand has yet been unrolled, the pioneers of civi-
lisation, and the majority of the English, Irish, and
Scotch settlers in the islands, have, with some few
exceptions, acted towards the natives in a spirit of
Christianity unknown to the Saxon colonists in
Ireland, the Norman invaders of England, and the
Spanish conquerors of America.'

It is to be hoped that the general restoration of
peace and the prohibition of inter-tribal wars; the
gradual individualisation of property in land now
held in common; the progress of trade and friendly
intercourse between the European settlers and the
Maoris; the increasing use of animal food and
wheaten flour; the schools, hospitals, roads, and other
institutions, by means of which the Colonial Government is endeavouring to promote the civilisation of
the natives;—will all contribute to arrest the further
decay of the yet surviving remnant of a most
interesting race.

Sir George Bowen visited Auckland,[1] the former
capital and most populous city of New Zealand, in
March 1868, and was welcomed with a 'magnificent
reception,' not only by thousands of his fellow

---

[1] The seat of Government was removed in 1864 from Auckland to
Wellington on account of the more central position of the latter city.

countrymen, but also by the principal Maori chiefs of the northern districts, 'headed by Eruera Patuone, who, with his brother Tamati Waka Nene, has ever been the firm friend of the English in peace, and their brave ally in war. While I was rowed ashore,' added the Governor, ' these chiefs, and the numerous assemblage of Maoris of both sexes that surrounded them on the pier, presented a sight in the highest degree picturesque and affecting; as they chanted their national songs of welcome, at the same time waving their mantles in the air, after the traditional custom of their race.'

During a visit to the goldfields of the province of Auckland, Sir George had the opportunity of meeting a large and representative gathering of Maoris, as he relates in the following extracts from a despatch:

To the Duke of Buckingham and Chandos.

Government House, Auckland: April 14, 1868.

There is one particular and suggestive fact connected with the town of Shortland at the goldfields, viz. that it is rising on ground belonging to the influential Maori chief Taipari. He declines to sell his land; preferring, with a view to its rapid increase in value, to let it in lots on building leases. But he has made liberal gifts of sites for churches for the Anglicans, the Roman Catholics, the Presbyterians, and the other principal Christian communions; as also for a public hospital, a cemetery, a park, and other public purposes. He employs Englishmen to survey and lay out roads and streets, and to construct drains, culverts,

and the like.   In short, he appears to me, on the one
hand, as capable of maintaining his just rights,
and, on the other, as desirous to improve his property,
as any English landlord.   Taipari's income, from rents
and mining licences, is already at the rate of nearly
4,000l. sterling yearly.   He has caused a commodious house, in the English style, to be built for himself on a slope commanding a beautiful prospect over
the sea, and the rising town.   Taipari's example, and
the knowledge of the wealth which he is acquiring by
allowing the colonists to occupy his land on equitable terms, are beginning to exercise a beneficial influence over many of his Maori countrymen, who
have hitherto lived in hostile isolation.

   I had at first intended to limit my tour on this
occasion to the goldfields ; but while I was at Shortland I learned that a large meeting of Maoris, composed partly of loyal tribes and partly of Hau-hau
fanatics, adherents of the so-called Maori King, had
assembled at Ohinemuri, about thirty miles up the
River Thames ; with the object, principally, of con-
sulting whether the miners should be permitted to
search for gold in that quarter.   I was advised by the
Government officers, and others best qualified to
judge on a subject of this nature, that much public
benefit might result from my proceeding, without
notice, to the place of meeting ; not to treat expressly
of public affairs, but, as it were, to receive, on behalf
of the Queen, the homage of the assembled Natives ;
many of whom had been recently in arms against the

Crown. Accordingly, I went up the River Thames in a small Government steamer, and anchored off the Maori encampment, which presented a very picturesque sight, with the flags of the several tribes flying over their tents. After a slight hesitation, all these flags were lowered before the Governor's flag; and I was invited by a deputation of chiefs to come ashore. I landed amid general shouts and songs of welcome from the Hau-haus as well as from the friendly Natives; and was conducted to a seat placed for me in the centre of the camp. On my right and left were ranged about four hundred of the loyal Ngatimaru and other tribes; while immediately in front was a nearly equal number of Maoris who were engaged against the Government in the war. The customary war dance, equivalent to a military guard of honour elsewhere, was led by Taraia, the famous chief of the Ngatitameras, who presided over the last great cannibal feast held (in 1843) in New Zealand, and who is one of the few survivors of times and manners which have now well-nigh passed away. Taraia afterwards excused himself to me for his rather feeble dancing, which he ascribed to his four-score years, and not to any want of loyalty on his part. On the conclusion of the war dance, I was addressed in the usual fashion by the leading Maoris present in a series of speeches.[1]   The Hau-hau chiefs

---

[1] It should be explained that at the *Koreros*, or conferences with the Maoris, the Governor and the native chiefs respectively speak each in his own language; and that the speeches are translated, sentence by sen-

avoided committing themselves expressly to any particular course of policy; but since my return to Auckland I have been assured that my visit and the speech which I addressed to the meeting have produced a favourable impression, and have paved the way to several arrangements and concessions calculated to preserve the peace of the district and to extend the authority of the law. In particular, it is stated that the minds of my audience were disabused of a prevalent notion that the arrival of the new Governor would lead to alterations in the law, and to a reversal of the policy pursued of late years by Her Majesty's Government. In my reply to their speeches, I reminded them, in their own figurative language (which is as necessary to produce a good impression on the Maoris of the present day as on the Scotch Highlanders of 150 years ago), that ' Governors and Maori chiefs, like other men, are mortal, and pass away, like the changes of the seasons; whereas the law remains the same for ever, even as the sun shines in heaven both in summer and in winter. I have come here to uphold the law. If any man be aggrieved, let him state his grievance in a lawful manner, and justice will be done him whether he be Pakeha or Maori.' And again : ' The Queen is always glad to hear that her Maori children are living in peace and harmony with her European children. It is, and always has been, the desire of the Queen

tence, by a Government interpreter. This system enables the Governor to watch the effect of his words, and to modify them accordingly.

that there should be one law for both Pakeha and Maori. The word of the Queen is that the Pakeha and Maori should be united as one people.' ·

We here quote an extract from a subsequent despatch respecting the Auckland goldfields :

'Most of the gold hitherto exported from New Zealand is the produce of the goldfields of the South Island during the last ten years ; but the earliest discovery took place so far back as in 1852, about twenty miles north of the mouth of the River Thames. Much excitement at that time arose among both the Colonists and the Natives, and fears of a dangerous collision between the two races were entertained. However, Te Taniwha, the principal chief of the district, convened a meeting of his countrymen to decide the terms on which the Europeans should be allowed to dig for the precious metals on Maori land. Lieutenant-Governor Wynyard, Chief Justice Martin, Bishop Selwyn, and other prominent English functionaries and settlers were invited to be present ; and, through the influence of Te Taniwha, an equitable arrangement was promptly made, the requisite permission being granted by the Maoris on payment of a moderate licence fee by each miner. Mr. Swainson, formerly Attorney-General of New Zealand, has put on record in his " New Zealand and its Colonisation," a graphic description of the remarkable scene presented by the above-mentioned meeting. He writes : " The presence of the aged

chief Te Taniwha,[1] his remarkable appearance, and
the occasion itself, gave to the assemblage an
unusual interest. Though bowed down and enfeebled
by age, the old man still retained the use of his
faculties, and in a remarkable degree possessed that
bold outline of head and face which formerly distinguished the chieftains of the country. There
stood the last living link between the past and
present of New Zealand; one who in time long past
had himself stood face to face with England's great
navigator, and who still lived to tell of Captain
Cook's first visit to New Zealand; how the natives
all thought that his ship was a whale with wings, and
that his crew were gods; how for some time he, Te
Taniwha himself, then but a little boy, was afraid to
go on board; how Captain Cook spoke little—less
than the other officers—but took more notice of the
children, patting them kindly on the head.[2] And
now this venerable chief, as the crowning act of a
long and eventful life, and confiding in the justice of
the British Crown, came forward to welcome the
Queen's vicegerent to the new-found fields of gold.
When the first specimens were shown him of the gold
discovered on his land he said he should now be
content to die; that he had lived many days, but
that this was the brightest of them all. He did not

[1] Te Taniwha died in 1853.

[2] On another occasion, Te Taniwha further related that Captain
Cook, on landing, almost invariably walked rapidly about, waving his
right hand to and fro, doubtless scattering the seeds of Europe in the
soil of New Zealand. (See Thomson's *New Zealand*, chap. 9.)

seem to value the consideration of the gain the discovery would bring him, so much as the thought that *his* land, the land of his ancestors, should be the first to produce the precious metal for which the white man so eagerly sought. Glancing at the time-honoured peak above him, and turning to the setting sun, he appeared to commune with the generation that he had outlived." '

The expected visit of the Duke of Edinburgh was unavoidably postponed by the attempt to murder him at Sydney by a Fenian assassin (named O'Farrell), who was tried before the Supreme Court, convicted, and hanged, though the Duke himself interceded for his life. Moreover, the New South Wales Parliament passed a very stringent Act which at once put an end to the Fenian movement in that Colony.

To the Earl of Belmore, K.C.M.G., Governor of
New South Wales.

Government House, Auckland, New Zealand: April 4, 1868.

My dear Lord Belmore,

I am much obliged by your kind letter of March 20, which brought me the first reliable intelligence we got here respecting the state of the Duke of Edinburgh. As in Australia so in New Zealand, the news of the murderous attempt on the life of His Royal Highness has excited general horror and indignation, and has called forth enthusiastic expressions, at public meetings and otherwise, of the loyalty and patriotism of the overwhelming majority of the community. Public opinion will support me in the most energetic measures to stamp out Fenianism at Hokitika, on the goldfields of the South Island—where a procession was held (before the arrival of the news from Sydney) in honour of the Manchester Fenians. I have sent thither H.M. ship 'Falcon' with a detachment of the 18th Regt. on board, to support the civil power in case of necessity. The ringleaders of the Fenians, and the editor of their organ, the 'New Zealand Celt,' have been arrested on a charge of sedition, and if the existing laws do not prove sufficient for the emergency, I have no doubt that the New Zealand Parliament will grant further powers.

Writing on the same subject to the Duke of Buckingham, Sir George said :

'There is a strong Fenian agitation among the Irish on our southern goldfields, and I have received notices that there is a secret society determined to assassinate the Governor, as such, and not from any personal ill-feeling! I am warned to adopt precautions for my safety. Lord Belmore writes to me that his life also has been threatened. Neither of us attaches much importance to these warnings or threats, though others do so. At all events, it would be worse than useless to adopt any precautions, for no man can protect himself against assassins, who, like O'Farrell, the Fenian who wounded the Duke of

Edinburgh at Sydney, are ready to sacrifice their own lives. I shall make no change in my manner of life, nor say anything publicly on the subject of the threatening letters.'

The Fenian ringleaders in New Zealand were tried, found guilty, and punished by fine and imprisonment; and the energetic measures adopted on this occasion stamped out the movement. It should be mentioned, as a characteristic trait of the loyal Maoris, that several of their chiefs expressed to the Governor their indignation at the attempt on the life of the 'Queen's Son,' and offered, when the Duke of Edinburgh should visit New Zealand, to seize the few Fenians in that Colony and carry them off to the mountains.

CHAPTER XV.

A VOYAGE in H.M.S. 'Brisk' to the Bay of Islands,
in the northern districts, proved singularly interesting. 'All the Maoris of the north,' reported the
Governor (May 4, 1868), 'that could be assembled
at short notice, met me, to the number of about
three hundred, at Waitangi,[1] on the spot where the
meeting of February 5, 1840—so momentous in its
results—was held.

'It will be remembered that the chiefs who first
addressed the meeting at Waitangi, in 1840, strongly
dissuaded their countrymen from the cession of their
national independence ; and that the majority yielded
at length to the authority and eloquence of Tamati

---

[1] 'Waitangi' means 'Weeping Water,' and is the picturesque
native name of the beautiful cascade near the spot where the cession
of New Zealand to the British Crown was agreed to in 1840. It has
since been remarked by a Maori chief that this name was prophetic of
the blood and tears which were shed in the two wars between the
Colonists and the Natives.

Waka Nene, who urged that the sovereignty of the
Queen would bring with it the blessings of Christianity
and of civilisation. It has been often stated, and
it is generally believed here, that without the
support of this celebrated chief, the British Government could not have been established in New Zealand in 1840, nor maintained during the war of 1845–
48. It was with deep interest that I and the other
Englishmen present at the recent meeting saw this
loyal subject of our Queen, this constant friend and
brave ally of our race—now in extreme old age—
arise, and striking his staff on the ground, proceed to
remind his Maori countrymen that, standing on that
very spot, he had counselled the fathers of the present
generation to place themselves under the shadow of
the Queen and the law; that he knew he had
counselled them well; and now exhorted the sons of
his former hearers to dwell in peace and brotherhood
with each other and with the Colonists.'

Writing three years later of the death of this chief,
Sir George Bowen made some well-deserved comments
on his services.

To the Secretary of State.

Government House, Wellington, New Zealand:
August 23, 1871.

My Lord,

It will be observed that, in the speech with which
I opened the present session of the Colonial Parliament, there occurs the following paragraph :—' You

will concur with me in regretting the death of the celebrated chief, Tamati Waka Nene, alike distinguished for his loyalty to the Queen and for his friendship with the English, and who, whether in peace or war, did more than any other chief in New Zealand to establish the Queen's sovereignty and to promote colonisation.' In their addresses in reply to my speech, both Houses reciprocated the feeling thus expressed, and the same sentiment is universal throughout this Colony.

Tamati Waka Nene, the principal chief and most famous warrior of the great clan of the Ngapuhis, long the most powerful in New Zealand, died at the Bay of Islands on the 4th instant, lamented alike by the English and by the Maoris. His age must have been above eighty years, for he was an elderly man when he procured the cession of the sovereignty of these islands to the British Crown, by the Treaty of Waitangi, in 1840, and when he fought so gallantly for the Queen in the Maori War of 1845–48. His last illness was short and not severe. A few weeks previously he had paid me a visit at Auckland, and he was then still erect in stature and unclouded in mind. His dying words were earnest exhortations to his countrymen to live in peace and union with the English; and his last wish was that he should be buried, not, like the old heroes of his race in heathen times, in a remote cavern of the mountains, but in the English churchyard at the town of Russell. This last wish was assented to by his family and his clan, and the funeral took place on the 11th instant, according to the rites of the Church of England, to which Nene had been, for more than thirty years, a sincere and faithful convert. His coffin was borne to the grave by twelve of the leading Colonists of the north, who have owed so much to his good offices, while his chief surviving clansmen and the Government officers of the district were pall-bearers. Had it been possible for me to leave Wellington during the session of the Colonial Parliament, I should have gone myself to the Bay of Islands to pay the last mark of respect to him.

In my despatch of May 26, 1870, written after my second visit to the northern clans, I gave some description of the Ngapuhis and of their country, and mentioned that Tamati Waka Nene always spoke 'with grateful emotion of the silver goblet presented to him several years ago by the Queen, in recognition of his services to the British Crown. As he has outlived his own children, he has bequeathed it as an heirloom to the family of the late Mr. Russell, a respectable settler at Hokianga, who married his niece, and there it will be carefully preserved. The best writer who has hitherto compiled the annals of New Zealand remarks that as many noble Spanish houses in Peru and Mexico boast of their descent from the Incas and from Montezuma; and as many leading families in Virginia are proud of the connexion of their ancestors with Pocahontas and the Red Indians of a former age; so the time may yet come when the descendants of some of the first English settlers in this country will be proud of having in their veins the blood of Tamati Waka Nene, and of other Maori chieftains and warriors who were the loyal friends and brave allies of their forefathers.'

In May 1868, the Governor made an official tour in the Waikato district, in the centre of the North Island. He was accompanied by Mr. Richmond, the Minister for Native affairs. 'The Maoris of the Waikato Confederation,' writes Sir J. E. Gorst,[1] 'have been of late years regarded as the most important in New Zealand. Their pre-eminence over other tribes is due, not to any intrinsic merit of their own, but solely to their geographical position. Their greatness has grown up with the settlement of Auckland, the richest in the North Island, which lies at their feet, and has been for many years at their mercy. The land on which they live is fertile, and difficult to be invaded; while at their backs they have a rugged, inaccessible country—a retreat where they can set our civilised armies at defiance. When New Zealand was first colonised, no one supposed that in the end we should have to fight the Maoris for the possession of the soil. The early settlers confidently pushed their way into the heart of native districts; homesteads of a few hundred acres, isolated in the midst of Maori villages, were bought without apprehension by European farmers, and inhabited in security by

---

[1] In his clever book entitled *The Maori King.* Sir J. Gorst was for some years a police magistrate in New Zealand.

their wives and children. The Government did not hesitate to purchase blocks of land cut off by intervening native territory from the main settlements, which were retailed in small farms to settlers, without a suspicion that the latter were being thereby doomed to ruin. And now that a quarrel has at last arisen between the races, the consolidation of our own territory and the formation of a defensible frontier between European and Maori land imperatively demand conquest, which must entail bloodshed and suffering upon both sides.'

Extracts follow from Sir George Bowen's despatch on the subject of his tour in the Waikato :

To the Duke of Buckingham and Chandos.

Government House, Wellington : June 30, 1868.

My Lord Duke,

It will be remembered that, after some severe fighting at Rangariri and elsewhere, during the campaigns of 1863 and 1864, General Cameron took possession of the great Waikato plain; and that military settlements have since been formed there on the plan adopted by the Colonial Legislature. I wish to draw attention to the field now open in the Waikato, especially for agricultural settlers of experience, and possessing some capital.

I was received everywhere throughout my recent tour, by the colonists and by the Maoris alike, with addresses of welcome and other cordial demonstrations of loyalty to the Queen and of good will to myself, as Her Majesty's representative. The principal settlers of this district, and also those Maori chiefs of the Waikato who have remained loyal to the Crown during the war, had assembled to meet me at Ngaruawáhia, the old Maori capital, which was occupied by the English troops in December 1863, and is now the centre of the military settlements. It is situated at the distance of about seventy-eight miles from Auckland, at the confluence of the rivers Waikato and Waipa; and the native name of Ngaruawáhia, commemorating this 'meeting of the waters,' seems likely to outlive the new official designation of Newcastle.   Here the triumphal arches formed of the beautiful ferns and flowering shrubs of the New Zealand forests, in the erection of which the colonists had vied with the Natives to do honour to the new Governor, the British cheers mingling with the Maori chants of welcome, and at night, the bonfires and fireworks of the Europeans lighting up the national dances of the Natives, all combined to present a most suggestive scene.

On the day after my arrival, the usual meeting was held by the Natives, when Wi te Wheoro and other leading chiefs addressed me in complimentary speeches, full alike of the shrewd diplomacy and of the figurative language of their race. This meeting was held near the tomb of Potatau te Whero Whero, who was elected in 1857 to be the first King of the Maoris. This tomb is much dilapidated; and I promised, on behalf of the Colonial Government, that it should be restored and kept in repair, 'in honour of a famous chief of the old time, who never made war on the Queen, and who lived for many years in peace and harmony with his English neighbours.' In my reply to the address of the Waikatos, I exhorted them to bury in the grave of Potatau all feelings of hostility to the English It will be recollected that Potatau died before the commencement of the late war, and that his son and successor, Tawhiao, a man of little force of character, soon fell into the hands of a few ambitious chiefs and fanatical native prophets, animated by bitter hostility against the Europeans, and setting the Queen's authority and laws at utter defiance.

From Ngaruawáhia I proceeded to the new township of Hamilton, where I was received by another body of the European settlers and by the Ngatihaua clan, to which belonged the eminent chief Tarapipipi te Waharoa, better know in parliamentary papers and official records by his Christian name of William Thompson, and by his *sobriquet* of the 'Maori Warwick,' or the 'King-maker'; for he was the leading and controlling mind of what is termed the 'King movement.' He died in 1867; and his clansmen, though mostly engaged against the Government during the war, have now returned to their villages, and are living on peaceful terms with the Europeans. His son, and the other chiefs of the tribe, came to welcome me at the Hamilton meeting; and it was interesting and gratifying to see the military settlers and the Ngatihauas, so lately arrayed in arms against

to perform all lawful acts, and that good may result
to all persons throughout the whole of this island.

Reply of the Governor.

' O my Friends!—I am very glad to see here
assembled the people of Ngatihaua, and I thank
you for coming so far to welcome me, and for your
loyal speeches. I have heard and read much of your
late chief Wiremu Tamihana, who was long foremost
among Maoris in the arts of peace. I have also heard
that none are more distinguished than your tribe for
bravery in war. War has now ended, and I see with
pleasure Maori and Pakeha meeting here in mutual
trust and friendship. The energies which have been
employed in strife may now again be directed to
those arts which Wiremu Tamihana once loved ; and
Pakeha and Maori may emulate each other in making
this beautiful land more beautiful still by covering it
with gardens and orchards—with cornfields, pastures,
and towns. This is the desire of the Queen, who has
sent me to be her representative ; this is my desire,
and the desire of the Ministers, of the Legislature, and
of all the Europeans in New Zealand. If my coming
among you can in any way bind closer the friendship
of the two races, it will be my greatest pleasure often
to visit the places where they dwell together. I hope
next year I may be able to see you in your own
villages, and to stay longer among you. Meantime
let your work be untiring to spread peace and good-
will—to bring back the stray sheep of the Maori race.

My hand and the hand of my Government is stretched out to receive them.

' I had hoped that the coming of the Prince, the Queen's son, might have been the occasion of ending all bitterness and anger. His visit has been prevented by evil men, but it will rejoice the heart of the Queen to know how wide and how warm have been the indignation and sympathy excited by the crime against her son. He has requested me to say to both races how great is his sorrow that he could not visit New Zealand.

' As for what was said by one of the speakers respecting the Waikato river, hearken ye to my word. The river is, and always has been, the common highway of both races—of the Pakeha and of the Maori. All who go up and down upon the river on their lawful errands will be protected by the law.

' With regard to what was said respecting the land, listen again to my word. The Government gave due warning that those who rebel against the Queen and the law, would be punished by the loss of their lands. But large reserves of land have been made in the Waikato, and also at Mangere near Auckland, and in many other districts, with the object of rewarding the loyal, and of providing homes and subsistence for all those who desire to return to the paths of peace and quietness. Let all such apply to the Government in the lawful manner, and full provision will be made for them.

' And now, O my friends! in conclusion, I thank

After this Maori *Korero* (a ceremony corresponding somewhat to the Durbars of British India), I visited the *pah*, or fortified village of Maketu, and the *whares*, or dwellings of the principal chiefs. I then inspected the school for their children, which has been established by the Arawas, assisted by the Colonial Government, under the provisions of the ' Act[1] to regulate and provide subsidies for Maori schools.' Though this school had been open for only seven months, and the teaching is entirely in English, the master being a former corporal of the 12th Regiment, I found the Maori children quite as proficient in reading, writing, arithmetic, and in the other branches of primary education, as English children of the same age, and under similar circumstances, would be. It was very gratifying to observe the intelligent interest evidently taken in the examination by the managing committee of fourteen Maoris, who were all present. No efforts will be wanting on the part of the Colonial Government to extend an efficient system of schools throughout the native districts.

After leaving Maketu, I visited Opotiki, also in the Bay of Plenty, as it was named by Captain Cook. Opotiki was the scene of the cruel murder, in 1865, of the Rev. C. S. Völkner (the resident Church of England Missionary), by the fanatical Hau-haus, under the prophet Kereopa, who devoured a portion of the body of his victim. To punish this and other similar atrocities (including the murder of Mr.

[1] No. 41 of 1867.

Fulloon, and his crew), an expedition of colonial Militia and friendly natives was organised. This force was completely successful, routing the Hauhaus at every point. A portion of their land was confiscated; and the township of Opotiki, with the fertile plain surrounding it, was allotted to military settlers. Owing to the frequent incursions of the Hauhaus and Urewras, it is still found necessary to maintain about eighty of these settlers on permanent pay, and to station them in two blockhouses, commanding the entrance of the passes leading from the mountains into the plain. Attended by a small escort of Volunteer cavalry, I rode over the confiscated land, which, when law and order shall have been fully established, will probably support a flourishing settlement. I also held a *Korero* with the small neighbouring tribes of the Ngaitai and Ngatiwhakatohea.

On my voyage from Opotiki round the East Cape, I landed on the curious volcanic cone, which rises in the centre of the Bay of Plenty. In the middle of the huge crater there is a lake of hot sulphureous water, and clouds of steam (whence the name of White Island) are constantly sent up from a number of boiling springs. There is no animal life whatsoever, and scarcely any vegetable life, on this lone and gloomy islet.

I visited next Turanganui, named Poverty Bay by Captain Cook, because the hostility of the natives prevented him from procuring supplies there. But a fertile plain extends behind the township situated

And now once more, O my friends! I thank you for your welcome, and I pray that God, the giver of all good, may grant you happiness and prosperity.

Any sketch of Sir G. Bowen's life in New Zealand would be very incomplete which should not refer to his friendship with Bishop Selwyn, who, like himself, felt a warm interest in the Maoris; and with the other Anglican Bishops, especially with Bishop Patteson, the head of the Melanesian Mission, whom he had known at Oxford, and with whom he maintained an affectionate intercourse. The Bishop had been an honoured guest at the Government House, before he sailed in 1871 on his last missionary voyage, when he met a martyr's death at the hands of the natives of Nukapu, a small island in the Melanesian group.

A remarkable incident occurred when Bishop Selwyn held his last Synod at Wellington, after his translation to Lichfield. Sir G. Bowen drove the Primate and his suffragan Bishops to the pier, where they embarked in a small coasting steamer which was to take them back to their respective dioceses. Reference was made to the belief of seamen (a tradition probably of Jonah), that a Bishop on board ship is likely to bring ill luck; and, strange to say, four hours after leaving Wellington, the steamer conveying the five Bishops struck on a rock near the shore, filled, and, in a short time, sank. Fortunately, Bishops Selwyn and Abraham had rowed in the Cambridge College races, and now got out a boat and brought their brethren on shore;—(humanly speaking) saving their lives, and the lives of those shipwrecked with them.

CHAPTER XVI.

RENEWAL OF THE MAORI WAR—TITOKOWÁRU AND TE KOOTI—
MASSACRE AT POVERTY BAY—POLICY OF THE GOVERNOR—HE
PROCEEDS TO WANGANUI, AND ADDRESSES THE ASSEMBLED
CLANS, WHO TAKE UP ARMS FOR THE QUEEN—DEFEAT OF
THE REBELS—CAPTURE OF NGATAPA—TRIAL OF THE MAORI
PRISONERS—THE GOVERNOR'S COMMENTS ON THE STATE OF
AFFAIRS, AND PRACTICAL SUGGESTIONS.

SIR GEORGE BOWEN reported in August 1868, that
the state of affairs which, on his arrival in New
Zealand in the previous February, he found existing
in the districts occupied by the hostile Maoris, was
described by the most competent judges as ' a doubt-
ful armed truce.' This truce was broken in the
latter months of 1868 by dangerous and simultaneous outbreaks on the West coast of the North Island
under Titokowáru, and on the East coast under Te
Kooti. The former chief at first gained some successes over the colonial Militia and Volunteers, re-
pulsing with severe loss their attack on his pah, called
Te Ngutu-o-te.Manu, or *the Hawk's Beak*. But a still
more dangerous outbreak was led on the East coast
by Te Kooti. This latter chief, with about two
hundred Maori prisoners of war, had been sent, under
the administration of Sir G. Grey, to the Chatham
Islands, a dependency of the Colony distant some
400 miles from Wellington. In October 1868,

that 'he supposed it was considered complimentary to the colonists to tell them that they were so free that they might change their allegiance and nationality at pleasure ; but that it would really have been more complimentary, as well as more constitutional and more patriotic, to tell them that England would spend her last soldier and her last shilling to keep them in the Empire, as the Northern States had told the Southern States in the recent Civil War in America.' [1]

After honestly stating his own opinion, Sir G. Bowen, directly he was instructed that Her Majesty's Government had finally decided on the entire removal of the troops, loyally acquiesced in that decision. He wrote: 'I hold it to be the paramount duty of every Governor to obey the orders of Her Majesty's Government, and that he should do this not merely ministerially, but loyally, striving his best to prevent any mischievous results which he may have foreseen.' Accordingly, the discontented party were

---

[1] Just at this somewhat inopportune moment, there happened to arrive in New Zealand, the United States' corvette 'Kearsage,' which a few years previously had sunk the Confederate cruiser 'Alabama.' Sir George Bowen invited the Captain to the Government House, placed a horse at his disposal, and asked him to join his riding party daily. 'Well, Governor,' said the Captain, 'I thank your Excellency ; but the fact is that I was never across an animal in my life, except once when I rode a donkey up Mount Vesuvius, and the cuss nearly kicked me off into the crater. However, I guess I can ride the cross-trees of a man-of-war against any British or other officer.' It is an interesting fact that Sir G. Bowen was informed by his guest, that after the sinking of the 'Alabama,' Captain Semmes was seen in the sea, keeping himself afloat by a life-belt and a plank. The victors could, of course, have easily made him prisoner, but they preferred to let him escape on board a passing English vessel, for they feared that in the then exasperated state of feeling in the Northern States, he might be tried and hanged for treason by the Civil Courts ;—a fate from which they wished to save a gallant enemy.

persuaded to await the decision of the Home authorities on the alternative proposal, viz. that England should guarantee a loan of a million sterling for the defence of New Zealand by the Colonial Government. This alternative was finally conceded. But immediate action was required in the very critical position of the Colony, at a moment when it was generally feared that the entire Maori race would unite against the colonists. Sir George Bowen successfully urged on his Ministers that the proper policy to adopt was practically that of William III. after the complete defeat of the English troops in 1689 at the battle of Killiecrankie, when the king entrusted Lord Breadalbane with a Commission and a sum of money ; —the result of which was that the victorious Highland clans either remained quiet, or joined the new Government. Sir George further determined to forthwith proceed in person, accompanied by his Prime Minister, Mr. Stafford,[1] to Wanganui, and there to address the assembled clans, calling on them to take up arms once more for the Queen. It was an anxious time ; for the rebel Maoris had advanced within a few miles of Wanganui, sweeping away the English settlements. However, the action of the Governor was completely successful. On November 17 he was able to report from Wanganui as follows :

' At this moment the head-quarters of the colonial forces, under Colonel Whitmore, are in a redoubt on the Kai-iwi River, about ten miles north-west of Wanganui. The head-quarters of the rebels under Tito-

---

[1] Afterwards Sir Edward Stafford, G.C.M.G.

This may be called the main turning-point of the Maori war. Reinforced by the loyal clans, Colonel Whitmore,[1] the commander of the colonial forces, was enabled to take the field again, and after several sharp skirmishes, to drive Titokowáru back into the forests of the West Coast. He then proceeded to the East Coast; and on January 10, 1869, captured Ngatapa, the chief stronghold of the rebels who had perpetrated the Poverty Bay massacre. We subjoin the despatch of the Secretary of State commenting on this exploit;

Downing Street: April 2, 1869.

Sir,

I have received your despatches, in which you report the operations of the colonial forces under Colonel Whitmore against Te Kooti and his followers, and the success which has attended those operations by the taking of Ngatapa. From the plans which accompany your despatches, this rebel stronghold appears to have been very formidable by nature, and strengthened by the defensive works which the Maoris throw up with a skill and precision closely allied to science.

The operations which have been attended with so successful a result were conducted in a skilful and energetic manner by Colonel Whitmore, who, profiting by his experience in savage warfare at the Cape and in New Zealand, appears not to have neglected the military precautions which professional training shows to be necessary on such service, nor to have failed to

---

[1] Afterwards Sir George Whitmore, K.C.M.G.

display the perseverance and determination essential to the accomplishment of a difficult enterprise.

I have read with satisfaction the reports of Colonel Whitmore in which he brings to notice the conduct of the colonial forces: their patient perseverance in approaching the place, and the energy and courage they displayed when the assault was given, reflect credit on all engaged; and Her Majesty's Government learn with great satisfaction that the colonial forces have proved that they are capable of successfully dealing with armed rebels.

The native chief Ropata seems to have largely contributed to the success of the enterprise; and his conduct and that of his people show how important and valuable the assistance of native auxiliaries may be made for all defensive purposes.

The presence of Mr. Richmond, a member of your Government, was no doubt a most useful assistance to Colonel Whitmore; and I gladly recognise the services rendered by that gentleman.[1]

It is satisfactory to know that the colonial force displayed the humanity and forbearance towards the women and children taken in the rebel stronghold which ought to distinguish troops under all circumstances. I consider the whole operation to have been skilfully and creditably conducted.

I cannot doubt that this success will have the

[1] When the driver of one of the Government ammunition carts was wounded at the capture of Ngatapa, Mr. Richmond, the Minister for Defence, himself caught the reins, and took the place of the disabled man.

effect of restoring security to the East Coast of the Colony, and of producing a very marked impression throughout the Maori country.

Te Kooti effected his escape from Ngatapa, and for some time carried on, like Titokowáru, a guerilla warfare in the mountains. But he was pursued and defeated by our brave Maori allies at Tokano and elsewhere. Moreover, the Colonial Government adopted the policy of Lord Chatham and General Wade, and pacified the Maori, like the Scotch Highlands, by engaging some of the clans to fight the rest, and by paying the natives generally (including hundreds of those recently in arms against the Crown), to make roads opening up their own mountains and forests, and thus rendering future rebellions difficult.

We here reprint extracts from the Governor's despatches respecting the trial before the Supreme Court of the Colony of the Maori prisoners from the bands of Te Kooti and Titokowáru. Sir George Bowen and his ministers adhered from the beginning to the maxim ' that the grass soon grows over blood shed on the field of battle, but never over blood shed on a political scaffold.' Accordingly, ' they determined that, under the peculiar circumstances of this country, no capital sentence should be carried out against Maoris convicted only of having carried arms against the Colonial Government.' They further rejected the proposals urged in many quarters for superseding (as had been done in other Colonies) the ordinary tribunals by the establishment of Courts-Martial. As Sir G. Bowen reported: ' To omit many other considerations, we felt that there was no reason to suppose that the Supreme Court and the Civil juries were unable or unwilling to administer, with a severity sufficiently deterrent, impartial justice to both races of the inhabitants of this country.

' Out of the total number of nearly one hundred prisoners, more than twenty of the least criminal were discharged, no evidence against them having been tendered on the part of the Crown; while the remaining seventy pleaded guilty, or have been convicted after long and patient trials before the Supreme Court.

' The Judge who presided (Mr. Justice Johnston) has written to me that the general result of these trials has been, in his opinion, " most satisfactory"; and that "they will prove of great service to the Colony, as showing the true intentions and objects of the rebels. The real nature of the West Coast rebellion has been made manifest—Te Kooti's professed object clearly having been to exterminate the adherents to the Government of both races, and to enjoy the plunder." Mr. Justice Johnston further reports that the prosecutions were very well conducted by the Attorney-General on behalf of the Crown; that the prisoners were very ably defended by the counsel provided for them at the expense of the Colonial Government; and that the demeanour of the jurors left nothing to desire.'

The Governor forwarded a copy of the Proceedings of the Executive Council, in which the sentences on the Maori prisoners were carefully considered.

'It will be seen,' he reported, 'that it was finally determined that the sentence of death should be carried into effect only in the person of Hamiora te Peri, the most aggravated case in the opinion of the Judge who presided at the trials. This man was not a Chatham Island prisoner, nor a member of Te Kooti's tribe. It could not therefore be urged, in palliation of his crimes, that he was avenging his imprisonment, or that he was influenced by the feelings of clanship. He voluntarily joined te Kooti soon after his landing, evidently from the mere love of blood and plunder, and was clearly proved to have taken an active part in the cruel murders of unarmed men, Europeans and Maoris, and of women and children, in the Poverty Bay massacre. These atrocities are as much abhorred by the natives generally as by the colonists, and the fate of Hamiora te Peri excited no sympathy among his own countrymen. He was executed on the 16th instant, within the precincts of the gaol at Wellington, and exhibited craven fear on the scaffold. I am assured that this is the only known instance of any Maori having ever met death, under any circumstances whatsoever, except with stern indifference or with calm and decorous fortitude.

'On the grounds fully explained in the enclosed Minute of Council, the capital sentences of three other members of Te Kooti's bands (Heteriki, Rewi, and Matene) have been commuted to penal servitude for life, with the prospect of further remission in the event of good conduct. These men will be kept to hard labour in the gaol at Wellington.

'The remaining convicts, seventy-three in number, being prisoners from the bands of Titokowáru on the West Coast, were not found to have been directly concerned in murders or other heinous atrocities; consequently, their sentences have been commuted, according to the measure of the guilt of each individual, to various terms of penal servitude,—in no instance exceeding seven years,—" on the understanding that there will be, after careful consideration of the special circumstances in each case, a further remission; and that if tranquillity is restored, with a reasonable prospect of permanence, and if these prisoners behave well, a general amnesty will be granted."'

The following extract from a semi-official letter will help to illustrate the preceding narrative:

To an Official Friend.

Wanganui, New Zealand : November 17, 1868.

I write to you from Wanganui, one of the earliest English settlements in New Zealand, and now a town of about 3,000 inhabitants, and the centre of the disturbed districts on the West Coast. Titokowáru has killed or driven off (indeed he is reported to have *eaten off* some of them) all the farmers within a short distance of this town. The survivors have fled into Wanganui. It is said in the local press

that the present state of this town vividly recalls
the descriptions of the European cantonments in
India during the Mutiny of 1857. But I apprehend
that long familiarity with danger has produced here
a certain amount of insensibility. One of the ladies
who, with her family, narrowly escaped from the
Hau-haus three days ago, when their house in this
neighbourhood was destroyed, said to me this morning that this was the fourth time during the last
twenty-five years that she had had to fly for her life
in New Zealand ; but that she knew that our English
race would prevail in the end. However, the massacre
of the settlers at Poverty Bay, on the 10th instant, was
as shocking as anything that ever occurred in India.

It may, perhaps, be asked why I have left perfect safety at the seat of Government at Wellington,
to come ' to the front ' at -this perilous crisis, when
Titokowáru has sworn that he will get my head, to
send it round to the various tribes, as a trophy of
victory, according to the ancient Scotch, and modern
Maori custom. I am aware, of course, that common-
places may be spoken on this subject, and that if
a civilian gets killed by exposing himself to danger,
people only remark, ' *Que diable allait il faire dans
cette galère?* ' The fact is that after the check experienced by Colonel Whitmore on the 7th instant,
mainly owing to the withdrawal of the native contingent, through the mutual jealousies of the chiefs,
our Maori allies all retired to their camp near
Wanganui. I was assured on all sides that my

presence here would go far towards restoring confidence to the panic-stricken townspeople; while it would afford the only chance of inducing the natives to take the field again on our side;—probably, of preventing them from joining the enemy.

Since the above was written, I have paid my visit to the camp of the Wanganuis and the other assembled clans; and I am happy to say that, in response to my address, Te Kepa Rangihiwhinui and several others of the bravest warriors sprang forward, and promised to take the field again with the colonial forces. The *Korero* was very Homeric. Kepa is the Achilles, and Mete Kingi the Ulysses of New Zealand; and their speeches and those of their respective adherents were very suggestive and characteristic.

Her Majesty's Government signified in emphatic terms their approval of Sir G. Bowen's conduct in proceeding to Wanganui at this dangerous crisis, and of the language which he addressed to the assembled clans.

The following despatch contains comments on the state of native affairs, with practical suggestions.

To the Duke of Buckingham and Chandos.

Government House, Wellington : December 7, 1868.

My Lord Duke,

It may probably be interesting to your Grace to read the opinion of the present condition of affairs in this Colony entertained by so able, experienced, and dispassionate a person as Sir George Arney, the present Chief Justice of New Zealand. He had lately been at Wellington, as President of the Court of Appeal, and on his return voyage to Auckland, where he generally resides, he encountered the vessel carrying some of the fugitives from the cruel massacre of English settlers perpetrated at Poverty Bay on the 10th ultimo. The Chief Justice sums up his opinion in the following terms : ' I will not venture to speculate on what may be done; but of this I feel convinced, that the Colony must brace itself up to hold its own until the time may arrive when the native race may feel constrained to respect us in our strength, as they now despise us in our weakness. Meanwhile, I do not envy you having to take up the government of this beauteous country at precisely that period of its history when, I believe, it has been left more embarrassed in its finances, more crippled, relatively, in its power, and more exposed, from its advanced settlements and increased cultivations, to the savagery of the Maori race than it has been left to any preceding Governor. I only hope that we may find our respite from destruction in the distracted counsels and divided allegiance of the natives ; the mass of whom know full well that they have received little wrong and much good from the settlers.'

Since the control of native affairs, including, practically, the conduct of the present and of future Maori Wars, was transferred in 1862 from the Governor

to the Ministers of the Colony for the time being,
a number of able public men have succeeded each
other in office in New Zealand, all doubtless animated
with a sincere desire to promote the welfare of their
adopted country. But if the exigencies of parliamentary government have sometimes embarrassed
elsewhere the conduct of even foreign wars, it will be
easily understood that those exigencies have created
still greater difficulties in the conduct of the internal
Maori war: when, as in New Zealand, the legislature
is so equally divided between the two conflicting
political parties that neither of them can make sure
of a working majority of more than two or three votes
in the House of Representatives ; when almost every
leading member of both Houses has a native policy of
his own, and is swayed by various kinds of personal
and local feelings and interests. Under such circumstances, as will be manifest without entering into any
details, there can be but little consistency of policy
or unity of action.

A portion of the population of the Northern
Island of New Zealand, under the pressure of the
long-continued Maori War and of the recent disasters,
would regard with complacency the suspension of
the existing constitution [1] in this island, or at least a
return to the system in force up to the year 1862,
under which the Governor personally possessed the

---

[1] A prominent member of the New Zealand Parliament lately exclaimed, ' What an absurdity it was to set up the British Constitution
in a country where all the landed gentry are savages, and, for the most
part, hereditary or relapsed cannibals !'

control of native affairs. Former experience, however, has proved that (in the words of Mr. Merivale) ' the suggestion of establishing in the same Colony responsible government for the settlers, and a separate administration of native affairs under the Imperial authorities, is unpractical. There cannot be two governments in the same community ; certainly not, unless some mode can be devised of having two public purses.'

It has often been observed that the immediate causes of the Indian Rebellion of 1857–8 were mainly : 1. Religious and national fanaticism. 2. The recent reduction in the number of the English troops employed in India. 3. The annexation of the entire territories of the King of Oude. So the main causes of the long continuance of the Maori War, which has now raged in New Zealand, with some periods of intermission, ever since 1860, are generally believed to be : 1. The outbreak of the Hau-hau fanaticism in connexion with the national, or (as it is termed), the 'native king movement.' 2. The removal of the English regiments before any tender of submission was made by, or any peace was ratified with, the Maori King, and the tribes which adhere to him. 3. The confiscation of a small portion of the territories of the rebel natives.

With regard to the first of these three causes, it may be observed that the religious and national fanaticism of the Hau-haus is analogous to the periodical outbreaks of a similar nature among the Malays (who are probably of kindred race with the Maoris), and among the Hindoos and Musulmans of India. It may not be altogether impertinent to mention that the ‘lily’ fills the same place in the mysterious proclamations of the Maori King, as the ‘lotus’ filled in the missives of some of the native princes in Hindostan.

With regard to the second of the causes mentioned above, it is often a matter of surprise, both here and in England, that two experienced generals, successively at the head of nearly 10,000 regular soldiers, and 5,000 of the colonial Militia, and with all the means and appliances of modern warfare, should not have succeeded in subduing King Tawhiao and his adherents, who are believed to have never brought into the field more than two thousand fighting men at the same time. But it should be recollected that, in the opinion of all competent judges, New Zealand presents as difficult obstacles as Abyssinia to an invading army attempting to penetrate the mountains and forests of the interior; while the Maoris are, beyond all comparison, more formidable enemies than the Abyssinians. It has often been observed that the British army did not lose a single man even at the capture of the royal fortress of Magdala, whereas the loss of the regular troops and of the naval brigade has been heavy before every Maori village and earthwork; while at the Gate Pah near Tauranga, in 1864, the 43rd Regiment lost more officers (fourteen out of twenty-four that went into action), than any single regiment lost at Waterloo. In a

word, it seems to be very generally agreed that the
conquest of King Tawhiao and the Hau-haus would
have been a much greater military feat than the conquest of King Theodore and the Abyssinians.

Few will probably be found to advocate another
aggressive war in the interior of New Zealand. It is
generally felt that we must content ourselves with protecting our existing settlements, and punishing the
cruel outrages and massacres recently perpetrated.
For these purposes, as also to prevent the horrors of a
war of race and extermination between the colonists
and the Maoris, to serve as a nucleus for the colonial
forces, and to maintain in the eyes of the natives the
prestige of the Queen's name and of Imperial power
and authority, a small garrison of Her Majesty's
troops is of proved value.

Of all the painful feelings excited by the present
condition of New Zealand, perhaps the most painful
is connected with the effect produced on the minds
of the loyal natives by the official announcement in
the midst of the most dangerous crisis that has ever
occurred in the history of this community, to the
effect that the last British soldier will be removed in
next February from New Zealand. It is, of course,
impossible to explain to the Maoris the grounds of
the complete change which has taken place of late
years in the views of the Imperial Government with
regard to the military protection of the Dependencies
of the Crown; or the mixed motives which induced
one of the conflicting parties in the New Zealand

Legislature to advocate the so-called 'self-reliant policy,' without taking any steps to create a permanent or effective defence force.

It may appear strange to superficial or ill-informed observers that the English settlers in the North Island are unable of themselves to subdue the Maoris, seeing that their numbers are nearly as two to one, about 80,000 colonists to 45,000 Maoris.[1] But it will

---

[1] We may compare the following remarks on this question of the author of *Greater Britain* (Part II. c. 5), who visited New Zealand during the war: ' Savages though the Maoris be, in irregular warfare we are not their match. At the end of 1865 we had of regulars and Militia 15,000 men under arms in the North Island of New Zealand, including no less than twelve regiments of the line at their " war strength "; and yet our generals were despondent as to their chance of finally defeating the warriors of a people which—men, women, and children—numbered little over 40,000 souls. Men have sought far and wide for the reasons which led to our defeats in the New Zealand wars. We were defeated by the Maoris as the Austrians by the Prussians, and the French by the English in old times, because the victors were the better men. Not the braver men, when both sides were brave alike; not the stronger; not, taking the average of our officers and men, the more intelligent; but capable of quicker movement, able to subsist on less, more crafty, more skilled in the thousand tactics of the bush. Aided by their women, who, when need was, themselves would lead the charge; and who at all times dug their fern-root and caught their fish; marching where our regiments could not follow, they had, as have the Indians in America, the choice of time and place for their attacks; and while we were crawling about our military roads upon the coast, incapable of traversing a mile of bush, the Maoris moved securely and secretly from one end to the other of the island. Arms they had, ammunition they could steal, and blockade was useless with enemies who live on fern-root. When they found that we burnt their pahs, they ceased to build them; that was all. When we brought up howitzers, they went where no howitzers could follow. It should not be hard, even for our pride, to allow that such enemies were, man for man, in their own land, our betters. All nations fond of horses, it has been said, flourish and succeed. The Maoris love horses, and ride well. All races that delight in sea are equally certain to prosper, empirical philosophers will tell us. The Maoris own ships by the score,

be remembered that the Maoris were not subjugated during the years when an English army of nearly ten thousand regular soldiers, in addition to the colonial forces, was employed in this island. Moreover, the great majority of the settlers in New Zealand are emigrants from the labouring classes in England, and had probably never carried arms of any kind until they found themselves enrolled in the colonial Militia. On the other hand, every Maori is a born soldier; strong, fleet, and intrepid; accustomed from his infancy to the use of weapons, and to the sight of blood; and trained to great skill in bush fighting by the guerilla warfare of the last eight years. Again, the colonists occupy settlements placed chiefly along and near the sea-shore. They occupy, as it were, the circumference of a circle, whereas the Maoris are entrenched in the almost impenetrable mountains and forests of the centre, whence they can send forth forays in every direction. It will be further recollected that, in 1745, 4,000 Highlanders easily conquered all Scotland, except the few fortified posts garrisoned by English troops, although the Lowlanders were infinitely more numerous in comparison with the Celts than the British colonists in New Zealand are in comparison with the

and serve as sailors whenever they get a chance; as deep-sea fishermen they have no equals. Their fondness for draughts shows mathematical capacity; in truthfulness they possess the first of virtues. They are shrewd, thrifty, devoted friends, brave men. With all this, they die. "Can you stay the surf which beats on Wanganui shore?" say the Maoris of our progress; and of themselves, "We are gone—like the Moa."'

Maoris; and though the Lowlanders were animated against their assailants by the animosities which spring from differences of race, language, and religion. In short, it is not to be denied that if the small British detachments which now hold some of the towns, and thus leave the colonial forces free to cope with the insurgent natives in the open field, are withdrawn, the main hope, under Providence, of the colonists in the North Island must lie in the hereditary feuds which have hitherto prevented the Maoris, like other races living under the tribal system, from acting together against the authority of the Queen. If the entire Maori people were to unite against us now, we could probably hold only the towns of Auckland and Wellington. So, British authority would have been practically annihilated if the British troops had been removed from Scotland during the rebellions of 1715 and 1745, and if the Hanoverian had joined the Jacobite clans. So, too, the English would have been driven out of all India (except, perhaps, the Presidency cities) in 1857, if the European army had been withdrawn, and if the Sikhs, together with the Nizam and the other loyal native princes, had joined the Sepoy mutineers. The late Primate of New Zealand, now Bishop of Lichfield (Dr. Selwyn), has remarked on more than one public occasion that there is, in the present condition of this Colony, nothing which is new to the student of the history of other countries where formidable aborigines had recently been brought into contact

with alien invaders or settlers. The social state of the Maori districts of New Zealand at the present day is analogous to that of the Celtic districts of Ireland down to the reign of George I., and of the Celtic districts of Scotland down to the reign of George III. In fact, it has often been observed with truth that those who wish to understand the present condition of the Maoris, should read with care the description of the Scotch Highlanders at the end of the seventeenth century, as contained in the 13th chapter of Lord Macaulay's ' History of England.' In my Despatch, No. 116, by this mail, I attempted a description of my visit to the Maori camp near Wanganui on the 17th ult.; but I should have drawn a much fuller and more vivid picture of what I saw there, and especially of the meeting between Colonel Whitmore and the Maori chiefs, if I had simply quoted the following passage describing the Highlanders under Dundee :—
' All that was left to the Commander under whom these potentates (the Highland chiefs) condescended to serve, was to argue with them, to supplicate them, to flatter them, to bribe them; and it was only during a short time that any human skill could preserve harmony by these means, for every chief thought himself entitled to peculiar observance, and it was therefore impossible to pay marked court to any one without disobliging the rest. The General found himself merely the president of a congress of petty kings. He was perpetually called upon to

hear and to compose disputes about pedigrees, about precedence, about the division of spoil. His decision, be it what it might, must offend somebody. At any moment he might hear that his right wing had fired on his centre in pursuance of some quarrel two hundred years old; or that a whole battalion had marched back to its native glen, because another battalion had been put in the post of honour. A Highland bard might easily have found in the history of the year 1689, subjects very similar to those with which the war of Troy furnished the great poets of antiquity. One day Achilles is sullen, keeps his tent, and announces his intention to depart with all his men. The next day Ajax is storming about the camp, and threatening to cut the throat of Ulysses.'

It was remarked above that, in the same sense in which the annexation of the entire territories of the King of Oude was one of the causes which led to the Indian rebellion of 1857, so the confiscation of a small portion of the land of the rebel Maoris may have been one of the causes of the continuance of the Maori war, which has now raged in New Zealand, with little intermission, since 1860. The map, which I transmitted with my despatch of March 17th ult., will show that the confiscated land embraces but a small part of the surface of the North Island. Much of it, moreover, has been already restored. It appears to be admitted on all sides that forfeiture of land was a just punishment for rebellion, accompanied with cruel murders and other horrible outrages; and that it was

also a punishment in accordance with Maori usage, as
well as with the laws of civilised nations. But it also
seems to be now generally admitted that it was imprudent at the present time to occupy with settlers
distant and isolated positions, in the immediate neighbourhood of the most hostile tribes, and of the most
impenetrable mountains and forests. In fact, what
the Secretary of State for the Colonies (Mr. Cardwell) foretold in his despatch,[1] of April 26, 1866,
to my predecessor, Sir G. Grey, has now come to
pass. Mr. Cardwell then pointed out that ' if the
proposed new settlements were too far advanced
beyond the country already occupied, it might prove
impossible to abandon them without discredit, or to
protect them without disproportionate expense.' On
the whole, I am disposed to concur with those who
argue that the military settlements ought to have been
placed mainly, if not solely, on the open and easily
defensible Waikato plain ; and to have been protected
by a line of posts drawn across the North Island
(advantage being taken of the nature of the ground)
from the sea at Aotea, or Whaingeroa, on the West
Coast, to the sea at Tauranga, on the East Coast. A
frontier might thus have been secured analogous to
the old Roman frontier between the Friths of Forth
and Clyde.

It is believed that in this, and in my previous
despatches on the same subject, I have given a full
and accurate account of the present condition of this

[1] See the *Parliamentary Papers* presented June 1866, p. 127.

Colony. It remains for me to suggest what should be done at this crisis, the most dangerous which has hitherto occurred (as the Chief Justice has observed), in the history of New Zealand.

It is generally hoped that the single battalion of Imperial troops which still garrisons four of the main centres of population (Auckland, Taranaki, Wanganui, and Napier), will be left here, in accordance with the earnest desire of the New Zealand Parliament, which is now pledged to pay the entire cost. Moreover, it will be recollected that New Zealand alone is already paying for native purposes, defence, and the interest of the war loan of three millions sterling, nearly four hundred thousand pounds annually, that is, far more than the aggregate payments for similar purposes of all the Australian Colonies put together; and that these burdens render necessary taxes at the rate of 6l. 5s. per head of the population, double the rate in the United Kingdom. It is trusted that one battalion will be left as some equivalent for this expenditure. But that battalion (the 2nd, 18th Royal Irish) numbers barely 750 effective officers and men, whereas there is good reason to believe that there are now as many Maoris in arms against the Crown as there ever were while there were 10,000 regular soldiers in the Colony; and the Government has received repeated warnings that the Maori King will probably, sooner or later, give the signal for a general rising of the hostile tribes, and a general massacre of the colonists. With the utmost efforts that can be used, my responsible advisers appear to be unable to raise in New Zealand a permanent force of above 2,000 really effective men, in addition to the Militia and Volunteers, who are practically available only for the defence of their respective districts. Each private in the permanent force is paid 5s. per diem, and, with his rations, clothing, arms, &c., costs the Colony at least 150l. per annum.

I am strongly inclined to agree with those who, from their long experience of the native character, believe that if a small garrison of Imperial troops, in addition to the colonial forces, were maintained in New Zealand for the next few years, as was maintained here from 1846 to about 1860 during the interval between the first and second Maori Wars; and if no further attempt were made to occupy lands in distant and isolated positions, or in the immediate neighbourhood of hostile tribes, this Colony would probably enjoy permanent peace and security. It will be remembered that the native race is rapidly diminishing, while the Europeans are as rapidly increasing in numbers. In 1848, only twenty years ago, the Maoris in the North Island exceeded 100,000; while now, in 1868, they are under 45,000. Consequently the Maori difficulty is a question of time, probably of the next ten years. During that period, every effort should be made to push roads into the interior. Experience has amply shown that the best weapons for the conquest of the Highlands of New Zealand in the nineteenth, as of the Highlands of

Scotland in the eighteenth century, are the spade and
. the pickaxe.

I will conclude by summing up my practical
suggestions, with the expression of a strong conviction that permanent peace and security may be
restored to New Zealand by adopting the following
measures :

a. The presence, in addition to the colonial forces,
of one regiment of regular troops (to hold the chief
towns, and keep up the *prestige* of the Imperial
power in the eyes of the Maoris).

b. The prohibition of fresh settlements in exposed
and dangerous districts.

c. A peaceful arrangement, not inconsistent with
the suzerainty of the Queen, with Tawhiao, the chosen
chief of the Maoris.

In his reply to the above despatch the Secretary
of State declared that the two latter suggestions
were 'clearly judicious.' As it has been already
stated,[1] it was finally arranged that the Imperial
Treasury should guarantee a loan of one million
sterling towards the cost of the defence of New
Zealand by the Colonial Government, instead of
allowing one regiment of Imperial troops to be
retained temporarily. To negotiate this question
with Her Majesty's Government, the Colonial Ministry
despatched to England as Commissioners two of
the ablest members of the Colonial Parliament, viz.

[1] See above, p. 333.

Messrs. Featherstone and Bell, afterwards Sir I. E. Featherstone, K.C.M.G., and Sir F. Dillon Bell, K.C.M.G. (now Agent-General for New Zealand in London).[1]

[1] It was stated in the Colony that the Home authorities at first tried to persuade the Commissioners to be satisfied with the guarantee of half a million sterling; to which arrangement one of them was inclined to agree, when the other (as he reported) 'floored it' by insisting on the guarantee of the whole million. A well-known New Zealand politician remarked on this point: 'Really our two Commissioners represent between them the Natural History of the Colony. One is the Fauna (*fawner*) and the other the Flora (*floorer*).'

CHAPTER XVII.

THE WAR BECOMES A GUERILLA—THE GOVERNOR CONTINUES HIS
OFFICIAL TOURS—LAST SURVIVOR OF THE MAORIS WHO HAD
SEEN CAPTAIN COOK—VISITS OF THE DUKE OF EDINBURGH—
EXPEDITION TO THE HOT LAKES—QUOTATION FROM ' GREATER
BRITAIN.'

AFTER the great successes of the Colonial forces and
loyal Maori clans at Ngatapa and elsewhere, the
war became merely an intermittent guerilla. The
Governor continued to visit personally every district
where his presence could be of advantage. The subjoined extracts from his despatches furnish details
and illustrations of his policy and action :

To the Duke of Buckingham and Chandos.

Government House, Wellington, New Zealand:
February 20, 1869.

My Lord Duke,

For some time past there have been rumours of
probable disturbances in the district of the Wairarapa, which begins at a distance of about thirty-five
miles east from Wellington. I thought it advisable
to choose the present time to pay to this district a
short official visit ; from which I returned yesterday.
I was accompanied throughout my tour by Commodore Lambert, commanding Her Majesty's naval

forces on this station; and by Mr. Featherstone, the Superintendent of the Province of Wellington.

The fertile and picturesque valley of Wairarapa stretches inland from Palliser Bay, and is about sixty-five miles in length, with a width ranging from fifteen to nearly forty miles. The European settlers amount to nearly three thousand souls; of this number about eight hundred are adult males, and of these I found above seven hundred, in fact, almost every man capable of bearing arms, enrolled in the local corps of Militia and Volunteers; I saw, moreover, fully five hundred horsemen assembled in one day at Greytown, the principal centre of population in the Wairarapa; and I was escorted through the district by a strong detachment of Volunteer cavalry. The usual addresses of respect and welcome were presented to me by both the Europeans and the Maoris.

There is a considerable Maori population, including many Hau-haus, in some parts of the valley, and of the slopes of the surrounding mountains. At the usual *Korero*, or native meeting, I was addressed in loyal and pacific speeches by the principal chiefs, who, however, did not conceal their apprehension of the possible invasion of the Wairarapa by the hostile natives, and of the disastrous consequences which would ensue should Tawhiao take the field and call the entire Maori race to arms against the English. There can be no doubt but that the natives generally are still watching the progress of events with gloomy irresolution, and that very much depends on the success of the negotiations recently entered upon by my Government with the view of securing at least the neutrality of the so-called Maori King.

Meanwhile the settlers in the Wairarapa, as in most other parts of this island, seem to be now fully prepared to defend, in case of need, their lives and homes. Nearly every able-bodied man in the valley is armed and drilled; while a redoubt and block-house have been erected in a central position as a place of refuge for the women and children in the event of an outbreak.

I may take this opportunity of mentioning that, on my journey back from the Wairarapa, I visited at his *kainga* (or village), about twenty miles from Wellington, the famous Ngatiawa chief, Táringa Kuri, the last survivor of those who had seen Captain Cook on one of his later voyages to New Zealand. The first English settlers in this country state that Táringa Kuri was a very old man on their first arrival here thirty years ago; and his age is now generally believed to exceed one hundred years. He is extremely feeble, but, in common with his people, he expressed much gratification at my visit.[1]

---

[1] Táringa Kuri died in the autumn of 1871; and by a singular coincidence two other leading chiefs, also closely connected with the early colonisation of New Zealand, Tamati Waka Nene and Te Puni, died within the same twelvemonth. See pp. 297-300; and 427-28.

To the Same.

Government House, Wellington, New Zealand:
February 22, 1869.

My Lord Duke,

I have the honour to transmit herewith a copy of the last report received from Colonel Whitmore, respecting the progress of events on the West Coast. It is the opinion of the most competent judges that there will be a tedious guerilla warfare in that quarter. Titokowáru appears to have retreated to a strong position in the forest, whence he sends forth marauding parties against the settlers, and lays ambuscades for the escorts and foragers of the colonial forces, often with fatal effect.

I regret to add that an official letter from the Superintendent of the Province of Taranaki reached Wellington yesterday, reporting the murder on the 13th instant, by a party of Hau-haus, of the Rev. John Whiteley (an aged and respected Wesleyan missionary), together with Lieutenant Gascoigne, his wife and three children, and two other settlers, at the White Cliffs, a place about thirty miles north of the town of New Plymouth. It is feared by many that these murders may be the commencement of a fresh outbreak in that quarter also, and there is great alarm felt at New Plymouth.

A detachment of Volunteers from New Plymouth has proceeded to the White Cliffs, and recovered the bodies of some of the murdered settlers. Every effort in their power will be made by the Colonial

Government, and by the local Militia, for the protection of the town and province of Taranaki.

The Governor visited in person shortly afterwards the province of Taranaki and New Plymouth, its chief town, riding through the disturbed districts, and inspecting the posts held by the Militia and the native contingent. The grand physical feature of this part of the Colony is the shapely snow-capped cone of the lofty extinct volcano, called Taranaki by the Maoris, but named Mount Egmont by Captain Cook. Bishop Selwyn once remarked that the people of this province were 'as fond and proud of their mountain as if they had created it themselves.' At the public dinner given in his honour, Sir G. Bowen, in proposing 'Prosperity to Taranaki,' said, 'As the standing toast in Shropshire is "All round the Wrekin," so here it should be "All round Mount Egmont."'

To the Earl Granville, K.G.[1]

Government House, Wellington, New Zealand:
March 12, 1869.

My Lord,

In continuation of my despatch of February 22nd ult., I have now the honour to forward herewith a memorandum submitted to me by Mr. Richmond, the Minister for the Native Department, showing the progress of the Maori War, and the general condition of native affairs at the present time.

It is generally felt that it would be unfortunate,

[1] Lord Granville had succeeded the Duke of Buckingham as Colonial Minister.

for many obvious reasons, if the last British soldier should be withdrawn on the eve of the Duke of Edinburgh's arrival. Moreover, the feeling of the principal Maori chiefs naturally resembles that of the great Indian princes. One of the most able and observant of the writers on British India[1] has remarked that ' Hyder Ali and Runjeet Singh, the Hannibal and the Mithridates of India, had often in their mouths the same phrase concerning the power of the English. They feared, they would say, not what they saw, but what they did not see. Jung Bahadour, the far-famed Mayor of the Palace of Nepaul, when the first dull rumour of the coming crisis began to be bruited, paid a visit to England on purpose to learn for himself what the state of the case really was, and returned firmly resolved not to take part against a power which could raise at a pinch hundreds of millions of money and hundreds of thousands of men.' So the single battalion of Imperial troops still left in New Zealand, though it is restricted to garrisoning the towns, and takes no part in the fighting, still is, in the eyes of the Maori chiefs, a symbol of the power and protection of the Queen.

In my despatch of January 7th ult., I added : ' In common with all the leading public men of this country, I am convinced that it is of vital importance to endeavour to come to a peaceful understanding, not inconsistent with the sovereignty of the Queen, with the so-called ' Maori King ' ; by which title his

[1] Sir George O. Trevelyan, Bart., M.P. See *Cawnpore*, p. 27.

adherents appear to mean nothing more than a great chieftain and magistrate, analogous to the semi-independent rajahs of British India. All feel that it would have been more satisfactory if Tawhiao could have been brought to submission while there was in New Zealand, in addition to the colonial forces, an army of ten thousand British soldiers ; but all agree that since his conquest was found impracticable then, it would be worse than folly to attempt it now, by the unaided efforts of the colonial forces alone.'

There can be little doubt but that the Maori King is himself disposed to peaceful counsels ; still he, like several of the Indian princes in 1857, when placed in a somewhat similar position, may ultimately have to yield to the violence of the barbarous warriors and fanatical Hau-hau prophets by whom he is surrounded.

To the Same.

Government House, Wellington : March 20, 1869.

Colonel Whitmore is cautiously but perseveringly forcing his way through the forests on the West Coast ; and on the 13th instant, after a night march, and under cover of a mist, he surprised Titokowáru's camp, and drove him from it with some loss. The small force under Colonel Whitmore's immediate command is gradually acquiring discipline, confidence, and skill in bush fighting ; but it will be recollected that, while the enemy is stronger and more experienced than ever, the colonial troops do not exceed one-fifth of the number of the regular soldiers lately employed in the same service. For it will be remembered that after the utmost exertions that could be used, and after recruiting throughout this Colony, and in Australia, the Colonial Government has been unable to raise its permanent force to above two thousand men.

The latest intelligence from the Waikato is still of an uncertain character. The movements of the Maori King, on whom so much depends, seem as yet undecided. It is stated that a large meeting of the King natives is to be held at the end of this month of March ; and that it will then be finally settled whether they shall declare for peace or for war.

Meanwhile intelligence has reached Wellington in confirmation of the report of the fresh outbreak on the East Coast. It appears that Te Kooti after his escape at the capture by Colonel Whitmore, in last January, of his main stronghold at Ngatapa (about thirty miles inland from Poverty Bay), retreated to the mountains of the interior, where he was joined by a portion of the wild and savage Urewera clan, the McGregors of the Maori Highlands. He has now made a foray against the settlements in the Bay of Plenty. In that quarter about five hundred Europeans of all ages and sexes are dispersed along a coast line of above one hundred miles; living intermingled with the natives, and in their own phrase 'under the Maori tomahawk'; just as the settlers near the Highland border, one hundred and fifty years ago, lived under the Celtic claymore. Of these five

hundred souls, there are about two hundred men able
to bear arms; who are enrolled in the Militia, and are
now holding the redoubts at Tauranga and Opotiki,
to which their families have mostly fled for refuge.
The English are supported by an equal number of the
Arawas,—a clan which has continued as loyal to the
Crown throughout the Maori rebellions as the Campbells remained during the Scotch rebellions of 1715
and 1745.

Te Kooti has already captured (though after
severe loss) a pah belonging to the friendly natives;
he has destroyed the settlement at Whakatáne; and
murdered, among others, Mr. Pitcairn, an English
surveyor, and M. Guerin, a Frenchman, long resident
in this country, who manfully defended his house, and
killed several of his assailants before he succumbed to
overpowering odds.

The Colonial Government has sent to the assistance of the settlers in the Bay of Plenty all the men
that can be spared from the other threatened points.

The indirect effects of these fresh massacres were
more reassuring than could have been anticipated. As
Sir George Bowen wrote to Lord Granville (July 5,
1869): ' The truth is that (as the tone of several of my
recent despatches will show), I have thought better,
and not worse, of the prospects of this Colony with
regard to the native rebellion, since the Poverty Bay
massacre, than I thought before that catastrophe. It

has caused the spirit of the colonists, and of the loyal
Maori clans, to swell up high and fierce. Moreover,
it was believed by many of those best acquainted
with the native character, that a bloody outbreak of
this nature would prove the signal (as on former
occasions) for a very extensive rising of the disaffected tribes, with the so-called Maori King at their
head; whereas Tawhiao and his adherents have
abstained from active hostilities for so many months,
that I now am inclined to hope that they will not rise
at all.'

———————

In the midst of these alarms—which were, however,
subsiding, as the colonial forces acquired strength
and discipline—the 'Sailor Prince' paid his first visit
to New Zealand. The recent attempt of a Fenian at
Sydney to assassinate him naturally intensified the
sympathy and loyalty of the colonists.

To the Earl Granville, K.G.

Government House, Auckland : June 7, 1869.

My dear Lord,
　　In my despatches by this mail, your Lordship
will find full and detailed reports of the very successful visit to New Zealand of the Duke of Edinburgh. After a stay of seven weeks in this Colony,
H.R.H. took his final departure on the 1st of June,
' a day,' as he observed, ' auspicious in the annals of
the British navy,' and is followed by the loyal affec
tion and hearty good will of this community, to all

classes of which he had endeared himself by his gracious tact and courtesy, and by his unaffected sympathy with the Colony in the difficulties against which it has been so long struggling. He visited all the chief centres of population, viz. Auckland, Wellington, Nelson, Canterbury, and Dunedin, spread along a coast line of above 1,000 miles ; and his sojourn here, while it passed over without a single *contretemps*, has done much public good by at once rewarding and confirming the loyalty of the friendly Maoris, by leading to pacific overtures from the hostile tribes, and by intensifying (if I may so speak), the personal attachment of the overwhelming majority of the colonists to the Queen and the Royal Family. We all feel towards the Captain of the 'Galatea' the sentiment of Horace : [1]

Sis licet felix ubicunque mavis,
Et memor nostri, GALATEA, *vivas !*

The Duke was good enough to say, and to show by his manner, that he 'felt quite at home' with Lady Bowen and myself during the seven weeks that he spent under our roof. He exerted himself zealously to entertain the society invited to Government House, bringing his stage scenery on shore from the 'Galatea,' and having it put up in the ball-room under his own superintendence. Lord Charles Beresford and others of his officers gave us capital private theatricals, the Duke himself leading his orchestra. As you are doubtless aware, he is an accomplished musician,

---

[1] *Carm.* III. 27.

and an excellent mimic and *raconteur*, when he finds himself among people he knows well and likes. He had not so much shooting as I had hoped to give him ; for Commodore Lambert took advantage of his being on the station to hold several naval courts-martial ; and His Royal Highness will never allow anything whatsoever to interfere with his professional duties.

If the Duke is charming as a guest, he is, if possible, still more charming as a host. He took me with him in the 'Galatea' on his visit to the southern provinces. It was observed that he gave the Governor all the honours as the colonial representative of the Queen, and seemed to regard himself, while afloat, simply as a captain in Her Majesty's navy serving in the waters of my Government. While keeping up strict discipline, he is beloved by his officers and men, who would follow him anywhere and everywhere. Commodore Lambert and the other senior officers here consider the Duke to be above the average of officers of his own age as a practical seaman, while there are few men in the Royal Navy who know more about steam machinery, naval construction, and what may be called the scientific part of the profession. Moreover, H.R.H. never forgets that, as Master of the Trinity House, he is, in a sense, the head of the mercantile marine of England ; and, as such, he is always anxious to promote in every way the interests of trade and commerce. He has made valuable practical suggestions for the improvement, lighting, and defence of several of the harbours of New Zealand.

Writing at a later period of the Duke of Edinburgh's second visit to New Zealand, in 1870, Sir George Bowen reported to the Secretary of State His Royal Highness' expedition to the celebrated Hot Lakes:

Government House, Auckland, New Zealand :
December 26, 1870.

My Lord,

I have the honour to report that on the 12th instant, His Royal Highness the Duke of Edinburgh, accompanied by myself and by several officers of H.M.S. 'Galatea' (including Lord Charles Beresford), left Auckland in the Colonial Government steamer 'Luna,' on a visit to the Lake District on the East Coast of this Island. On the following morning we landed at Tauranga, the principal port in the Bay of Plenty, where His Royal Highness was enthusiastically welcomed by 700 chiefs and warriors of the clans of the Arawas and Ngaiterangis.

From Tauranga we proceeded to Maketu, the principal *kainga*, or settlement, of the Arawas, and celebrated in Maori tradition as the spot at which their ancestors, some twenty generations back, first landed in New Zealand. No Europeans have as yet settled in the inland districts of this portion of New Zealand ; but His Royal Highness was as safe among the Arawas in their own country as he would be

D D 2

among the Gordons in Aberdeenshire. We were,
however, attended by a guard of honour, consisting
of a strong escort of the clansmen in arms for the
Queen. The Duke of Edinburgh and his officers
were much interested by the many striking scenes
and incidents of life in a Maori camp, especially by
the war songs. chanted by the Arawas around the
watch-fires which they kindled every night in front
of our tents. On the other hand, the native warriors
were delighted by His Royal Highness' power of
enduring fatigue ; by his good horsemanship and
swimming ; by the skill and vigour with which he
paddled his canoe across their lakes ; and by his
constantly wearing the kilt, which is the favourite
dress of the Maori as of the Scotch Highlanders.

I shall not detain your Lordship with an account
of the hot lakes, solfataras, and geysers of this
Island, for they have been fully described by other
writers. Suffice it to say that, on the 14th instant,
we rode from Maketu to Ohinemutu, the principal
inland settlement of the Arawas, a distance of nearly
forty miles ; the road leading us along the shores of
the beautiful Lakes Rotoiti and Rotorua. It will be
remembered that (as I reported at the time) this road
was spontaneously made by the Arawas, the chiefs
and clansmen labouring together, for the use of the
Duke of Edinburgh more than two years ago, when
his visit was first expected. On the 15th instant,
after swimming in the tepid waters of the solfataras,
and inspecting the principal geysers, we rode over

the hills to Lake Tarawera, which we crossed on the following day in native canoes, encamping for the night on the famous 'terraces' of Lake Rotomahana.[1] After examining the wonders around, we returned on a subsequent day to our previous camp at Ohinemutu, where we spent quietly Sunday the 18th instant. The Rev. S. Spencer, a missionary clergyman resident at Maketu, who had accompanied our party, read the service of the Church of England in the open air on the shore of Lake Rotorua. It was a calm and beautiful day, and the scene was highly picturesque and suggestive ;—the little knot of Englishmen surrounding the 'Son of the Queen,' and the large congregation of Maoris repeating the responses and joining in the hymns of our Church in their own sonorous language ;—amid some of the finest prospects of lake and mountain, and near some of the most wonderful natural phenomena in the world ;—in the very heart, moreover, of the native districts of New Zealand, and of the country most renowned in Maori song and legend; and on a spot where, in the memory of men still living, human victims were sacrificed, and cannibal feasts were held.

On the 19th we rode back from Ohinemutu to Maketu ; and thence returned by sea to Auckland.

---

[1] The fairy-like 'Pink,' and 'White' Terraces were unfortunately destroyed by the terrible earthquake of 1886.

The following despatch relates the progress of events, and quotes a graphic description from 'Greater Britain':

To the Earl Granville, K.G.

Government House, Wellington: September 19, 1869.

My Lord,

Te Kooti has again attacked the friendly natives near the central lake of Taupo, and there have been several skirmishes in that quarter. Reinforcements from the armed constabulary and from the native contingent have been sent up from Napier on the East, and from Wanganui on the West Coast. Titokowáru, with the remnant of his band, is supposed to be still in the dense forests near the base of Mount Egmont, not far from Taranaki, where it is believed that he is seeking aid from Wiremu Kingi te Rangitaki, the William King of Waitara, who began the present war in 1860. In short, the hostile clans are now planting their crops, and endeavouring to recruit their stores of ammunition. They have been hitherto supplied, to a large extent, by rene-gade European dealers. But some emissaries of the rebels were lately captured in the Waikato; and it is hoped that the organised police which the Colonial Government is now creating may be able to stop effectually the illegal sale of arms and gun-powder. The Maoris have a proverb similar to that of old respecting the 'time when Kings go to war.' Like the Red Indians of North America, whom, as it has been often observed, they closely resemble in many respects, the Maoris are accustomed to renew hostilities in the late summer, when their crops have been gathered. Fresh raids on the settlements may then be expected in New Zealand as in the Western States of North America ; but such partial outbreaks can be dealt with by the colonial forces and by the loyal clans. I remarked in a previous despatch that the part of ' Greater Britain ' which relates to New Zealand is admirably true and graphic : and I would venture to request attention to a typical Maori speech therein recorded : [1] ' O my guests !' said Kawana Hunia of the Ngatiapas, ' when ye return to our great Queen, tell her that we will fight for her again as we have fought before.

' She is our Queen as well as your Queen—Queen of Maoris and Queen of Pakeha.

' Should wars arise, we will take up our rifles, and march whithersoever she shall direct.

' You have heard of the King movement. I was a Kingite, but that did not prevent me fighting for the Queen—I and my chiefs.

' My cousin, Wiremu, went to England, and saw our Queen. He returned——

' When you landed in this island, he was already dead.

' He died fighting for our Queen.

' As he died, *we* will die, if need be—I and all my chiefs. This do you tell our Queen.

[1] See *Greater Britain*, Part II. chap. 4.

' I have said.'

This passage, spoken as Hunia spoke it, was one
of noble eloquence and singular rhetorical art.   The
few first words about Wiremu were spoken in a half
indifferent way; but there was a long pause before
and after the statement that he was dead, and a sinking of the voice when he related how Wiremu had
died, followed by a burst of sudden fire in the ' as he
died, *we* will die—I and all my chiefs.'

I may observe that speeches to a similar effect
have often been addressed to me by the loyal Maoris.

CHAPTER XVIII.

THE fire of war was gradually dying out, but to prevent its embers from being rekindled, the Governor continued his visits to the chief Maori clans. The following extract from a despatch describes his official tour in the district of Kaipara.

To the Earl Granville, K.G.

Government House, Auckland : October 25, 1869.

My Lord, . . .

Kaipara is a large inlet of the sea on the West Coast of the North Island, into which run several rivers, all navigable for many miles by vessels of considerable tonnage. On the banks of these streams there are forests of the Kauri pine (*Dammara Australis*) and other valuable timber trees ; while there is also an amount of fertile soil which would support a large agricultural population. As yet, however, the Europeans who have settled in the Kaipara district do not exceed one thousand (including women and children), while the Maoris, once numerous along these beautiful rivers, have now dwindled down to little more than seven hundred. With the exception of some Ngapuhis on the Wairoa, they are the remnant of the clan of the Ngatiwhátuas, to whom the country around the present site of Auckland formerly belonged, and who have always been firmly attached to the English. The Ngatiwhátuas occupied the country lying between the two most powerful and warlike clans in New Zealand, the Ngapuhis and the Waikatos, who were constantly at war with each other, and generally chose the intervening territory for their battle-ground. To quote from Sir W. Fox:[1] ' As these invasions were annual, the position of the Ngatiwhátuas became something worse than that of Belgium used to be among the belligerents of Europe. In short, as they told me on one occasion, ' if you English had not come, they would have eaten us up between them.' When we did come, the Ngatiwhátuas pressed on our acceptance the district where Auckland stands, and by getting us to occupy the intervening tract, they obtained the best possible security against the renewal of the raids through their own country, which had kept it in a continual state of desolation and alarm.'

Here it may be observed, in passing, that it seems to be generally forgotten in England that the colonisation of New Zealand, while it has led to temporary wars between the settlers and the natives

[1] *War in New Zealand*, p. 26.

in some parts of the North Island, has at the same
time stopped the savage and internecine strife which
formerly raged throughout the country among the
Maoris themselves.   During the last quarter of a
century the influence and mediation of the Colonial
Government have repeatedly prevented bloody struggles between the rival clans, and have thus signally
promoted the cause of humanity.   The principal
chiefs of the Kaipara receive among them about five
thousand pounds annually for the sale and rent of
their lands, and for licences to cut timber and procure Kauri gum—a valuable article of export from
the north of this island.   They are thus enabled to
live in comfort, and to hire European mechanics and
labourers to build them good houses and boats, and
to cultivate their farms and gardens.

We spent Sunday the 17th inst. at the *kainga* of
the influential chief, Arama Karáka, who has been
educated by the missionaries ; and we attended Divine
Service at his house.   Surrounded by his children and
clansmen, with their wives and families, he read
prayers in Maori, and afterwards delivered extempore
an excellent address from the text, 'Fear God and
honour the king'; enforcing the duties of obedience
to the law and the civil magistrate.   Nothing could be
more impressive than the devout manner in which
the responses were made and the hymns sung by the
entire congregation in their own sonorous language.

It so happens that I am the first Governor that
has ever visited Kaipara; and this fact alone was

sufficient to secure me a warm welcome from the
natives of the soil. The following is a full and literal
translation of the speech of one of the chiefs, and
conveys the sentiments expressed in similar terms
by the rest : ' Welcome, O Governor! salutations,
O Father! from all our tribe. Welcome to your
children at Kaipara. You are the first Governor
that has ever visited Kaipara. We welcome you
even as that bird so beloved by the Maoris, the
kotuku (i.e. the white crane of the Southern Seas,
rarely seen in New Zealand), which visits us but once
in a lifetime. This our country of Kaipara has
always been held as *tapu* (i.e. forbidden ground) by
former Governors, but now you have made it acces-
sible to all. The former Governors have treated it
as an abode of slaves ; but you have treated it as an
abode of chieftains (*Rangatira Kainga*). And yet
we have held fast the keys of our rivers, and refused
to open them to Heke, the fierce enemy of the Pakeha,
when he desired to advance through our tribe and
destroy Auckland.[1] And now, O Ngatiwhátuas! my
second sight (*takiri*) was true. I saw in my visions
the Governor arrive among us ; and lo! he is here.
Hearken, O spirits of our forefathers, of Tinana, and
of all the mighty dead [calling on the names of departed
chiefs], hearken! The Governor at last is here. O Governor ! we Maoris are passing away, even like the waning
moon ; there is little now to welcome you but the
everlasting hills and the ever-flowing rivers. [A *waiata*,

[1] i.e. during the first Maori War in 1845-8.

or traditional song of welcome, was then chanted.]
We hail you, O Governor! whose face our forefathers
yearned to see in the days that are gone.   The
hearts of us, the remnant of our people, the scattered
sheep of the Maori fold, have long been dark, but
they are now light.   We rejoice that you have brought
hither the *mana* (i.e. sovereign grace and power) of
Queen Victoria, to support and protect us.   Evil
men from among the Hau-haus have tried to tempt and
mislead us ; but now we shall hold fast unto death
the sovereignty of the Queen.   There are two things
to which we shall cleave,—the law of God, and the
law of the Queen.   If any man among us shall be
guilty of any crime, he shall be given up to the
law, even though he should be the son of a chief.
The rest of our island has been filled with raids, and
burnings, and blood ; with the screams of evil birds
of prey, with the howling winds of war and murder ;
but here, in Kaipara, there is the voice of peace, calm,
and sunshine.'   [Another *waiata* was then sung.]

My visit to the North is stated to have been
opportune, for Hau-hau emissaries have lately endeavoured to persuade or terrify into joining the rebellion the hitherto loyal or neutral clans, which had
begun to feel themselves neglected.

The firm but conciliatory policy adopted by Sir
George Bowen and his Government towards the Maoris
gradually brought about a much improved condition
of affairs.   As the Governor reported :

To the Same.

November 25, 1869.

It will be recollected that, on my first visit to the Waikato, I caused the tomb of his father, Potatau te Whero Whero, the first King of the Maoris, at Ngarua-wáhia, the old Maori capital, to be repaired; and I have been assured that this act produced a very favourable impression upon the mind of Tawhiao. Subsequent friendly overtures and negotiations, the success of the colonial forces against Te Kooti and Titokowáru in the field, and the moral support afforded to the Colony by two Queen's ships on the coast, have combined to keep the 'Maori King' and the clans that adhere to him, from open hostility, though (as it has been truly said) 'they have long been hanging on the central mountains of this island like a thunder-cloud, ready to burst at any moment on the English settlements.'

The general policy recommended by me in my former despatches was pronounced to be 'clearly judicious,' and was formally approved and sanctioned by your Lordship.[1] It was also adopted (as we have seen) by the Colonial Government. At the beginning of the present month. Mr. McLean, the Minister for Native Affairs, was permitted to cross the *Aukáti*, or 'pale,' and held a very satisfactory conference with the principal chiefs who have per-

---

[1] See Secretary of State to the Governor of New Zealand, February 26, and May 21, 1869. (*Parliamentary Papers*).

sisted during many years past in active or sullen
hostility—in particular, with Tamati Ngápora, the
uncle and chief councillor of King Tawhiao, and
with Rewi Maniapoto, the formidable warrior who
commanded the Maoris against the British troops
under General Cameron at Rangariri, Orákau, and
throughout the Waikato campaigns of 1863 and 1864.

Mr. McLean is convinced that Rewi was sincere
when he said that their recent interview was the
' streak of light before the dawn, which would soon
spread,' and that ere long King Tawhiao himself will
consent to meet the Governor at a formal conference,
when the foundations of permanent peace and tranquillity will be laid. Meanwhile, there is little doubt
that we need be no longer apprehensive of a general
rising of the hostile Maoris. The only favour which
Tamati Ngápora and Rewi asked was that their
relative Te Hura, and a few other natives still con-
fined at Auckland, under a sentence of the Supreme
Court, for their participation in the outbreak on the
East Coast in 1865, should be released and given up
to them; and to this request I readily consented.
In return, the chiefs of the 'King party' undertook
to be answerable for the future good conduct of these
men, and to assist the Government and the loyal clans
in putting down murder and brigandage. The Maoris
rarely fail to perform promises made at their public
Koreros, or meetings.

In April 1870, the Governor paid another visit to the northern tribes of the Ngapuhis and Rarawas;

To the Same.

Government House, Auckland : May 26, 1870.

My Lord,

I have the honour to transmit herewith a brief but accurate summary of my recent official visit to the great Maori clans of the North, viz. the Ngapuhis and the Rarawas. This account was written by a professional reporter connected with the colonial press, who took down in shorthand the substance of the speeches delivered by myself and by Mr. McLean (the Minister for Native Affairs), as also by the principal chiefs at the *koreros*, or general assemblies, of their tribes, held to welcome me.

It will be observed that the Maoris appeared highly pleased at seeing the representative of the Queen visiting their *kaingas*, or villages; and that I was everywhere received by them with strong and repeated assurances of their loyalty to the Crown, and of their good-will towards their British fellow-subjects. These feelings were expressed with equal warmth by the chiefs who fought against the English in the first Maori War (1845–8), and by Tamati Waka Nene and the other chiefs whose influence induced their countrymen to cede the sovereignty of New Zealand to the Queen by the Treaty of Waitangi, in 1840, and who have since supported Her Majesty's authority against their disaffected countrymen with constant devotion and gallantry. Cavalcades of mounted chiefs met and escorted me through each district; while, on my arrival at each *kainga*, I was received by the assembled clansmen with shouts and chants of welcome, and with the striking war dances of the Maoris, their traditional equivalent for military guards of honour.

The Statistics of New Zealand for 1867[1] show that when the last census was taken in the December of that year, the population of the long, narrow peninsula which stretches north of the city of Auckland was estimated to consist of nine thousand Europeans, and about the same number of Maoris. There has been little change during the past two years in the relative proportion of the two races in this part of the Colony. It is to be borne in mind, however, that the Europeans are chiefly settled in the country of the Ngatiwhátuas, that is, in the southern half of the peninsula; while in the country of the Ngapuhis and of the Rarawas, that is, in the northern half of the peninsula (comprising the districts of the Bay of Islands, Hokianga, and Mongonui), the Maoris are still by far the most numerous. In these last named districts they probably outnumber the Europeans in the aggregate by four to one; while in the extensive region watered by the Hokianga River and its tributaries, it is estimated that there are now fully two thousand natives and only one hundred Europeans.

[1] Any good map of New Zealand will show all the places referred to in this despatch.

Under these circumstances, it is not to be denied that, in the phrase addressed to me by one of the principal settlers in the north, ' the English there are living under the Maori tomahawk'; for their few and scattered homesteads are entirely at the mercy of the populous *kaingas* and *pahs* (native villages and forts) in their neighbourhood. However, notwithstanding —indeed partly (perhaps) in consequence of the weakness of the colonists in this quarter,—perfect mutual confidence and good-will exist between them and the Maoris. It will be remembered that the first Maori war was waged with a portion of the Ngapuhi clan under the chiefs Heke[1] and Kawiti; while the remainder of that tribe, under Tamati Waka Nene, fought in support of the sovereignty of the Queen and in alliance with the English troops. Even during that war the settlers were never molested by the hostile section of the Ngapuhis, who indeed prided themselves on carrying on the contest in a most chivalrous manner. It has been often repeated, for instance, how, when Heke captured a convoy of cattle on its way to the English camp, he not only allowed it to proceed, but actually sent some of his warriors to assist in driving the sheep and oxen through a difficult pass in the hills; observing that

[1] Heke has been dead for many years, but I was hospitably entertained at a feast given in my honour by his widow, the daughter of Hongi; who, in right both of her father and her husband, is regarded by the Ngapuhis as a great chieftainess. The elder Kawiti is also dead, but his son, Maihi Kawiti, who fought against the English in the first war, and lost two brothers in action with our troops, came to welcome me, and afterwards returned with me to Auckland.

he knew that English soldiers could not live, like
Maoris, on yams and fern-root;—that they could not
fight unless they were well fed on beef and mutton;
and that he had no wish to take them at a disadvantage; for, in that case, their defeat would reflect
no honour on his arms.

A main cause of the friendly feelings existing
between the natives and the colonists in the north
is doubtless the fact that several of the leading
settlers in early times, gentlemen of character and
education, married the daughters of Maori chiefs;
and that their children are now regarded as adopted
members of their mothers' tribe, and thus entitled to
its respect and protection. Again, a powerful influence has been exercised by the families of some of
the early missionaries, born in the northern districts,
and intimately acquainted with the language and the
customs of the people among whom they have lived
from their childhood. The result of these combining
influences is shown by the language of the address
presented to me by the English settlers, and by the
speeches of the Maori chiefs.

The settlers said: 'May it please your Excellency,—We, the European inhabitants of the Wai-
mate and its vicinity, beg to offer you a cordial
welcome to our district. Most of us are sons of the
soil, few of whom have seen our fatherland; but we
assure your Excellency that we glory in being an
integral part of the British nation; while in attachment to the throne and person of our gracious

Sovereign, and in veneration for the British Constitution, we yield to none of Her Majesty's subjects.

'Your Excellency will be pleased to learn that from our earliest days we have always lived with our fellow subjects of the Maori race on terms of perfect amity. We gladly avail ourselves of this opportunity of bearing testimony to their loyalty to Her Majesty's Government; and we have every confidence that it will be maintained.'

On the other hand, the speeches of the Maori chiefs of the North were full of assurances of their devoted loyalty to the Queen; of their affection for their European neighbours; and of their obedience to the law. It is a significant fact that the only two petitions which they made to me were: (1) That towns should be founded in their districts, so that more Europeans might come to live among them, and trade with them; and (2) that gaols should be built in the north, 'for the punishment of the evil doers of both races.' The Resident Magistrates find small difficulty in carrying out the law in this part of the island, though they have no armed force at their disposal, and could do little without the support of the native chiefs. Mohi Tawhai (the principal chief of Hokianga) welcomed me in the following terms on my arrival at his river:—
'Welcome, O Governor! Behold your canoe now floating in the waters of Hokianga.[1] It is not now

---

[1] This is the Maori form of placing a river at the disposal of the Governor.

only that we have joined the Queen. We were devoted to her in former years, and still remain so. Welcome, O Governor! and bring peace to us your children, that your laws may be a garment to spread over us, and that we may live under the shelter of your laws.' The other chiefs everywhere spoke to the same effect ; and their sentiments may be said to be summed up by Tiopira in the following terms :— 'Welcome, O Governor! in times of peace and quietness. I have only one word for you: Love, Love, Love. All we want is peace and good-will. . . . . . There is nothing we desire but that we should be all as one with the Europeans and the Government. Salutations to you, O Governor!'

That these professions are sincere has been abundantly proved by those of the northern Maoris who have so freely shed their blood for the Queen, and without whose support the English (in all probability) could hardly have held their ground in New Zealand during the first Maori War. And there are two eminently suggestive facts to record with respect to the altered feelings of those who fought against the Crown in that contest:

(a) It will be remembered that the object of the first Maori War (1845–8), as also, indeed, mainly of the second War which began in 1860, was to dispute the sovereignty of the Queen as recognised by the Treaty of Waitangi. Heke and Kawiti, at the head of a portion of the Ngapuhis, commenced the first war by cutting down the flagstaff at Kororareka in the Bay of Islands, for they regarded it as the symbol of the supremacy of the Crown. At the conclusion of the hostilities in the north it was not thought prudent (as I am informed) to replace this flagstaff; but a few years ago, Maihi Kawiti and others of our old enemies spontaneously re-erected it at their own expense and with their own labour; at the same time tendering to the Government a large grant of their land as a sign of permanent peace and good-will.

(*b*) When I visited, during my recent tour, the pah at Ohaiawai, in the attack on which, in July, 1845, the British troops[1] suffered a severe repulse, with heavy loss both in officers and men, I was much gratified to find that the Maoris who then fought against us had voluntarily, and entirely at their own cost, erected a pretty church among the now decayed palisades and rifle-pits; and that they had reserved the whole of the once fortified area as a cemetery, the natives who fell during the struggle having already been interred therein. When the Bishop of Auckland shall have consecrated this new burial-ground, the Maoris intend to remove into it the remains of our soldiers who now lie in unmarked graves in the neighbouring forest, and to erect a monument over them; so that, as an aged Chief,

---

[1] Consisting of detachments of the 58th, 96th, and 99th regiments and of seamen and marines from the men-of-war on the coast. An excellent account of the first Maori War, based on the Parliamentary Papers and official records, will be found in chapters 8 and 9 of Dr. Thomson's *Story of New Zealand*, published in London, 1859.

formerly conspicuous among our enemies, said to me, 'the brave warriors of both races, the white skin and the brown,—now that all strife between them is forgotten,—may sleep side by side until the end of the world.' I question if there be a more touching episode in the annals of the warfare of even civilised nations in either ancient or modern times.

It is, of course, well known that the Ngapuhis have always been the most powerful tribe in New Zealand, and that, about forty-five years ago, under their chief, Hongi Hika (who had been to England to request George IV. to assume the protectorate of New Zealand, and had been graciously received there), they invaded and overran the country of the Waikatos; whom they defeated with great slaughter. Both in their public speeches at the *Koreros*, and in their more private conferences with myself and Mr. McLean, the leading Ngapuhi chiefs condemned in emphatic language the conduct of the 'King of the Waikatos' (as they somewhat contemptuously style Tawhiao) in renouncing his allegiance to the Queen, and in virtually relapsing into heathenism by his adoption of the Hau-hau creed. This general sentiment was explained in one of the Maori speeches :—'Welcome, O Governor! I rise to tell you that myself and my tribe are attached to the Queen and to the Government. I wish you to have no doubts respecting our loyalty. Other tribes will speak for themselves. I speak on behalf of my own tribe. Do not suppose that I sympathise in any way with the

Waikato king. What has he done for me? Nothing at all. We are of one skin and of one blood, but our thoughts differ. The ancient trees of the forest [alluding to the chiefs of former days] have disappeared; we are a young people, growing up in their stead. From my youth up I have experienced nothing but kindness from the Queen. [The chief here took from his pocket a sovereign.] I hold in my hand the image of the Queen. It was this increased my civilisation, and supplied me with food and clothing. Had it not been for this [i.e. for the progress of civilisation under the sovereignty of the Queen], I should have no food nor clothing. Why, then, should I recognise the Waikato king, or sympathise with him? I adhere to the law of the Queen.'

At the same time, the Ngapuhis signified their entire concurrence with the policy shadowed forth in several of my despatches, and adopted by the Colonial Government; i.e. 'to make a peaceful arrangement, not inconsistent with the sovereignty of the Queen,' with Tawhiao and his adherents; and to leave him undisturbed so long as he confines himself to his own immediate territory. While the Ngapuhis are willing to give their mediation and good offices (if requested by the Colonial Government) to maintain tranquillity, they assured me and Mr. McLean that if Tawhiao and his Waikatos should hereafter attack the English settlements, 'the only feeling of the Ngapuhis, in the event of such violation of peace, would be to go in a body, and fight on behalf of the Government.'

Mr. Maning (the author of 'Old New Zealand,' and now one of the Judges of the Native Land Court), who has lived among the Ngapuhis for forty years, assures me that they could still bring into the field 'fully two thousand picked warriors.' In his opinion, the Ngapuhis, unlike the rest of the Maoris, are not materially decreasing in numbers. He thinks, indeed, that, in the district of Hokianga, they have positively increased of late years. He ascribes this satisfactory result mainly to their improved and civilised habits of life; and to their general use of good food and clothing, which the sale of their timber, flax, and kauri gum enables them to procure from the English traders settled among them. Moreover, several of the leading chiefs make strenuous efforts to prevent the spread of indulgence in spirituous liquors and of other vices, which have everywhere proved fatal to savage or semi-civilised races.

I may here mention that the leading Maori chiefs of the north, together with their wives, attended the ball which I gave at the Government House on the 24th instant in honour of Her Majesty's birthday. On that occasion, Kawiti and others of our former enemies were observed sitting near the widows of the Colonels who commanded the 58th and 96th regiments in the first Maori War, and in friendly conversation with several retired officers of those corps who have settled in the Colony.[1]

[1] When one of the formerly hostile Maori chiefs was told that the

On the whole,—so far as any certainty can be said to exist respecting a country circumstanced as is New Zealand, and respecting such a race as the Maoris—the colonial authorities feel a confident assurance that permanent tranquillity will be maintained in the north, and that they may rely not only on the friendship, but also, in case of need, on the active support of the Ngapuhis, the most powerful native tribe. All those best acquainted with the Maoris believe that my visits to the principal clans have produced a good effect, and that the general sentiments of the natives were truly expressed in the *waiata*, or chant of welcome, with which I was received at Hokianga :—'Lo! now the Governor has at length arrived. My heart has longed to see him, —whom our tribes, far and near, have united to acknowledge and recognise in terms of friendship and love. Welcome, O Governor! . . . In days gone by, the laws of God and the laws of the Queen stood side by side. Under the shadow of those laws our tribes take sweet repose, free from danger and surprise. Now at length the Governor has appeared. We see him in person. We speak with him face to face. Now, O Governor! this your presence at Hokianga will be the means of cementing in one bond of unity and fellowship the tribes of the

widows of these colonels were in the ball-room, he asked to be presented to them ; and, bowing low, thus addressed them : ' Ladies, when I was young I fought against your gallant husbands; I am now old, and I hope that I shall ere long meet them in Paradise, for they were indeed noble *toas* (warriors).'

Pakeha and the tribes of the Maoris, so that they shall henceforth live together in peace and friendship under one law and under one Governor.'

An interesting scene took place at Wellington on the anniversary of the Queen's accession, June 20, 1870, in the ceremony of presenting the swords of honour sent out by Her Majesty as tokens of recognition of the valour and loyalty of Te Kepa, Ropata, Mokena, and four other loyal chiefs. The chiefs having advanced for the purpose of receiving the swords, the Governor, who was attended by his Ministers and Staff, said:

'My friends, Te Kepa, Ropata, and Mokena,— The Queen has sent out from England swords of honour to be presented to you and to certain other Maori chiefs, in recognition of your loyalty to her Crown, and of your gallant services in support of her Government and of the cause of law and order in New Zealand. Her Majesty has commanded me, as her representative, to invest you with these swords, as tokens of her royal favour. I now proceed to perform this honourable duty on this day, June 20, which is the 33rd anniversary of the accession of the Queen, who, soon after she ascended the throne of England, became, through the Treaty of Waitangi, the Sovereign also of this country. I am glad, more- over, to carry out the commands of our Queen, by bestowing on you these marks of distinction in the presence of the Ministers and other chief officers of the Government, and of many members of the Parliament. And now to you, Te Kepa, I deliver this sword. Never shall I forget how, when I went to Wanganui, in November, 1868, at a time of much danger and distress, and called upon your tribe again to take arms for the Queen and the law, reminding you of the dying words of your great chief and near kinsman, Hori Kingi te Anaua; never shall I forget, I say, how you, Te Kepa, sprang forward, with the gallant spirit of your ancestors, and declared that you were again ready to take the field. Since that day you have been almost constantly on active service against the enemies of the Queen; and your march across this island, from Wanganui to Opotiki, in spite of many and great difficulties, is an exploit thoroughly appreciated both here and in England. You have been ably and bravely assisted by your friend Topia Turoa, on whom also a mark of the approval of the Queen's Government will be hereafter bestowed. Te Kepa, here is your sword. It bears on the blade this inscription—'Given by Queen Victoria to Te Kepa for his unfailing loyalty and valour.' May you long wear it in health and honour. To you, Ropata and Mokena, I now present, in the name of the Queen, these swords, which also bear your names and similar inscriptions with that presented to Te Kepa. Your tribe, the Ngatiporou, have rivalled the Wanganuis in loyalty to the Crown, in goodwill to your English neighbours, and in gallantry in war. Your services in many a severe conflict on the East Coast since 1865, as well as at Ngatapa and elsewhere, and your late expedition through the Urewera country, are well known and thoroughly appreciated; and I am confident that you will continue your efforts, in co-operation with the other forces of the Government and with the other loyal Maori tribes, until peace shall have been permanently established throughout this island. Here, Ropata and Mokena, are your swords, presented to you by the Queen. May you also long wear them in health and honour. And now, my friends, I trust that the ceremony of this day may be auspicious, and that, by the blessing of God, before another anniversary of the Queen's accession shall arrive, her heart may be gladdened with the tidings that the clouds of war and evil have passed away from this fair land, and that both races, the Pakeha and the Maori, are dwelling together under equal laws and in friendship and prosperity.'

Te Kepa Rangihiwhinui then replied in Maori, of which a *verbatim* translation is given :—O Queen Victoria! by the grace of God long may you live. May your children, the Prince of Wales, the Duke of Edinburgh, and the Princesses live long. I thank Victoria, Queen of this world, for casting her eyes in this direction, upon us, this dark-skinned people, this distant people. I thank the Queen heartily for sending me this proof of her love across the billows of the great sea. Here it is,—the sickle with which evil is to be cut down. Your ancestors, the Kings, have been protected by God, and so also yourself. There you stand on the most sacred place of your ancestors—the Kings of great fame of old. And now you have caused the sun to shine over this our island. It is very good that the elder and younger brother should live together, as they did in the Ark. Afterwards, the elder and the younger brother were divided. Now,

in this year for the first time they are again united.
I and my tribes are under the authority of the
Queen. This was Hori Kingi's last word to me,
and to all his tribe : ' When I am gone, remain quiet
under the authority of the Queen : be loyal to her.'
And to me especially he said : ' Be strong in putting
down evil, that peace may be secured in the future.'
Well, now that this pledge of your affection is here
before me, I trust that peace will always be with
you, O Queen Victoria ! and with your children.
May peace be with you, O Governor Bowen ! with
Lady Bowen, and your children. May peace be with
the Government of New Zealand. Let love be in
your hearts.

*To the Earl of Kimberley, Secretary of State for
the Colonies.*[1]

Government House, Wellington : August 23, 1870.

My dear Lord,

My plan of engaging the friendly clans to fight on
the side of law and order, and to make roads through
their own mountains and forests, while the so-called
Maori King and his adherents were given to understand that they will be left undisturbed so long as
they remain quiet within their own territory, was at
first unpopular in many quarters. Indeed, a year
ago, my Ministers and I were attacked in a portion
of the Press for arming the loyal clans, making a
peaceful arrangement with Tawhiao, and for refusing to
proclaim martial law, or (under the peculiar circum-

---

[1] Lord Kimberley had succeeded Lord Granville at the Colonial
Office.

stances of the Colony) to hang the Maori prisoners, unless proved guilty before the Supreme Court of murder or some other atrocity, in addition to carrying arms against the Government. But now our success has made the Parliament and public agree that we were right, and the result is almost perfect political quietude.

The Maoris are certainly a most interesting race. As Scholars as well as Statesmen, your Lordship, Mr. Gladstone, and many of your colleagues would delight in seeing a *Korero*, or meeting of the natives. It is very Homeric. I send herewith photographs of my friends Te Kepa and Ropata, the chiefs who have fought so gallantly for the Crown since my appeal to them when I went to Wanganui in November 1868, at the time of the Poverty Bay massacre.[1] Te Kepa is a chief of very high birth, and can count his pedigree from the time when the Maoris, led by one of his ancestors, first landed in New Zealand about 600 years ago. He is very gentlemanlike in manners and appearance, and not darker than most Portuguese nobles. Indeed, if he were in a London drawing-room, people would ask ' Who is that distinguished foreign officer ? ' The Duke of Edinburgh was much struck with him. When he dined with me to meet the Duke, he was suffering from inflammation in his eyes, caught through exposure in the field while in arms for the Queen. When the Duke expressed his regret for the suffering which his loyalty had brought on him, he ex-

[1] See above, page 334-35.

claimed to the interpreter : 'Tell the Prince that I care not how soon I become even blind in fighting for his mother, now that mine eyes have seen the son of my Queen.' Is not this the sort of speech that Cameron of Lochiel might have made to Charles Edward at Holyrood in 1745 ? I am informed on high authority that the Queen was much interested and gratified by this incident.[1]

I have had a very arduous task here, for I have had to contend with a very formidable outbreak of the Hau-haus (i.e. of the Maoris who have renounced their allegiance to the Queen, and relapsed into heathenism), without any aid from England, though there were lately as many insurgent Maoris in the field as during the period when there was an army of 10,000 regular troops in this country. And, more recently, as will be seen from the New Zealand press, and from the debates in the New Zealand Parliament,

---

[1] Another incident occurred at the dinner referred to above. Among the loyal Maori chiefs invited to meet the Duke of Edinburgh was one of the original signers of the Treaty of Waitangi in 1840, and who had ever since been a firm friend of the English. One of the Anglican Bishops afterwards said to the Governor : ' Do you know, sir, the antecedents of that old heathen ? ' ' No, my dear Bishop,' was the reply, ' but I do know that he brought five hundred of his clansmen into the field to fight for the Queen, so I invited him to meet the "Queen's Son." ' ' Well,' continued the Bishop, ' when I first arrived in New Zealand, that chief came to me and said that he wished to be baptized. I knew that he had two wives, so I told him that he must first persuade one of them to return to her family. He said he feared that would be difficult, but that he would see what could be done, and come back to me in two months. When he returned, he exclaimed, " Now, Missionary, you may baptize me, for I have only one wife." I asked, " What have you done with our dear sister, your first wife ? " He replied, smacking his lips, " *I have eaten her !* " '

I have had to struggle with a very general spirit of disaffection to the Imperial Government, arising out of the removal of the last Imperial regiment while the native war was still raging, though the Colonial Parliament had engaged to pay its entire cost. But I am thankful to say that I believe the worst is now over. The Hau-haus see that the colonists and loyal clans are too strong for them, and the Maoris generally believe that it will be more pleasant and profitable to trade with the English than to fight with them. On the other hand, the concession of the Imperial guarantee of the loan of a million sterling for colonial defences; and, above all, the kindly and sympathetic language of the Secretary of State in his recent communications, are fast causing the revival of the old loyalty of New Zealand.

To the Same.

Government House, Wellington : September 24, 1870.

My dear Lord,

I am very grateful for your most kind and encouraging letter of July 17, which reached me by the last mail. I read to the Colonial Ministers those paragraphs in which you express your sympathy with this Colony and your appreciation of the very difficult position in which I am placed, further assuring the colonists that the policy of England 'is not a mere selfish one, but is believed to be really the best for the interests of the Colony itself'; and that 'you greatly admire the promptitude and energy, worthy of men of English descent, with which the colonists have recently dealt with the native difficulty.' These words had a most happy effect. Mr. Fox,[1] the Prime Minister, and others of the leading public men here, say that they have a grateful recollection of the valuable assistance which you gave twenty years ago to the Canterbury Association, and, somewhat later, towards the passing of the New Zealand Constitution Act. The concession of Lord Granville about the guarantee to the loan ; his personal courtesy to the New Zealand Commissioners in England ; and, above all, the completely altered tone of the despatches from the Colonial Office during the last few months, had caused the tide of feeling here to turn ; and now your letter has carried it to the flood. What is the immediate result ? Why, that even those who four or five months ago were all agog for separation from England, and annexation to the United States, are now loyal again, and the Ministers asked me to include·in the Prorogation Speech a congratulation to the Parliament on the cordial relations re-established with the mother-country ! It is national sympathy and not dry logic which keeps a great Empire

[1] Now Sir William Fox, K.C.M.G. Sir George Bowen was his guest in November, 1868, at Rangitikei, some thirty miles from Wanganui, but only one mile from a large village of Hau-haus, who 'plainly told Mr. Fox that they would rise and kill him and all the other Pakehas in the district if so ordered by King Tawhiao.' In the following year Sir G. Bowen was again the guest of Sir W. Fox, when the Governor and his Prime Minister rode together from Wanganui to Taranaki through the country recently laid waste by Titokowáru, but where they were loyally received by Hone Pihama, and other chiefs formerly in rebellion.

together; and, whatever may be the future destiny
of the British Colonies, all would allow it to be a
grave misfortune to permit the separation to be so
precipitated, or matters so to 'drift,' as to produce
in Australasia the bitter and lasting rancour against
England so long prevalent in America.

In a recent letter (1889) to an English Statesman,
Sir G. Bowen wrote as follows :—

'I have always retained a deep sense of the
steady support which I received from Lord Kimberley
on all occasions, and especially during the manifold
difficulties which I had to encounter while Governor
of New Zealand.   Other Governors have expressed a
similar feeling.   Above all, the greatest of our living
Proconsuls, the Marquis of Dufferin and Ava, once
made to me this striking remark: " While Lord
Kimberley was Secretary of State I always felt, in
difficult times, like a man fighting with a strong wall
at his back." '

CHAPTER XIX.

FINAL CLOSE OF THE TEN YEARS' WAR—THE GOVERNOR'S RIDE
THROUGH THE INTERIOR OF THE NORTH ISLAND FROM
WELLINGTON TO AUCKLAND—SUBMISSION OF THE FORMER
REBELS—ALBERT VICTOR POMARE—LETTER TO SIR T. M.
BIDDULPH—MAORI MEMBERS IN THE COLONIAL PARLIAMENT.

THE just and politic measures of the Government
and Parliament, and the gallantry of the colonial
forces, both English and native, finally brought
to a close, towards the end of 1870, the Maori
war, which had lasted as long as the war of Troy—·
for ten years since 1860. As it was remarked
at the time : 'a judicious mixture of firmness and
conciliation has at length subdued those formidable
foemen :—

Quos neque Tydides nec Larissæus Achilles,
Non anni domuere decem, non mille carinæ : [1]

That is, whom neither Generals Cameron and Chute,
with their army of 10,000 regular troops, nor the
strong squadron of men-of-war, with its naval brigade
on shore, had succeeded in conquering during the
war of the last ten years.'

Subjoined are reports of the Governor's visits to
the lately disturbed districts :

[1] Virgil, *Æn.* II. 197.

To the Earl of Kimberley.

Government House, Wellington, New Zealand :
December 12, 1871.

My Lord,

I have the honour to report that I proceeded by sea to Wanganui on November 27th ult., and returned thence to Wellington overland on the 5th instant.

The immediate cause of this expedition was the invitation of the provincial and municipal authorities, and also of the Maori chiefs of the district, that I should open the iron bridge which has now been completed over the river Wanganui. This is an important public work, being only about one hundred and twenty feet shorter than London Bridge. It was designed by the eminent civil engineer, Mr. George Robert Stephenson; and the materials were chiefly constructed in England, but they were put together and erected on the spot by a colonial contractor.

It will be recollected that Wanganui is one of the earliest European settlements in New Zealand, dating from 1842. Situated near the mouth of the principal river, and in the centre of the most fertile districts in the western portion of the Province of Wellington, it would have made rapid progress had it not been for the almost constant Maori wars and disturbances which have frequently threatened its very existence. However, the town, situated on the right bank of the navigable river Wanganui, and about four miles from

the sea, already contains nearly four thousand
European inhabitants; and, now that permanent
tranquillity appears to have been established, it has
every prospect of a successful future. On the left
bank, nearly opposite the town, is Putiki, the principal *kainga* of the great Maori clan of the Wanganuis, of which Te Kepa is the leading chief.

In my reply to the address of the settlers, I spoke
as follows: ‘ This, gentlemen, is my third visit to
Wanganui. I have not forgotten that, in the address
presented to me on the occasion of my first visit, in
November, 1868, you expressed your regret that I
“ should have arrived among you at a time when a
native insurrection was raging within a few miles of
this town, and when your hearts were saddened by
the loss of no inconsiderable number of your fellow
settlers, who had gallantly shed their blood in the
defence of the throne and of their adopted country.”
Permit me now to congratulate you on the very
striking improvement which has taken place in the
condition and prospects of your town and district
during the brief period of the last three years. In
November, 1868, a formidable rebellion had broken
out in your immediate neighbourhood, and the rebels,
after devastating the whole country to the west,
had advanced to within ten miles of your suburbs.
Under these circumstances, I came among you myself, having been assured that my presence at that
perilous crisis would prove of public advantage, especially in stimulating the zeal of your Maori allies,

who, indeed, headed by the gallant Te Kepa, took up arms at my call.

'My second visit to Wanganui was in September, 1869, when I rode overland from this town to Patea. All pressing danger had then passed away, but there still existed a general feeling of insecurity. Now, on my third visit, I find that the wisdom and firmness of the Legislature, ably seconded by the gallantry of our local forces, both European and Native, and by the public spirit of the population at large, have established what I trust will prove permanent tranquillity and confidence. The settlements laid waste by the rebels have been reoccupied and extended; and a public coach is now running from Wanganui to Taranaki, through the country which four years ago could not be safely traversed even by a very large force of Imperial and Colonial troops. The facts to which I have referred are well known to all who now hear me; but it seems expedient to place them on record for the benefit of those at a distance who are deeply interested in the welfare of New Zealand.'

The address of the natives was read on the bridge by the gallant Te Kepa, surrounded by the chiefs and clansmen of his tribe. He wore his uniform as a major in the Colonial Militia, and the sword of honour presented to him by the Queen. During my stay at Wanganui, on this as on former occasions, I paid a special visit to the Maoris at their own *kainga* of Putiki, and was again received with the customary war dance and chants of welcome. In

the *Korero* which followed, and which was attended
by several chiefs recently in arms against the Crown,
all the speeches were of the most loyal and peaceful
character ; and I was assured that I might always
rely on the active support, alike in peace and in war,
of the Maori clans which have already fought so long
and so bravely for the Queen.

The Maoris asked permission to row Lady Bowen
and myself, together with my family and suite, in
their war-canoes up the beautiful Wanganui River.
Except in the immediate neighbourhood of the town,
no Europeans have as yet settled on its banks, but
they are studded with picturesque native villages,
at each of which the Governor and his party were
greeted with shouts and songs of welcome. At night
we encamped under tents at one or other of these
kaingas, our Maori hosts gathering for us the flowering shrubs of their country, which form a soft, elastic,
and fragrant couch. The scenery of the upper part
of the Wanganui River resembles in many of its
features that of the Rhine between Cologne and
Mannheim. The old towns and castles are, of course,
wanting here, but the vegetation of Germany is far
surpassed by the magnificent and almost tropical
luxuriance of the New Zealand forests. Nothing can
be more striking and suggestive than the sight of a
fleet of Maori war-canoes, such as that which conveyed
and escorted us. The prow and stern of each canoe
ends in a highly curving peak, carved in fantastic
shapes, gay with streaming pennons of divers colours,

and profusely decorated with the feathers of the kiwi
(*Apteryx*) and albatross. Each canoe is rowed by
from twenty to fifty kilted warriors, while in the
midst stands a chief, with the spear (*taieka*) and
greenstone sceptre (*mere punamu*) of his rank, guiding and encouraging his clansmen by voice and gesture,
and marking the time for the rhythmical stroke of the
paddles and for the wild chants with which it is
accompanied.[1]

Although all is now calm and peaceful on the
Wanganui River, it will be recollected that much
sharp fighting took place on its banks in both the
first and second Maori Wars, and especially in the
years 1864 and 1865. In the early part of the
former year a large party of Hau-haus from the interior attempted to descend the river, with the object
of sacking and burning the town; but they were
met and utterly defeated by the loyal Maoris in the
fiercely contested battle of Moutoa (May 14, 1864).
A handsome monument has been erected in the
market-place of Wanganui by the Provincial Government of Wellington, to the memory of the Maoris
who fell at Moutoa.[2]

On my return last week overland from Wanganui
to Wellington, I found everything tranquil and prosperous, where, on my previous journey through the

[1] A sketch of a Maori war-canoe is given in the frontispiece to Sir
George Grey's *Polynesian Mythology*.

[2] A full account of the fighting near Wanganui in 1864 and 1865 will
be found in Sir W. Fox's *War in New Zealand*, chaps. 9 and 14, and
in the Parliamentary Papers of those years.

same districts in November, 1868, all was confusion
and terror. The colonists are everywhere improving
their homesteads and steadily extending their farms;
while the Maoris, who were recently on the point of
coming to blows among themselves respecting the
ownership of some land at Horowhenua, near Otaki,
have listened to the advice and exhortations of myself
and of Mr. McLean, and agreed to submit their pre-
tensions to arbitration.

The above and some shorter tours were followed
by Sir G. Bowen's ride through the interior of the
North Island, which was regarded at the time as
another turning-point in the history of the Colony.
He reported (April 1, 1872):

'I propose to ride across the centre of the North
Island, from Wellington to Auckland, by Napier, the
great central lake of Taupo, the Hot Lakes, and the
Waikato. This journey will probably occupy from a
fortnight to three weeks, and much of it will necessarily be of a very rough nature, as lying beyond the
limits to which colonisation has hitherto extended.
But it is expected by those who know the Maoris
best, that a visit from the representative of the
Queen to the native tribes of the central interior will
be productive of much political advantage; while
confidence in England as to the permanent tranquillity
of New Zealand will be confirmed when it is known
that the Governor has himself crossed in safety so
many of the recently hostile and disaffected districts.'

The following letters give some description of this anxious but very important journey :

To R. G. W. Herbert, Esq., Permanent Under Secretary of State for the Colonies.

Lake of Taupo, New Zealand: April 9, 1872.

My dear Herbert,

I wrote to you from Wellington on the eve of my departure on my overland journey to Auckland through the centre of this island and the heart of the native districts. Many persons, although all agreeing on the great importance of the Governor undertaking this expedition, felt anxious about its difficulties and dangers; and, as I told you, I was not myself without some presentiment of evil. But this day I have the great happiness of writing officially to Lord Kimberley from the shores of the great central lake of Taupo; which was as little known to the first settlers of New Zealand thirty years ago as the great lakes in the interior of Africa are now known to the Europeans resident at Alexandria and the Cape of Good Hope. Moreover, until within the last few months, the natives of these central districts were devoted to the so-called Maori King, and (with the single exception of the Chief Poihipi, the friend and guide of the late Lt. Meade [1]) they were hostile to the Queen and to all white men. In 1869, they joined the rebel leader Te Kooti, when there was much hard fighting at Tokano and elsewhere (as described

---

[1] See the excellent account of his adventures in *A Ride through New Zealand*, by Lt. the Hon. H. Meade, R.N.

in my despatches at the time), between the insurgents and the colonial forces, and the loyal clans led by the gallant Te Kepa. Last night I slept at Opepe, ten miles from my present quarters ; where in June, 1869, a detachment of the colonial forces was surprised and slaughtered by Te Kooti; and I have been received with shouts of joy and welcome in the country where Lt. Meade had literally (as he says in his book) ' to ride for his life.' The chiefs and tribes so lately in arms against the Queen, assure me that they are now convinced of the good intentions towards them of my Government, and that their true interest is to live in peace and harmony with the colonists. They are quite clamorous to be employed on the roads which are gradually but surely creeping up from the coast into their mountain fastnesses, and which will soon render all future rebellions practically impossible. Several chiefs have taken contracts for making, by the labour of their clansmen, the road of ninety miles from the port of Napier to Lake Taupo. Half of it is already finished; and, strange and incredible as such a statement would have been only two years ago, it will be completed within six months from this date ; and a coach, subsidised by the Government, will then run twice a week into the heart of the (lately) rebel country. The Lake of Taupo is of about the same size (200 square miles of water) with the Lake of Geneva, which it much resembles. From the hut in which I am now writing, there is a glorious view across its waters to the burning mountain of Tongariro (6,200 feet) and the peak of Ruapehu (9,200 feet high), both covered with snow, and glittering in the bright sunshine and pellucid air.   To-morrow I cross over to Tokano, the scene of the fiercely contested battle of October, 1869, but where our late enemies are now assembled to give me an enthusiastic welcome.   They like seeing the Governor coming among them with only one aide-de-camp, two officers of the Colonial Government, and a few mounted orderlies.   There is nothing in Italy finer than the scenery through which we have been riding during the last few days.   On our return from Tokano, we shall continue our ride overland to Auckland, a ride of about a fortnight now, but which will be a drive of four or five days before long.[1]   The Maoris are waiting outside for a *Korero* with the Governor, so I must conclude.

P.S. The speeches of the Maori chiefs were quite enthusiastically loyal.   They placed their villages, their lands, their arms, everything they have, at the disposal of the Queen, and of the Governor, *à vendre et à pendre*, in the sentiment of the old French saying.

To the Earl of Kimberley.

Lake of Taupo, New Zealand: April 12, 1872.

My dear Lord,

My last despatches will have informed your Lordship of my intended journey across the centre

---

[1] Now, in 1889, railways run over most of the country through which Sir G. Bowen rode in 1872.

of this island; to which great importance is attached on public grounds; and also of my successful arrival at the great central lake (or as the Maoris call it, ' Sea '—*Moana*) of Taupo.

On the 9th ultimo I wrote that, after an enthusiastic reception by the Maoris at the north end of the lake, one of whom, Poihipi, is among the few survivors of the chiefs who signed, in 1840, the treaty of Waitangi, ceding the sovereignty of New Zealand to the British Crown, I was about to cross over to Tokano at the south end, where a large number of those lately in arms against the Queen were assembled to give their submission. I received a still more enthusiastic greeting from these ex-rebels, who assured me that they had returned to Christianity as well as to their allegiance to the Queen, a fact which they wished to prove by quoting largely (though not at all in a profane tone or manner) from Scripture; stating, for example, that they should be admitted to favour ' like the labourers who came in at the eleventh hour,' and hoping that the Government would act on the principle of the text, ' that there is more joy in Heaven over one sinner that repenteth, than over ninety-and-nine just persons who need no repentance.' Herman Merivale says somewhere that colonists bear no malice, however fierce their temporary quarrels, against 'Downing Street,' as they always call the Colonial Office; and really Maori rebels seem to be equally forgiving. One chief, who was our guide at the south end of the Lake, had lost an eye and a hand in fighting against our forces; and one old chieftainess, who was almost too affectionate in her welcome to me, had lost a brother and two sons in the war. I addressed the assembled warriors at some length, fully explaining the gracious intentions of my Government; and I was answered in very loyal speeches. The chiefs said that they had only the following requests to make: 1. To have ' Queen's flags' (i.e. Union Jacks) to hoist in all their Pahs, instead of the rebel, or Hau-hau, flags, which they have everywhere destroyed. 2. That a township might be founded on the shores of the Lake, and called 'Bowen,' after my name. 3. That they might be employed in making roads through their own country. 4. That the Government would place a steamer on the lake, so that there might be easy access to all their settlements for the officers of Government, and for colonists desirous to lease or buy portions of their land. It will be easily understood that no objection was made on my part to any of these requests.

I rode from Tokano to the beautiful Lake Rotoaira at the foot of the burning mountain of Tongariro. This is, speaking geographically, one of the most interesting spots in New Zealand, for here nearly all the principal rivers of the North Island have their sources within a few miles of each other: the Waikato flowing to the north, the Wanganui to the south, and so forth. I was reminded of that famous pass in Pindus, whence flow the Achelous, the Peneus, the Haliacmon, and the other chief rivers of Northern Greece, and where Aristœus

Omnia sub magnâ labentia flumina terrâ
Spectabat diversa locis.[1]————

From the south end of the Lake of Taupo stretches away a vast extent of rich and beautiful plains and valleys at present almost without a single inhabitant of any race. But now that peace is firmly established, the sheep-farmers are already in treaty with the native owners for leases enabling them to depasture stock. As I rode along in the shadow of the mighty Tongariro with one of the Maori lords of the soil, he said that he had lived to see many changes, and that he still hoped to see the primeval forests felled; the fair plains and valleys before us dotted with tens of thousands of sheep and cattle; English steamers rushing over the lakes; English towns and villages springing up on the banks of the rivers; so that the sale and rents of his domains might enable him to spend his old age in comfort, and to educate his children in the language and learning of the English. I thought of Longfellow's 'Hiawatha:'

I beheld too in that vision
All the secrets of the future,
Of the distant days that shall be.
I beheld the westward marches
Of the unknown crowded nations.
All the land was full of people,

[1] Virgil, *Georg.* IV. 366.

Restless, struggling, toiling, striving,
Speaking many tongues, yet feeling
But one heart-beat in their bosoms.
In the woodlands rang their axes,
Smoked their towns in all the valleys,
Over all the lakes and rivers
Rushed their great canoes of thunder.

From Lake Taupo Sir G. Bowen continued his ride through the territories of the native clans to Auckland. On May 15, 1872, he wrote to Lord Kimberley :

' I have now the satisfaction of reporting that the second half was as prosperous as the first half of my expedition; and that I reached Auckland on the 24th ultimo, at the end of what has been truly called " an important and memorable journey." All those who are best acquainted with the Maoris and with this country generally agree with the opinions expressed in the annexed leading article of one of the principal journals of New Zealand :

' " The tour overland through the extensive tract of country chiefly owned and occupied by the native tribes of New Zealand, which has just been accomplished so successfully by His Excellency Governor Sir G. F. Bowen, will go farther to reassure the people of England with respect to the satisfactory settlement of the native difficulty than a thousand arguments and *ex parte* statements on the subject. Throughout the entire distance traversed by His Excellency and the few attendants who accompanied him from Wellington northward till they reached the

Upper Waikato, the most cheerful demonstrations of welcome and good-will were everywhere accorded to the Queen's representative. Not only by the influential chiefs who remained firm in their allegiance to the European cause in days gone by, when the Colony stood so much in need of their assistance, but by many who were at one time prominent leaders among the most determined of our enemies, the same hearty desire was expressed that the past should be forgotten, and that all occasion for differences between the races should be carefully guarded against for the future." '

The Earl of Kimberley to Sir G. Bowen.

Downing Street: August 21, 1872.

Sir,

I have to acknowledge your despatch of the 9th April, written from the Lake of Taupo, in the course of your expedition from Wellington to Auckland, and your further despatch of the 15th of May, announcing the completion of your journey.

I have much pleasure in congratulating you upon the success of this expedition, and upon the satisfactory evidences which you received at each place of the intentions and disposition of the Maoris.

These despatches afford striking confirmation of the success of the native policy adopted by your Government.

The following letter will be read with special interest :

To Major-General Sir T. M. Biddulph, K.C.B.,
Private Secretary to the Queen.

Wellington : August 12, 1872.

My dear Sir,

In your last letter to me, you were good enough to say you would like to hear occasionally about the welfare and progress of Albert Victor Pomare,[1] the Maori boy whom the Queen supports at the Orphan Home near Auckland. I was lately there, and made it my business to visit this interesting child at his school, and to see him elsewhere. He is in excellent health and seems quite happy. The matron and teachers of the Orphan Home, as also Lady Martin (the wife of the late Chief Justice), Mrs. Cowie (the wife of the Bishop of Auckland), and other ladies who visit and manage it, all speak in high terms of the good conduct and good disposition of the little Albert, and of his general progress. All recommend that he should remain where he is for at least two years more ; and I entirely concur in this view. He is very grateful to his royal benefactress ; and, as I mentioned in a former letter, the great clan of the Ngapuhis, to which he belongs (and which is as powerful in New Zealand as the Campbells are in Scotland), has a loyal and dutiful sense of Her Majesty's bounty to a child of the clan.

It appears from your last letter, that you take an interest in the progress of affairs in New Zealand ; and, indeed (if I mistake not), some members of

---

[1] The orphan son of a loyal Maori chief.

E E 2

your family took an active part in the foundation of this Colony. Accordingly, I venture to send you a brief account of my late journey from Wellington to Auckland, across the central Highlands, and through the recently hostile districts. This account was drawn up from notes taken at the time by one of the officers of the Government who accompanied me.

My journey overland is considered by all the best judges to be a fresh turning point in the history of this Colony, and to afford the best proof of the establishment of permanent tranquillity. Soon after my arrival in New Zealand in 1868, I pointed out in my early despatches to the Secretary of State (many of which have been presented to the Imperial Parliament) that the state of the Maori Highlands at the present day closely resembles in many respects that of the Scotch Highlands one hundred and fifty years ago. The Maori clans were lately divided into the loyal subjects of the Queen, on one side, and, on the other, the followers of the so-called 'Maori King'—a sort of Polynesian 'Lord of the Isles'—just as the Scotch clans were formerly divided into Hanoverians and Jacobites. I saw that the policy which gradually pacified the Scotch Highlands would prove to be the proper policy for this country also; and it has been adopted by the Colonial Government and Parliament. We are steadily pursuing the system of Marshal Wade in opening up the country by roads, and of Lord Chatham, in employing the disaffected clans on

public works, and in regiments and companies raised
for the Crown. About three thousand Maoris, most
of whom were lately in arms against us, are now
garrisoning posts for the Government, or are working
on the roads, which open up their own mountains
and forests, and will soon render rebellion impossible
in the future. Everywhere in the recently hostile
country I was received as the representative of the
Queen with the most loyal and cordial respect; and
saw the 'Union Jack,' the symbol of submission to
the authority of Her Majesty, hoisted by the natives
themselves over the *pahs* (i.e. fortified Maori villages)
where the rebel flag had floated for several years.
There was one very striking scene of this nature.
One pah in the interior of this island is held by an
old chief, who had the reputation of being a sullen
and obstinate rebel; and as my route lay about half-
a-mile from it, I was advised by the loyal chiefs to
pass it by without a visit. However, when my little
cavalcade of five or six horsemen came in sight on
the brow of the nearest hill, we saw the 'Union
Jack' run up at the flag-staff; while from the tree-
ferns, palms, and all the beautiful and semi-tropical
underwood of the New Zealand forests around us,
a number of the clansmen sprang up, not in mute
defiance like the clansmen of Roderick Dhu, in the
famous scene of the 'Lady of the Lake,' but with
the soft musical tones of the *Haere Mai*, the Maori
chant of welcome. Soon afterwards, the old chief
himself came forward, and welcomed me to his

country with that dignified courtesy which Maoris and Red Indians know so well how to assume.

In fact, the feeling in favour of a native king is fast dying out here, just as Jacobitism died out in Scotland a hundred years ago. And as the Farquharsons, Mackenzies, and other Highland clans, once Jacobite, are now enthusiastically attached to the House of Hanover, so many of the Maori tribes, once 'Hau-hau,' or rebel, are now loyally (in their own phrase) 'reposing under the shadow of the Queen.'

Anthony Trollope is now visiting New Zealand. It is to be wished that he may do for the Maoris what Walter Scott did for the Highlanders, and Fenimore Cooper for the Red Indians. He might find here materials for several novels, which would preserve the memory of a very interesting race. I visited again on my recent tour the famous Hot Lakes and springs (resembling the *geysers* of Iceland) which I visited in 1870 with the Duke of Edinburgh. His Royal Highness has left a most favourable impression behind him in New Zealand, and is regarded with affectionate respect alike by the colonists and by the natives, who often ask after the 'son of the Queen.' I may here mention that (as I have officially reported to Lord Kimberley) the intelligence of the illness of the Prince of Wales called forth throughout New Zealand a general sympathy, which proves (if, indeed, any proof were wanting) the strength of the loyal attachment of all classes in this community to the Crown and to the Royal Family.   I appointed by proclamation a day of general thanksgiving for his Royal Highness's recovery; and it was observed as in England.   It was everywhere kept as a close holiday; and appropriate services were held in the churches of all the religious communions, and attended by crowded congregations.   I added in my official despatch to Lord Kimberley:

'It has been remarked here that in the old French Monarchy the children of the Sovereign were called the children of France (*les enfans de France*); and that although the English people do not use the same graceful phrase, they feel thoroughly the sentiment which it expresses.   It has been my agreeable duty to report in several previous despatches, the enthusiastic welcome with which the Duke of Edinburgh was received in New Zealand on his visits in 1869 and in 1870; and I now assure your Lordship, that it has been truly observed in the public press that there is scarcely a household in this Colony in which the illness of the Prince of Wales was not deplored almost as would be that of an honoured relative.'

————————

To the Earl of Kimberley.

Government House, Wellington, New Zealand:
September 7, 1872.

My Lord,

I have now the honour to forward a translation of the report, sent to the Colonial Government by the

Maoris present, of a great native meeting held in last July at one of the places lately visited by me, viz. Mataahu, near the East Cape, the *kainga*, or settlement, of Ropata te Wahawaha, the principal warrior of the powerful clan of the Ngatiporos, and one of the six chiefs to whom the Queen has presented swords of honour.

The main object of this meeting was to erect, with great ceremony, a flagstaff, and to hoist on it the ' Queen's flag '—i.e. the Union Jack—in token of the permanent establishment of peace, and of the return of the entire native population of the East Coast from rebellion to their allegiance to the Crown, and from the Hau-hau fanaticism to Christianity. There were also carried by the representatives of the several clans other banners bearing devices symbolical of the loyalty and Christian faith of the Maori people.

The speeches of the leading Maori chiefs present at the meeting will repay perusal; especially that of Ropata te Wahawaha, who wore his uniform as a major in the Colonial Militia, and the sword of honour presented to him by the Queen for his long-continued services in the field in support of Her Majesty's authority and the cause of law and order. He began in these words :

' To all the tribes and chiefs I offer thanks because we have all met here together to witness the raising of our " Power " (the flagstaff), and the sign of our union in this our great security, and to enable me to show you these swords, which you have not before had an opportunity of seeing. These swords are a mark of honour from the Queen for your steadfast loyalty to her; a token of her love and approbation conferred upon you for your bravery in putting down the evil and upholding the good; and this flag also is a token of the support afforded you by the Government for your bravery in suppressing evil.'

After explaining the position of the Maoris at the present time, and exhorting them to peace and union, he concluded his address as follows:

'Let us all rejoice and be glad under this our flag (the Queen's flag), because we are able to breathe freely during this period of rest and security under the protection of this new power. Therefore, let us also be energetic and active in making roads in our districts, erecting schools for our children, building churches, and promoting Christianity; and let us also hold on to the law as a protecting fence round about us.

'Now I have explained to you, O ye people, the objects of our present assembling together, and which may be condensed under two heads: First, the command of Christ to deny ourselves, take up our cross, and follow Him. We shall then be His children indeed, and co-heirs with Him in His kingdom. Taking up the cross, we should pray always, both in prosperity and in adversity.

'Secondly; this is our power and strength (*mana*) which waves above us [i.e. the British flag]. If we do good we shall by it be increased and exalted; but if we do evil—that is, if we return to Hau-hau practices and principles, or take up arms without due legal authority—we shall be crushed entirely.

'God preserve the Queen, and you, her people, and take you under His divine protection.'

It will be further seen that the ceremony ended by the natives opening a subscription among themselves for the erection of a new school-house for their children.

The admission of Maori members into the Colonial Parliament—an important political measure always strongly advocated by Sir G. Bowen—is referred to in the subjoined despatch:

To the Same.

Government House, Wellington, New Zealand:
October 21, 1872.

My Lord,

In my despatch of September 20th ultimo, and on previous occasions, I have reported that the experiment of admitting Maori members to the House of Representatives had proved completely successful, and that it had been decided to admit them also to the Executive and Legislative Councils;—a resolution approved by all parties, both within and without the Legislature.

As your Lordship is aware, the Maoris in the House of Representatives are elected by their countrymen; but as the members of the Executive and Legislative Councils are nominated by the Governor, the selection from among the principal Maori clans and chiefs was a matter of delicacy, requiring careful consideration. With the advice of my Ministers, I have now summoned to the Executive Council two of the leading Maori members of the House of Representatives; and to the Legislative Council—

(1) Mokena Kohere, of Waiapu, in the province of Auckland, a chief of high rank and commanding influence in the great clan of the Ngatiporos, and who was recently presented by Her Majesty with a sword of honour for his long and gallant services in fighting for the Crown during the second Maori War.

(2) Wiremu Tako Ngatata, of Waikanae in the province of Wellington, the foremost chief of the clan of the Ngatiawas. When the first English colonists, under the auspices of the New Zealand Company, arrived in this country in 1840, they found this chief living in a pah on what is now the site of the city of Wellington. Together with his friend and relative, the celebrated Te Puni (whose death was recently lamented by both races),[1] Wiremu Tako Ngatata

---

[1] Sir G. Bowen reported (December 24, 1870) that 'the Government ordered a public funeral for Te Puni. Several of the colonial Ministers and other leading settlers of all political parties were pall-bearers, together with the principal clansmen of the deceased; the Bishop of Wellington read the Burial Service of the Church of England; Mr. McLean, the Minister for Native Affairs, delivered an eloquent address in Maori; and the Volunteer Rifles and Artillery fired the customary military salutes over the grave of the old warrior. Several of the colonial journals have made appropriate comments on the death of Te Puni. The subjoined extract will suffice to show the general sentiment: " The old settlers of Wellington did themselves honour in paying the last mark of respect to Te Puni; and the Government

cordially welcomed the early settlers, made over to them large grants of land, and protected them from the attacks of the hostile natives. I have already borne my testimony to the assistance which he afforded to me personally at the very critical period of the dangerous outbreak on the West Coast of this island in 1868.

Both of the above-mentioned chiefs are universally recognised as good representatives of their race. They have taken their seats in the Legislative Council, and have already begun to show, like their country-men in the other Chamber, an intelligent and active interest in the debates, and in the general business of the Parliament.

A Government interpreter is always present in both Houses to translate the speeches of the Maori

deserves thanks for assistance, without which it would have been im-possible to carry out the arrangements for the funeral in so satisfactory a manner. The frank acknowledgment of Te Puni's claims upon the gratitude of the colonists, and the manner in which they were alluded to by Mr. McLean, must have had a very gratifying effect on the Maoris who were present, and may exercise a salutary influence in other places. The ceremony in itself was striking and suggestive; vigorous civilisation laying the head of decaying barbarism in the earth gently and with reverence; not (as is usual in the case of the aborigines of other countries) with rude and careless contempt. Te Puni's burial in European fashion, with Europeans standing round his grave, and European guns firing over it, is typical of the not distant time when all the savage powers of obstruction yet latent among the Maoris will be buried in a similar manner, and the work of colonisation will proceed uninterrupted. It also suggests the thought of another hour, sooner or later to arrive, when the last Maori will be laid to his rest by European hands; and his race, so remarkable for its chequered character of good and evil—so much that is noble and striking, and so much that is savage and revolting—will remain only in the history and traditions of the past." '

members sentence by sentence.   They rarely speak, except on questions of land tenure, native laws and customs, and other subjects with which they are perfectly acquainted; and they are always heard with respect and attention by their English colleagues.

There can be no doubt that the admission of Maoris to the Executive Council and to the Parliament has been felt by them as a proof that they are now regarded as having equal rights with the colonists.   It was a most salutary measure.

CHAPTER XX.

OFFICIAL TOURS IN THE SOUTH ISLAND—CANTERBURY—JOHN ROBERT GODLEY—THE 'CANTERBURY PILGRIMS'—OTAGO—HOKITIKA—SOUTHERN ALPS—FJORDS OF NEW ZEALAND—MILFORD SOUND—LAKE WAKATIPU.

THE complete termination of the Maori disturbances in the North Island enabled the Governor to make some lengthened official tours in the South Island, which contains the great majority of the English settlers, but only a few hundred natives. Hitherto he had been unable to absent himself from the scene of hostilities, except during his brief voyage with the
• Duke of Edinburgh.

We subjoin some extracts from the Governor's reports of his Southern tours :

To the Earl of Kimberley.

'As the local journals observe: "A heartier or more universal demonstration could not have been made"; and I may add, that the good taste was equally conspicuous with the warmth of the welcome accorded to me by the Superintendents, by the Provincial Governments, and by all classes of the community.

'It will be seen that, in replying to an address presented to me in Canterbury, I spoke as follows:

" I thank you heartily for the welcome which your loyalty to our Sovereign has induced you to accord to me as Her Majesty's representative on my arrival in this great Province.

' " I am fully conscious that your cordial greetings are paid to me in my official character, and that I can have as yet but little claim to the personal regard of the people of Canterbury, unless, indeed, it be as an early friend of one whose memory will for ever be held in high honour and affection among you ; I mean John Robert Godley. Nearly twenty years have now elapsed since I first discussed with him his schemes for the foundation of this settlement, which he even then called the work of his life. You all know how well he performed that work. I will only add that it would have cheered his gallant spirit, in his sufferings from failing health, if he could have foreseen the rapid but solid progress, almost without precedent elsewhere, which you have achieved."

' It will be recollected that several of the New Zealand settlements, and especially Canterbury, were, in the words of Mr. Merivale,[1] " founded under good auspices, and in a spirit of enthusiasm unequalled in modern colonial enterprise, which carries the mind back to the days of Raleigh and his adventurous contemporaries." [2] In much of the society, in many of

---

[1] *Colonisation and Colonies*, p. 128.

[2] We may here quote a story often told : It will be remembered that the late Mr. Gibbon Wakefield took a very active part in the first colonisation of New Zealand ; and that it was his policy to utilise the religious movements at home to help in creating new settlements at the Antipodes. Thus the ' High Church ' movement in England was used

the fine public buildings of Canterbury, and in all that truly English tone and aspect of the community, which strike every visitor, the character of its first founders may still be traced ; while the remarkable progress of the settlement is a proof of the energy and perseverance with which they and their successors have turned to account the natural advantages of a region comparatively free from forest, and where the expense of clearing and of first communications was comparatively small ; containing also wide and fertile plains, singularly adapted to pastoral enterprise, and adjacent to districts eminently suitable for agricultural occupation.[1]

'I was everywhere most hospitably entertained at the houses of the leading settlers, many of whom have acquired very large estates in freehold ; and although colonisation in this part of the country dates from only twelve or fifteen years back, they already live in good houses, surrounded by all the comforts and

to found Canterbury ; while the ' Free Kirk ' movement in Scotland was used to found Otago. So advantage was taken of a dispute among the Independents to induce a number of them to emigrate to a district named Albertland. Mr. Gibbon Wakefield even conceived the idea of establishing a separate settlement of Jews ; for it was recorded in the early annals of the Colony that ' at this period one single Hebrew was painfully making his way among the Scotch at Otago.' Accordingly, Mr. Wakefield consulted an eminent Hebrew merchant about his proposed experiment. ' Would it not be a good thing to have a settlement of Jews in New Zealand ? ' ' Oh, capital,' was the reply; ' but how about the Christians ? ' ' Well, we have a settlement of High Church people at Canterbury, and of Free Kirk people at Otago ; why should not the Jews found a settlement of their own ? ' ' What, without any Christians ! No, Mr. Wakefield, that will never do; *we could not live.*'

[1] The first settlers in Canterbury, who arrived in 1851, are known as the *Canterbury Pilgrims.*

nearly all the luxuries enjoyed by country gentlemen in England. Not only have the best breeds of cattle and sheep been imported, but the acclimatisation of English deer, pheasants, partridges, and other game, together with thrushes, blackbirds, and other singing birds, is also rapidly progressing. It will be recollected that the native difficulty does not exist in the Middle Island.' . . .

'At the end of my tour, I spoke as follows: "Thus I close at Greymouth my present official journey through the greater portion of this Island— from Invercargill to Dunedin, from Dunedin to Christchurch, and from Christchurch to Westland. I hope to return next summer, and then to visit Nelson and Marlborough, and those parts of the southern Provinces which my limited time would not allow me to see during the past three months. These tours enable the Governor to make himself personally acquainted with the varies resources of the Colony over which he presides, and thus to make known authoritatively in the mother-country the vast field which it offers for emigration and for the investment of capital. Moreover, I have often been told that as the Queen is the connecting link between the provinces of the Empire, so the Governor is regarded as the connecting link between the several provinces of New Zealand. Certainly in the southern settlements during my present tour, as in the northern settlements during previous tours, the colonists of all political parties, and of all social classes, have gathered round me with

simple and spontaneous loyalty, but with no abate-
ment of the manly and intelligent independence of
the colonial character, to assure me of their devoted
attachment to our Sovereign and to the British
Empire, and of their respect and esteem for myself.
Such demonstrations, while most satisfactory on
public grounds, cannot fail to be gratifying to me
personally, and encouraging to every public officer
who may hereafter fill my place, for they are a practical proof that if he will only perform his duty
towards both the Crown and the Colony with firmness and honesty, his fellow countrymen, the people
of New Zealand, will be sure to rally round him." '

We here give an extract from the despatch describing Sir G. Bowen's visit with Commodore Stirling in
H.M.S. 'Clio' to the far-famed Sounds, or *Fjords*, of
the West Coast :

'These arms of the Great Southern Ocean,
cleaving their way through the massive sea-wall of
steep and rugged cliffs, reach far into the wild
solitudes of the lofty mountains which form the
cordillera or "dividing range" of the South Island.
These mountains attain their highest elevation further
north in Mount Cook, a snowy peak rising 13,200 feet
above the sea-level, and visible in clear weather at a
distance of more than a hundred miles to the mariner
approaching New Zealand; thus forming a noble
monument of the illustrious navigator who first recommended the planting of an English settlement in this

country. Though Milford Sound far surpasses the others in wild magnificence of scenery, these inlets have many features in common. To quote Admiral Richards : " A view of the surrounding country from the summit of one of the mountains bordering the coast, of from 4,000 to 5,000 feet in elevation, is perhaps one of the most grand and magnificent spectacles it is possible to imagine ; and standing on such an elevation rising over the south side of Caswell's Sound, Cook's description of this region was forcibly recalled to mind. He says : 'A prospect more rude and craggy is rarely to be met with, for inland appeared nothing but the summits of mountains of a stupendous height, and consisting of rocks that are totally barren and naked, except where they are covered with snow.' We could only compare the scene around us as far as the eye could reach, north to Milford Sound, south to Dusky Bay, and eastward inland for a distance of sixty miles, to a vast sea of mountains of every possible variety of shape and ruggedness ; the clouds and mist floated far beneath us, and the harbour appeared no more than an insignificant stream."

' The following extract from Dr. Hector's account of Milford Sound shows the probable mode of its formation : " Three miles from the entrance of the Sound it becomes contracted to the width of half a mile, and its sides rise perpendicularly from the water's edge, for from 2,000 to 5,000 feet, and then slope at a high angle to peaks covered with perpetual snow. The scenery is quite equal to the finest that

can be enjoyed by the most difficult and toilsome
journeys into the Alps of the interior ; and the effect
is greatly enhanced, as well as the access made more
easy, by the incursion of the sea, as it were, into
these alpine solitudes. The sea, in fact, now occupies
a chasm that was in past ages ploughed by an
immense glacier ; and it is through the natural progress of events by which the mountain mass has been
reduced in altitude, that the ice-stream has been
replaced by the waters of the ocean. The evidence
of this change may be seen at a glance. The lateral
valleys join the main one at various elevations, but
are all sharply cut off by the precipitous wall of the
Sound, the erosion of which was no doubt continued
by a great central glacier long after the subordinate
and tributary glaciers had ceased to exist. The
precipices exhibit the marks of ice-action with great
distinctness, and descend quite abruptly to a depth
of 800 to 1,200 feet below the water-level. Towards
its head the Sound becomes more expanded, and
receives several large valleys that preserve the same
character, but radiate in different directions into the
highest ranges. At the time that these valleys were
filled with glaciers, a great 'ice lake' must have
existed in the upper and expanded portion of the
Sound, from which the only outlet would be through
the chasm which forms its lower part." '

'On account of the great depth of water in these
inlets, and of the sudden storms of wind rushing down
from the mountains above, vessels are generally

obliged also to moor to trees or pinnacles of rock, whenever they reach a cove in which an anchor can be dropped. Accordingly, while we were in Milford Sound the " Clio " lay only a few yards from the shore, and moored head and stern to huge trunks of trees. Immediately above rose Pembroke Peak to the height of above 7,000 feet, covered with perpetual snow, and with a glacier reaching down to within 2,000 feet of the sea. The lower slopes of the mountains around are covered with fine trees, and with the luxuriant and evergreen foliage of the tree-fern and the other beautiful undergrowth of the New Zealand forests. Two permanent waterfalls [1] of great volume, one 700 and the other 540 feet in height, add picturesque beauty to the gloomy and desolate grandeur of the upper part of Milford Sound. During a storm of wind and rain which prevailed during three days of our stay there, avalanches were frequently heard thundering down from the snow-fields above ; while a multitude of foaming cascades poured over the face of the lower precipices, bringing down with them masses of rock and trunks of trees. In a word, Milford Sound combines the dark forests and winding channels of the *Fjords* of Norway with the snowy peaks and glaciers of Switzerland.' [2]

---

[1] Since named the ' Bowen ' and ' Stirling ' Falls.

[2] In the summer of 1889, Sir G. Bowen visited Norway and the ' Land of the Midnight Sun,' proceeding as far as the North Cape, and satisfied himself that the Fjords of Norway are not so grand as those of New Zealand, and especially as Milford Sound.

To the Earl of Kimberley.

Dunedin, Otago, New Zealand: January 7, 1873.

The residence of my family and myself in Dunedin during the past fortnight has been a source of constant satisfaction and pleasure to us,—not only from the heartiness of our reception on our arrival here, —not only from the public balls and other festivities given in our honour,—not only from the marks of respect and esteem showered upon us by all classes of the community,—but still more from the universal aspect of great and growing prosperity by which we are here surrounded.

It will be remembered that Otago was originally an almost purely Scotch settlement. On the 1st instant, I was invited to the annual meeting and games of the Caledonian Society, when an address of welcome was presented to me in the presence of above six thousand spectators.

My reply was as follows :

' Gentlemen,—I thank you for this address, which is very gratifying to me, in the first place on account of your expressions of loyalty to our gracious Sovereign ; and, secondly, on account of the assurance of your good will to Lady Bowen and myself. I have read with much pleasure the constitution and rules of the Caledonian Society of Otago, and cordially sympathise with its objects, which have been carried out here with so much energy and perseverance.

Indeed, it is hardly too much to say that this province itself was originally one great Caledonian Society. It is certainly a noble monument of the industry and enterprise of its founders. The official statistics prove the rapid strides with which it has advanced since the first difficulties inseparable from a new settlement were surmounted. It appears that the population of Otago, which in 1860 was in round numbers under 25,000, is now above 75,000; that the public revenue from all sources, actually raised in the province, which in 1860 was under 100,000*l.*, now exceeds half a million sterling; that the trade (including exports and imports) has risen in value during the interval between 1860 and 1872, from less than 400,000*l.* to nearly three millions; and that the increase in live stock and cultivation during the same period has been more than fivefold. Nor is it less satisfactory to observe the steady progress of education. In 1860 there were only twenty schools in this province, all of an elementary character. Now there are above 130 schools, including two high schools for boys and girls respectively, four grammar schools, and a school of art: while the University of Otago, with its able and learned professors from the Universities of Great Britain, crowns the noble scheme of public instruction. These are facts and figures which should be made widely known in the mother-country, and to which I am determined to give official circulation there. In this, as in the other provinces, a continuous stream of immigration—that

life-blood of a new country—is absolutely necessary
for the maintenance and extension of the progress
already achieved, and for the success of the public
works sanctioned by the Colonial and Provincial
Legislatures. In conclusion, gentlemen, I accept, with
much satisfaction, the honour which you propose to
confer on me, by enrolling my name as one of the
patrons of the Caledonian Society of Otago.'

To the Same.

Government House, Wellington, New Zealand:
February 20, 1873.

My Lord,

In continuation of my despatch of the 7th
January ultimo, I have the honour to report that
I left Dunedin on the 10th ultimo, and reached
Wellington on the 4th instant, after a rapid journey
through a large portion of the provinces of Otago
and Canterbury, during which I visited the goldfields
of the former province; its mountain lakes, exceeding in grandeur the lakes of Switzerland and Italy;
and the glaciers of Mount Cook,[1] the Mont Blanc
of the Southern Alps, which, like the Andes, rise
directly from the shore of the ocean.

I was accompanied throughout their respective
provinces by the Superintendents; and I take this
opportunity of recording my deep sense of the
heartiness and hospitality of my reception every-

---

[1] Mount Cook reaches 13,200 feet above the sea-level. Its summit
was recently ascended for the first time by Mr. Green, a member of
the Alpine Club, assisted by two Swiss guides.

where, by the local authorities and by all classes of the community. Among the numerous addresses of welcome were two from the Chinese gold-diggers, 'who take this opportunity of declaring their loyalty to Her Most Gracious Majesty Queen Victoria, and their appreciation of the happiness which they have experienced during the time they have resided under British rule; and for the consideration and protection afforded them in their various pursuits, by the justice and equity of the laws which here exist, and by the way in which they are administered.'

The pressing affairs of the North Island had prevented me from visiting the southern goldfields at an earlier period of my administration; and the miners, together with the rest of the population, were aware that I was on the eve of my final departure from New Zealand. In short, I was a man whom they had never seen before, whom they knew they would never see again, and who had enjoyed no opportunity of rendering them any special services; and yet in every district and township I was most cordially greeted as the representative of the Queen. Such demonstrations cannot fail to be satisfactory on public grounds; for in these self-governing Colonies the Governor is regarded as the main visible link of union with the Throne, the mother-country, and the Empire at large, and the marks of respect paid to him are intended as proofs of national loyalty and patriotism.

It is of course impossible to give, within the compass of a despatch, any adequate description of the goldfields of this Colony. I would, however, refer to the concise and accurate account contributed by Dr. Hector, F.R.S., to the 'Transactions of the New Zealand Institute,' Vol. II., pages 361–374. The official returns show that the aggregate value of the gold hitherto exported from New Zealand exceeds in value twenty-six millions sterling; and that the annual production averages between two and three millions sterling.

Gold-mining has now become a settled industry in this country. The miners have very generally brought their wives and families with them, purchased land, and made for themselves comfortable homes. The good order which is everywhere maintained amid the temptations of so exciting a pursuit is above all praise.

Agriculture is fast progressing on the plains of Canterbury, and in the valleys and lowlands of Otago. Long-woolled sheep of several kinds, and the best breeds of cattle, have also been imported in large numbers, and thrive admirably. The hills and uplands of both provinces are still occupied chiefly by flocks of the merino sheep, which find there a climate and country resembling, in many respects, their original home in Castile and Estremadura.

It is a journey of about two hundred and twenty miles from Dunedin to the great inland lake of Wakatipu, which is fifty-two miles long, with a breadth averaging from two to five miles. It is 1,070 feet above the sea level, and is surrounded by lofty mountain ranges capped with perpetual snow, and rising precipitously from the water. Lakes Wanaka and Hawea, and the other mountain lakes of Otago, are mostly similar in physical formation and in grandeur of scenery.

It is a remarkable fact that Lake Wakatipu was not known to the colonists at Dunedin and elsewhere on the sea coast of Otago before 1860. There was a tradition among the Maoris of the existence of a vast mysterious lake in the interior ; but an enterprising settler (Mr. William Gilbert Rees) was the first European who reached its shores, in the January of the above-mentioned year. Already there are two flourishing townships (Queenstown and Kingstown) on Lake Wakatipu, and steamers ply regularly on its waters. The mountains and lakes of this part of New Zealand are becoming the resort of an annually increasing number of tourists from the neighbouring Colonies. In fact, they will soon be for Australasia what Switzerland is for Europe.

After leaving Otago, I crossed the River Waitaki into Canterbury, and travelled to the foot of the glaciers on the western side of Mount Cook. The distance is about one hundred and ten miles from the seaport town of Timaru ; the first seventy miles— that is, as far as Lake Tekapo—can be traversed in a carriage, and the remainder on horseback. We encamped for two days in a tent close to the great Tasman glacier, which Dr. Hochstetter [1] describes as

[1] Hochstetter's *New Zealand*, chap. 21.

'surpassing in magnitude by far those of the Hima-
layas and European Alps,' and which is said to be
the largest in any temperate region of the world
with the exception of some glaciers recently discovered in Thibet. Moreover, the semi-tropical luxuriance of the foliage is another feature in which the
Alps of New Zealand far surpass the mountain
ranges of Europe.[1]

[1] We may here quote on this subject the opinion of the author of
Greater Britain (Part II.) : 'The peculiarity which makes the New
Zealand scenery the most beautiful in the world to those who like
more green than California has to show, is that here alone can you find
semi-tropical vegetation growing close up to the eternal snows. The
latitude and the great moisture of the climate bring the glaciers very
low into the valleys ; and the absence of all true winter, coupled with
the rain-fall, causes the growth of palm-like ferns upon the ice-river's
very edge. The glaciers of Mount Cook are the longest in the world,
except those at the sources of the Indus, but close about them have
been found tree ferns of thirty and forty feet in height. It is not till
you enter the mountains that you escape the moisture of the coast, and
quit for the scenery of the Alps the scenery of fairy land.' And again,
of the view from Hokitika at sunrise, it is said : 'A hundred miles of
the Southern Alps stood out upon a pale blue sky in curves of gloomy
white that were just beginning to blush with pink, but ended to the
southward in a cone of fire that stood up from the ocean ; it was the
snow-dome of Mount Cook struck by the rising sun. The evergreen
bush, flaming with the crimson of the rata-blooms, hung upon the
mountain side, and covered the plain to the very margin of the narrow
sands with a dense jungle. It was one of those sights that haunt men
for years.'

CHAPTER XXI.

PROMOTION TO VICTORIA—THE NEW ZEALAND UNIVERSITY—
FOUNDATION OF THE 'BOWEN PRIZE'—THE GOVERNOR'S
SPEECH AT THE COMMENCEMENT OF THE RAILWAY SYSTEM IN
THE NORTH ISLAND—FAREWELL VISITS—APPROVAL OF HER
MAJESTY'S GOVERNMENT.

As Sir George Bowen's term of office in New Zealand
drew towards its close, he received a signal mark of
approbation by his appointment to what is often
called the 'blue ribbon' of Colonial Governments,
—that of Victoria. Lord Kimberley announced the
promotion in the subjoined despatch:

Downing Street: November 21, 1872.

Sir,—I have the satisfaction of informing you that
the Queen has been pleased to mark her sense of the
success and ability with which you have administered
the Government of New Zealand by appointing you,
upon my recommendation, to the Government of
Victoria, which is about to become vacant by the
retirement of Viscount Canterbury on the expiration
of his term of office.

Sir G. Bowen announced the name of his successor (the Right Hon. Sir James Fergusson, G.C.M.G.)
in a speech to the Scotch at Otago, in the following
terms:

'Permit me to congratulate you on the nationality of the gentleman appointed to succeed me in New Zealand on my promotion to the Governorship of Victoria. Sir James Fergusson has many personal as well as official claims to your respect and confidence. He is a soldier, who has seen active service in the Crimea, and was wounded at Inkerman. He is a Statesman, who has for several years been a member of the House of Commons, and has filled more than one administrative office of importance. Finally, he is a Governor of large ability and experience, whose manifold qualifications and accomplishments will not be the less popular in this community because they are united in a Scotchman.'

The restoration of peace enabled the Government and Parliament to give their attention to two important objects; viz. the establishment of the New Zealand University; and the commencement of a system of railways in the North as well as in the South Island. Sir George Bowen had the satisfaction of inaugurating both these schemes before his departure. On February 24, 1873, he reported:

To the Earl of Kimberley.

My Lord,

I have the honour to transmit herewith, for your Lordship's information, copies of the letters which have passed between the Chancellor of the University of New Zealand and myself, respecting the foundation

by me in that University of an annual prize, to be
called 'The Bowen Prize,' for the best English essay
on a subject to be determined upon every year under
Regulations of the Council and Senate, or of the
Council alone.

It will be seen that (in the words of my letter),
'I am desirous to connect my name in this manner
with the Colony of which I have been Governor
during an important and critical period of its history.
I yield to no permanent colonist in affection for
New Zealand, and in lively interest in its progress
and welfare.'

The Chancellor (Mr. Tancred), in accepting my
gift, writes as follows :

'Permit me, as the Council is not now in session,
to take upon myself the grateful duty of expressing
my appreciation of your Excellency's kindness and
liberality in making so valuable a provision for the
encouragement of learning. I feel assured that in
thus tendering my warmest thanks for this proof of
regard not only to this University, but, through it,
to all in the country who are interested in the cultivation of the mind, I am only anticipating the action
of the Council.

'Such an evidence on the part of your Excellency of good-will to the Council, and of the well-
known interest which your Excellency has always
taken in the cause which it is our duty to advance,
will, I feel sure, keep your name in the grateful
remembrance not only of the present generation, but

of those who in future times, when New Zealand shall have become a great nation, shall wish to recall to memory their earliest benefactors.'[1]

With regard to the railways, we subjoin the reply of the Governor to the address presented to him at Wellington when he 'turned the first sod' of the first railway in the North Island. Now (in 1889), railroads extend over both Islands.

' Gentlemen,—

' I thank you for your address; and I assure you that it affords me sincere pleasure to perform the duty which I have been requested to undertake this day. Invitations to the Governor to inaugurate railways and other great public works and institutions cannot fail to be satisfactory and gratifying, for it is well known that such invitations are intended simply as marks of loyal homage to the Queen, and that they in no wise identify Her Majesty's representative with any of those differences of opinion which here, as in all other free countries, must be expected to arise upon every subject of public importance.

' The commencement of the general scheme of public works and immigration, which has been sanctioned both by the present and by the late Parliament

---

[1] There has not been space to reproduce any of the speeches of Sir George Bowen in New Zealand respecting the promotion of education, science, and literature, nor of his addresses at the meetings of the New Zealand Institute, which will be found in the *Transactions* of that body.

of this Colony—and which we celebrate this day—is indeed a memorable event in the history of New Zealand. It appears to be acknowledged on all sides that the two most urgent needs of this entire country are the improvements of our internal communications, and the settlement of our land, which now maintains a scattered population of less than three hundred thousand, but which, according to Hochstetter and other eminent authorities, could easily support twelve millions of people. It will be within the recollection of many who now hear me that a few years ago the Imperial Government despatched an able and experienced engineer to the United States of America, to report on the railway system there adopted, with special reference to the pressing requirements of our own Colonies. His principal conclusions were :

' " (1.) A railway would appear to be the best road for arterial lines of communication in a new country.

' " (2.) In making railways in a new country, bearing in mind the high rate of interest which money commands, the outlay for construction should be as small as possible, consistent with safety and economy of working ; the object being to devote the money to be spent to extending the mileage and opening up the country, rather than to making any solid works, or to obtaining high speeds."

' The decision of all questions of this nature must, of course, rest, so far as New Zealand is concerned, with the practical wisdom of the Colonial Parliament.

Meanwhile, let us thankfully acknowledge that the application of the steam-engine to the various arts in the nineteenth, is as important as the invention of the printing-press in the fifteenth century. It has been said, without any exaggeration, that what printing did for the development of the intellectual faculties, steam is doing in the promotion of the material welfare of our race; that within the last hundred years engineering science has trebled the mechanical power, and far more than trebled the resources of mankind; while it has reduced the dimensions of the globe, as measured by time, to less than one-fourth of what they were even in the days of the last generation.

'I earnestly hope that the ceremony of this day will prove auspicious to all concerned. May the public works now inaugurated throughout this country realise the hopes of the Ministers and Parliaments that undertook them; may they reward the skill and enterprise of the contractors and engineers; may they help to consolidate friendly relations between the Colonists and the Maoris; in a word, may they, under the favour of Divine Providence, endure throughout the great future of New Zealand as a source of permanent and ever-increasing prosperity.

'Finally, let me again, as on a previous occasion of a like nature, address a few words of friendly sympathy to the artisans and working men, who will soon erect in our several Provinces structures scarcely more honourable to the heads that have planned than to the hands that will execute them. I trust that thousands of the men employed on our railways will ultimately become permanent settlers on the broad and fertile lands of this Colony, and that their success will cause them to be joined by tens of thousands from the old home. I am confident that the new comers will emulate their fellow colonists in that respect for law and order which is one of the most prominent characteristics of our race. Let them recollect, moreover, that it is from their ranks that have sprung,—the Boltons and Arkwrights, the Telfords and Stephensons, and most of the chieftains of art and industry—

" Of the railway and the steamship, and the thoughts that shake mankind." [1]

Let them remember also that under the expansive freedom of our colonial institutions, even more surely than in the parent isles, Britain opens for all her sons a noble prospect of success and honour to genius combined with energy and with virtue. Only let it never be forgotten that what is needed here is not so much a new society, but rather the old society in a new country. On the broad and deep foundations of British principles, British feelings, and British institutions, let the fabric of the material prosperity of New Zealand be erected, and over it let the spire of education, learning, and religion be raised towards heaven.'

---

[1] Tennyson, *Locksley Hall.*

The addresses at the Governor's farewell meeting with the Maoris of the Waikato deserve to be recorded. The official despatch of March 15, 1873, reports:

On the 11th instant I proceeded to Ngaruawáhia, whither I was accompanied by the Chief Justice, Sir George Arney (who will on my departure become the Administrator of the Government pending the arrival of my successor), by Mr. McLean, the Minister for Native Affairs, by the Superintendent of the Province of Auckland, and by other functionaries and officers of Government. This was my fourth visit to the Waikato, which I have fully described in previous despatches.[1]

On my arrival at Ngaruawáhia, I was received with loud chants and songs at once of welcome and farewell, by the most numerous assemblage of Maoris which has been known for many years past. The loyal chiefs and clans were fully represented; and there was also a large number of Hau-haus, recently in arms against the Queen, but whose leaders now laid at my feet the embroidered mats which are the recognised token of submission and peace.

The terms of my official address to the Maoris on this interesting and important occasion were, of course, carefully concerted beforehand with Mr. McLean, the Minister for Native Affairs. In common with other leading men of all parties, Mr. McLean had, during the last session of the Colonial Parlia-

[1] See above, pp. 300-316.

ment, expressed the opinion that, since tranquillity appeared to have been permanently established, the time had come to take into consideration the propriety of proclaiming ere long an amnesty for all past offences of a political character committed by the Maoris. I entirely concur with this view. As your Lordship is already aware, no Maori now remains under confinement for any political offence ; but the arrangements deemed necessary by Mr. McLean prior to the proclamation of a general amnesty have not yet been completed. It will be a happy circumstance if my successor in the Government of New Zealand should find himself in a position to inaugurate his administration by the performance of this act of grace.[1]

The following is a translation of the address from the assembled Maoris :

This is a farewell address to you, O Father, our Governor ! Welcome, O loving parent the Governor of the chiefs and tribes of Waikato ! before you leave for the place which has been appointed for you by our gracious Queen. We are very sad on account of your departure. We will not forget what you said on your first visit to Waikato in May, 1868, that the Maoris and Europeans should bury their animosities in Potatau's tomb. There have been many troubles and evil deeds done in Waikato, but you have not been hasty to take action; you have been patient, and have not forgotten your word. The administra-

---

[1] A general amnesty was proclaimed shortly afterwards.

tion by you during your term of office of the affairs
of this Colony has been very just. You have not
caused any evil; the evil has been done by other
Governors before you. You and your advisers have
been energetic in the suppression of evil. You
leave us free from any blame; and we pray God
to conduct you, Lady Bowen, and your family, safely
to the place whither you are sent by the Queen.

The next address of welcome was presented by
a great Chief—a kinsman of the Maori king. The
following is a translation :

O Friend, the Governor! salutations to you. Welcome to Waikato, before you depart, to see these
tribes of yours, and your friends the chiefs of this
portion of the great and noble tribe of Waikato, who
live in this island. They have been justly punished
for their offences. Although there are living many
who did evil, there are many who have remained
quiet up to the present time; and we are still
dwelling together with our European friends as
brothers on this river Waikato. When you first
came here as a perfect stranger to see us, you
paid your respects to the tomb of your friend, our
great chief, Te Whero Whero, who lies in his grave
at Ngaruawáhia. You then made an important
statement, namely, that the animosities of the Maoris
and the Pakehas should be buried in the grave
of that old chief. Your word has been fulfilled.
I, his kinsman, and these chiefs, are carrying
out what he said when he was living. Although
others of his family may have gone astray, I have
adhered to what he said, and am still doing so. Do

not think that this tribe is the only one that has
done evil in this island; all the tribes have taken
part in what has resulted in the destruction of my
people and loss of my land. Although this tribe of
yours may have been forgotten by the Government,
and others may have been favoured, we, the chiefs,
will never forget your words. I shall bequeath them
to my children, for it was I who strengthened your
hands at the commencement of the great fighting in
this island. I had no grievance against any other
tribe. I fought against my own people for the suppression of evil. I am sorry that you did not see
the other portion of my tribe and my relatives.
Welcome, O Governor! welcome. Farewell to you
and your lady, and your children. Go to your new
Government under the authority and love of our
Queen, the mother of our future King, who was protected by God and brought safely through his severe
illness. We are very glad, and feel honoured on
account of the visit to us of his brother (the Duke of
Edinburgh), the descendant of great chiefs. Go, O
my father! in peace to your new home. May God
protect you, and keep you in health.

The speech of the Governor in reply to the Maori
addresses is thus reported:

'O my friends, chiefs and people of all the tribes
whom I now see before me! salutations to you all.
When I first arrived in New Zealand, five years ago, I
came among you at Ngaruawáhia, and you received
me with a hearty welcome, as you have also done now.
Then as now, we met near the tomb of Potatau te

Whero Whero, a noble chief of the olden time, who never made war against the Queen, but was ever loyal to the Crown and friendly to the Europeans. Thereupon both races, the English and the Maoris, delighted to honour him. Five years ago, standing on this spot, I said that the two races should bury any remaining animosities in the tomb of Potatau, and my word has proved true; you have buried your hatreds. The two races now live in peace and friendship together. So too I said on my first visit that the Europeans and the Maoris should grow into one people, even as the rivers Waipa and Waikato mingle their waters at Ngaruawáhia,—the old Maori capital; —and has not this been so? Do not Europeans and Maoris sit together in the Councils which govern this country; in the Executive, in the Legislative Council, and in the House of Representatives? The vote of each Maori is equal to the vote of each European in framing the laws which govern both races.

This is my fourth visit to the Waikato, and I should have been glad to have seen more of Potatau's descendants. I have given every proof of my desire to do so. And now, my friends, I have come to bid you farewell. Wherever I go I shall always cherish my love for you and for the glorious country which you share with your English friends and fellow-subjects. I am about to become Governor of the neighbouring Colony of Victoria; but I shall not there be far from you, and I shall always watch your progress with affectionate interest. My parting advice to you is to give your aid in support of the law, and also of the schools which the Government is establishing throughout these islands for the education of your children. There they will learn to be good citizens, and by acquiring the language and arts of the English, they will be able to take their part in the public affairs of the Colony, and to assist in developing its resources. I am very glad to leave on my departure this Colony prosperous and tranquil. On his visit to New Zealand the Queen's son, the Duke of Edinburgh, expressed his hope that the clouds of war would soon pass away, and the sun of peace would shine forth; and this is now so. The Colonial Government have recognised the establishment of peace. Already all Maoris who were in confinement for political offences have been set at liberty by me; not one remains in prison. And hearken, O my friends! to these words. So soon as the necessary arrangements can be made, it is proposed to proclaim, in the name of the Queen, a general amnesty for past acts of rebellion and other political offences. It is hoped that this act of grace will further cement the friendly relations now happily existing between the two races. Finally, O my friends! remember that the law is the best and most impartial arbiter for adjusting all the differences that may arise among the Maoris themselves, or between Maoris and Europeans. The law is no respecter of persons; it protects the weak as well as the strong; and you will find it your best shield and guide in future. It is my earnest advice that you should devote your attention henceforward to the arts of peaceful industry, and re-establish the name of Waikato as a country supply-ing the markets of the towns with grain, fruit, and other produce. Thus you will secure for yourselves and for your families the comforts enjoyed by the Europeans. And now, once more, O my friends! farewell. May Heaven pour its choicest blessings upon you. Be assured that my successor, Sir James Fergusson, will feel the same sympathy for the Maoris that I have always felt; as will also the Chief Justice, Sir George Arney, who will administer the Govern-ment immediately after my departure and until the arrival of the new Governor. Once more, farewell!'

To the Earl of Kimberley.

Bay of Islands, New Zealand: March 19, 1873.

My Lord,

I have the honour to report that I took my final departure from Auckland yesterday afternoon. My family and I were accompanied to the place of embarkation by the principal public functionaries and local authorities, by the public bodies, by the friendly societies, and by many thousands of all classes of the community. The demonstrations of regard for us, and of regret at our departure, were very lively and affecting.

This morning the steamer which is conveying me to Melbourne, stopped for a few hours (as had been previously arranged) at the Bay of Islands, to enable me to unveil the monument erected by the Colonial Government over the grave of Tamati Waka Nene. The ceremony was performed in the presence of the chiefs and clansmen of the Ngapuhi and of the other Maori tribes of the north; and of a large concourse of the leading colonists, who had assembled to pay honour to the memory of their firm friend and gallant ally. It is an interesting fact that my last despatch from New Zealand should be dated from the Bay of Islands, which has filled so prominent a place in the early annals of this country; and that my last public act here should be a mark of respect to the memory of the Maori chief who was mainly instrumental in procuring the cession of the sovereignty of these islands to the British Crown.

So ended Sir George Bowen's memorable government of New Zealand at the most critical period in the history of that great Colony. We have seen that, under his auspices, and through the policy which he recommended and supported, and which was ably carried out by Sir Donald McLean and other Ministers,[1] there was established between the two races a peace which has not since been seriously dis-

[1] Sir G. Bowen's despatches and letters bear frequent testimony to the abil'ty and public spirit of the members of his successive Ministries in New Zealand, without distinction of party. Of Sir Donald McLean he wrote: 'Himself born a Scotch Highlander, he thoroughly understood the principles and feelings of clanship, and thus exercised a powerful influence over the Maoris, whose language he spoke as fluently as his native Gaelic.'

turbed. All danger has now (1889) passed away, seeing that the Europeans in New Zealand are already a fast increasing population of 620,000, while the Maoris are a dwindling people of little over 40,000.

Her Majesty's Government thus for the second time expressed its sense of Sir George Bowen's services in New Zealand :

The Earl of Kimberley to the Officer administering the Government of New Zealand.

Downing Street: May 31, 1873.

Sir,

I have read with interest Sir George Bowen's account of his parting interview with the northern Maoris at Ngaruawáhia, as affording a further proof of the friendly relations which exist between the English settlers and natives in the Waikato, and of the satisfactory condition of native affairs.

I have to add that Her Majesty's Government are fully sensible of the success and ability with which Sir George Bowen administered the Government of New Zealand.

END OF THE FIRST VOLUME.

PRINTED BY
SPOTTISWOODE AND CO., NEW-STREET SQUARE
LONDON